Not All Mothers
Love Their Baby

(Well, not straight away at least)

Kirsty Mac

Not All Mothers Love Their Baby
(Well, not straight away at least)

Written by Kirsty Mac

@honestkirsty
#notallmothers

Edited by Mhairi Murray and Kristina Reynolds

Book cover by Alison Meloy

Poor human suffering my relentless questions about all things publishing and IT related, Stuart Learmonth

Self-Published on Amazon

This book is dedicated to those that need to read these words. For yourself, your partner or a loved one. Parenthood is hard, but it need not be lonely. Keep going. You are not alone.

xXxXx

Contents

Introduction

I crashed into parenthood, headfirst, frazzled, and utterly bewildered at the witching-hour screaming and naps that lasted a grand total of 20 minutes at a time. This wasn't what we had signed up for; babies are adorable, sweet, a fountain of youth and never ending snuggle buddies, no? Not quite. My fantasy of cutesy lunch dates, followed by laughter-filled play dates dissipated before my eyes, not that I could see anyway. A heavy, dense, powerful storm of Postnatal Depression blinded me, making my only focus surviving during a time that should have been 'once in a lifetime' enjoyable memories. In the whirlwind, my enjoyment was stolen, my life torn from its foundations, tossed into the air and landing in a hostile world I did not recognise.

I did not love being a mother. I did not love motherhood. I endured it - all of it. Yet, I stayed within it to care for my baby, giving her all that she needed and more. The adoring mother. That's what I wanted to be, what I wanted to emulate. To be like everyone else. Not this failure of a mother who screamed at her newborn and believed her partner was repulsed by her postpartum body, so disgusted he satisfied his 'appetite' elsewhere.

I acquainted myself with my illness, postnatal depression: a secret disease of new parents, hidden behind a veil of shame, guilt, pain, taboo and misunderstanding. Causing mothers (and fathers) to wail in despair - *'Why am I like this?'*, *'I am failing my family'*, *'I'm toxic to everyone', 'My baby would be safer without me here...'* An illness so powerful it aids in mothers taking their own life, just weeks after giving birth. A decision I related with, longing to be free from the noise in my head. The voice dragging me down, making my life insufferable and utterly painful. I looked at my newborn with disdain more than love, my partner even more so.

"Enjoy every moment. The days are long, but the years are short" I was told, *'thank fuck'* I thought, wishing my life away as I waited for the glorious day that 'things get easier'. But that day did not come, not for years. Deeper into a hole of depression I fell, my mind becoming more warped, more disconnected, more delusional. Until I made (okay, was heavily pushed to make) the decision to fight back. It was that or, well, my name would have been added to the mortality statistics of mothers taking their own life in a bid to free themselves and their family from the beast which resided within them.

In my battle against this *hidden* illness, I found it to be more common than many of the studies state. Mothers and fathers struggle en masse, yet not knowing it. Consumed by comparison on social media, chasing false ideals and being beaten by the stick of guilt when they feel that are not 'parenting enough'. This environment in which we live, a fast-paced era of social media, abundant in perfection and lies, has created the optimum breeding ground of mental illnesses, especially when combined with parenthood. Parents are weeping behind their phone screens, roaring in frustration, bewildered with repressed emotions and trauma, as they crash into parenthood, seemingly failing when compared to everyone else who 'has it all together'. But does anyone actually have their shit together?

The truth is, parenthood is hard and we all struggle at some point (or, like me, all the points when struggling with postnatal depression). The problem is we often find it hard to express ourselves. To admit how we feel about the change, our bodies, our partners, our babies. We presume we are the only one with these thoughts, a deadly place to be - alone. So, I share my excruciating story to let others know what life is really like being a parent and suffering with the cruel and heartless illness that ripped my baby from my heart, while instilling numbness and suspicion within me. I share it so others need not feel alone. More importantly, I share it to show there can be hope, a way back to a happy life, to a place of pure love and acceptance, of yourself. Not an easy path, but then again, there has been nothing easy about my path since having my vagina ripped like crepe paper during giving birth, so why make it easier now, eh?

So sit back, get the tissues; it's going to be emotional (to put it lightly) and let me take you on a fucked up, warped journey of a mother's mind lost to the helm of depression, as she comes face to face with her demons and kicks the shit out of them, one brutal therapy session at a time - and not just those with the qualified therapist. There's nothing taboo for me, nothing too shameful to reveal. From 5th labias to hypothetical love affairs and sex aversion, I want to tell you it all. I NEED to tell you it all. So no other parent endures the vice of isolation in parenthood or the heartache they feel crying in the shower when the force of parenting pushes them to despair, when they just can shake the thought of how much they are fucking this all up, when everyone else is 'nailing it'. They aren't.

Chapter 1

We Are Having a Baby! Let's Begin...

Late November 2014, I watch as two pink lines appear. I'm pregnant. Yikes!

For the best part of a year, my partner and I had discussed having a baby. As a young working couple, we had our reservations. What would life be like? Could we afford it? Should we wait and save more money? Maybe buy a house first? Was saving and planning the right thing to do? The truth is, if you are having those conversations and debates, then the decision has already been made.

We both **really** wanted a baby. We had been together for 10 years, sharing our own relationship defining moments in that time. We had both been to university together, spent that time drinking enough alcohol to blank out the memories that deserved to be forgotten (thankfully). We had good jobs and had met great friends in the process. We really did have a great life; pissing all our money away on dining out and fattening up our retro gaming collection. Even better, we were rich in free time. *Free time.* Lucky fuckers.

Lucky in life, falling pregnant was no exception. *Bish, bash, BOOM!* job done. Literally. This is no *Playboy* article; I just mean we fell pregnant VERY quickly. The *"bish, bash, BOOM"* isn't a review on my partner's seductive skills. Which will be about the only personal detail I keep close to my chest, as we progress through this book.

I told my partner the terrifying news; that we, as mere children ourselves, in our late 20s with nothing to do other than work and go for a pint, would be having a baby later the following year. We could not believe our luck, falling pregnant so quickly. It had only been a month since I confessed that I wanted nothing more than to carry his baby, and all this back and forth was eating me alive, expressing how we both felt, yet too shy to commit to. Now I stood in front of him with a positive pregnancy test, pleading that we go to the store to buy those overpriced tests, the ones that would estimate how many weeks along we were.

I was 2-3 weeks pregnant. We couldn't believe it. How lucky are we? Ridiculously so! Naturally, my partner saw this as a great achievement; a mark of his strength, manliness, his prowess. Joking for the next few weeks - and until infinity - that he must possess some form of manly 'superpowers' (I'll spare you the term he created). All but beating his chest as he bragged about our quick impregnation, boasting his touch - or even his glance - would get any woman within a 10-mile radius pregnant (I'm getting a migraine from eye rolling as I type…).

Throughout the following nine months, my strutting partner and I prepared to introduce our baby girl into the world. This basically meant I ate anything in sight and turned into a **HUGE** hormonal bitch, crying on my partner's shoulder, staining one of his precious Italian cloth shirts with wet mascara in the process. For what reason I was so upset, who knows. Maybe it was the time he ate my chocolate mousse I had saved. I had been dreaming of it the whole day, only to return home to an empty fridge and the brass neck of a man who complained that he *"didn't even like it"*. Apeshit I went.

Darn right. He ate my snack **AND** had the balls to complain it wasn't delicious. I'm glad I cried all over those 'darling' shirts of his. And I am even gladder he had to explain the mascara stains to the owner of the dry cleaners. Making a poor, tired, helpless and hangry pregnant lady cry, and all for a snack he didn't even like. Not so strutty now, are we, Mr '*Superpowers*'?

For the most part, I enjoyed being pregnant. There were no complications. No overly huge bump that threatened to burst at any moment. No niggles or worries. No bump straps mixed with crutches to support an aching pelvis. No planned caesarean section because the pregnancy was assaulting my body. Nothing. I got off lightly when compared to the tales from other mothers, and the issues they had endured during the baby baking.

Being pregnant brought us closer together as a couple. At times it was difficult: I would cry, out of frustration, anxiety, and being unsure of the future, we both found it hard to adjust to the new responsibility and the needs it created for each other. Silly things when I look back now. Arguing with my partner that 11 p.m. was too late a time to return home from the pub when we both had work the next day, and he knew fine well I can't sleep without him in the bed. I went apeshit on that one too. To be fair, that was probably hormone fuelled, but still - off he went with another black stained shirt to the dry cleaners, and yet another reason why he had made his suffering pregnant partner cry.

Hiding From Childbirth

It wouldn't be unfair to say I went into childbirth clueless. Everyone speaks about birth like it is a run of the mill, everyday occurrence. Which it is. It's just something women do and get on with. Why would I presume there was anything else to it? The baby comes out one way or another, and that's it. You get up, you move on. End of. Neither my partner nor I were prepared for birth, not that any amount of preparation will help, in some cases. I avoided birthing classes, antenatal groups, videos and books, mainly because I couldn't entertain the notion of people telling me anything about the unknown, filling my head with ways it should be when the event had yet to unfold. I also thought I knew what birth would be like anyway, so I didn't want extra things to think or stress about.

I did attend one pregnancy session, *'Aqua Bumps'*, or something to that effect. A bunch of eager and heavily pregnant women floating around a pool on pool-noodles, enjoying the relief and support the water brought to their expanding bodies while they performed some light exercise, guided by the rather energetic trainer on the sidelines.

During the class, we were instructed to pair up, find an equally excited mum-to-be and perform whatever joint exercise it was. The lady I teamed with struck up conversation. She asked how many weeks pregnant I was and when I was due. She was due a month or so before me. I remember her face beaming as we spoke, clearly very excited about her impending arrival. I was excited to meet my baby too, but I could do without this awkward class and all of these strangers if I'm honest. Having never been keen on doing things like this on my own at the best of times, even worse; being in predominantly female surroundings has never been easy for me. I've never felt that I fit in with women; my humour is too crude, too quick, and too close to the bone for the girls I have encountered. I grew up on a diet of teasing and competing with my brothers, being treated as their equal, subjected to *Robocop* and Schwarzenegger films on the daily. I know more about *Total Recall* than I do *My Little Pony*. Not exactly the classic traits of a 'little girl'.

After what I can only presume was pool buoyance tests (why else would they force heavily pregnant women to 'balance' on a pool noodle?), the pregnant swarm of ladies dried off and met to discuss all things pregnancy. Rushing to get dressed and manoeuvre my large pregnancy bump in a small changing cubicle, I was the last one to arrive at the seated circle of nightmares. The room was big, filled with women at all stages of pregnancy, sitting on the floor in a circle where the dreaded introductions would begin:

"Hi, my name is Kirsty and I'm 28 weeks pregnant".

Arguably, this experience is more uncomfortable than having a midwife's hand rammed up your fanny* (*British slang for 'vagina' and not the butt, just so we are all clear. Although, I'd still say having a hand up your *arse* would be more pleasant than attending that group). I remember the room being filled with false plastered-on smiles strangers give each other. Not insincere, but not genuine either; more than likely all feeling just as awkward as each other.

There was one lady there about to pop with her second child; either it was her due date, or very close to it. I remember this because there was some form of discussion about an injection, and if she would be having it this time around. I just sat there; not having a clue what they were on about, becoming quite freaked out that all these women seemed so excited and 'motherly'. Meanwhile, panic was rising inside of me. I felt like that kid who comes out the exam, listening to everyone talk about which answers they put down. Only to realise, I had given a completely different answer from everyone else in the group, at every question. The whole scenario filled me with dread, I felt like I had no idea what I was doing, or if I would ever be as 'motherly' as these women.

I'll Be Back... Actually, No I Won't

I didn't relate to, or 'click', with any of the 'Masters of Motherhood' in this group. In fact, I hated the whole fucking thing and could not wait to leave. And what the fuck was this injection they spoke of? Why was it such a big deal? Should I be thinking about this? I had no idea, and so I nodded along like the rest of them, listening as this woman spoke of her first birth story while she rubbed her baby bump tenderly. I now know it was the Syntocinon injection, offered straight after birth to help contractions of the uterus. Still, I have no idea what the debate was about; all I know is I wanted out of that room, and quickly. That was the first - and last time - I would try out any of that antenatal class nonsense. Too much excitement. Too many animated smiles and wide eyes. Far too much baby talk and not enough flatulence debating for my liking.

I went about the rest of my pregnancy with blinkers set firmly around my eyes, seeing only what I wanted. Unfortunately, blinkers don't work on the ears. The duty of all mothers before us is to share their birth stories, coupled with that twang of upset and anger. The stories of midwife neglect and the extraordinary length of time each women endured her labour. How they screamed and reached for the closest shears to cut off those devil man balls, grinding them into powder, to ensure this act of Hell never occurs again.

There is no way to avoid hearing why you will be pleading for an epidural after 12 hours of labour, no matter what you say to this 'been there before and know it all mother', who seems so intent on scaring the life out of a first-time expectant mother. There's no way to rebuff the bragging mothers before you who want to puff up their chest while reliving the birth of their children. (Well, no socially acceptable way at least.) You can't exactly tell her why, as a first-time pregnant mother, you don't want to hear about her 3 days of labouring hell, only to culminate in a genital explosion requiring a seamstress amount of stitching, to give her anything that resembles human genitals. Hard pass on those stories, thank you very much.

So with the very much unwanted bragging rights of mothers before me, and the crazy ecstatic faces of the soon-to-be mothers, I was firmly set against wanting to know anything more about childbirth. My turn had yet to pass, and either way, I didn't want to fuel my worries by being around mothers or soon-to-be-mothers. I just wanted the day to arrive, so I could get my own birth story and pass down the torch of 'I was ripped from arse to elbow when I gave birth' to expectant parents after me.

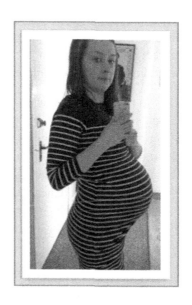

Chapter 2

The Most *'Magical'* Day of My Life

For two days I experienced contractions before giving birth. It was hot outside, it was hot inside; a real rare occurrence in Scotland. Although, to be fair, being 40 weeks pregnant, I could be sitting in the Arctic and still complain it was too hot.

One day past our due date, we took the car for a valet. Being first-time parents, we had the belief that everything must be as clean as possible as to prevent infection or harm to our baby. Which of course meant the car would be cleaned to within an inch of its life.

After dropping the car off to be cleaned, we walked (I waddled) to the local supermarket. It all seems irrelevant, but it's part of the story; I knew I was having contractions and knew my mucus plug was about to pop. And it did, as I discovered in the supermarket toilet. Totally one of those cringe things I'll be saying to my daughter in years to come, hoping to make her squirm. Me, positively proud in nostalgia; her, disgusted with my fond memory that I came bundling out the supermarket toilet, beaming that my mucus plug had started to drip out of my body!

I couldn't sleep that night on account of the surges pulsing through my back and groin. Finding my only comfort sitting upright, I made a pregnant lady 'nest' of sorts on our corner sofa, cushions propped up behind me to provide at least some form of support to my aching back. I pulled all the electronic necessities close to me, in the hope they would get me through a night of patchy sleep, at best. The TV remote and phone were now my distractions, my lifelines in-between the minutes of intense tightening of my pelvis, as my partner slept peacefully in the bedroom nearby. I wanted to be alone, in my happy place, watching *Friends* episodes while I tried my best to doze in and out of sleep. I remember the pain being bearable, coming and going, no structure, no patterns, just tightening of the back, almost like period pains, but far more intense in nature.

The following morning at 10 a.m., I had a midwife appointment to drag my tired, leaking arse to. After arriving and making some small talk, I told her about the 'show' and dreadful night's sleep. All music to any midwife's ears, she quickly popped the question that every tired, aching pregnant lady, loves to hear:

"Shall we have a look?"

Knees bent, with my long navy-blue summer dress ruffled up under my arse, she did what all midwives do and had a good old peep inside my genitals. To my utter delight, I was 2cm dilated, and so I jumped (metaphorically) at the prospect of a membrane sweep, in the hope it would encourage labour to begin. I was so thankful the sleepless night and all that pain had all been for something - a whole 2cms! I was happy with that. I recall the midwife saying I would have this baby soon; she would be seeing me in a few days with my newborn. Not one to enjoy disappointment (who does?), I mentally doubted her words and disagreed; I'd still be pregnant this time next week.

After the midwife ~~'high fived' my diaphragm~~ gave me a membrane sweep, I met my parents to walk around the local shopping centre and grab a bite to eat. My contractions had become **exceptionally** intense by this point. Looking back, I'm not sure why I ever doubted I was in labour. Yes. *I really did doubt it!* 2cms dilated, experiencing pains that caused me to stop what I was doing, face turning red, unable to speak, going within myself, pushing out all other sounds while I focused on my breathing, and I *actually doubted* I was in labour at all. I know. *I'm an idiot.*

Walking around the shops, I held in the pain and gave off an air of *'I'm fine'* - in the exact way Ross Geller was *"fine"* when he so clearly wasn't. I was out in public, so I didn't want to be that crazy pregnant woman holding on to shelves for dear life and threatening strangers with a full-blown Fanny Show, as if I was about to give birth there and then. My poor concerned parents kept asking if I was okay, and did I want to leave? Of course, I replied with *"No, I'm fine, I just need to wait a minute. It will stop".* They did side-eyed each other a few times, bewildered at my behaviour and reluctance to go home, but they know better than to try *tell me* what to do. In rebellion, I would have set up camp in that bloody shopping centre and crossed my legs so hard, the baby would never be born!

As if shopping while in the early stages of labour, with your first child, totally clueless, wasn't enough, my partner and I had arranged for our mortgage broker to visit the flat. Falling pregnant gave us the boot up the arse we both needed in order to purchase our first house. We had been renting for years with a view of buying our own place one day. That "one day" kept getting pushed back, further and further, as we found new ways to piss our cash away. But man, did we have a beastly retro gaming collection! That was all about to change. Soon after seeing those two pink lines, we decided to embark on one of the most stressful things a person can do; buy a home and move, all whilst having our first child. Combining two of the most stressful life events to take on at the same time? Well, is it any wonder *why* I was so prone to Post Natal Depression (PND)…?

Continuing with our 'genius' vibe, we arranged for the mortgage broker to finalise our first house purchase and sign off on all the documents - 2 days after our due date. *Excellent timing.*

After perfecting my contorted strain face - the likes you'd expect to see from the World's Strongest Man as he picks up an aeroplane with one hand - it was time to leave the shops and head home to meet the mortgage broker. He was a lovely man but **very** chatty. The contractions had upped their game quite a bit by the time he arrived to our flat. Not only could I no longer could I hold a conversation, but I didn't want to listen to the conversation either. He spoke for what felt like a week and a half - about what, I have no idea. Something about the mortgage and no going back? No clue. Couldn't give a shit at this point. I could have signed over my unborn child to his care for all I knew.

Again, like out with my parents, I sat there and smiled, nodding along with the conversation, willing him to get out the fucking door so I could moan and rock back and forth to my wide, swollen, pregnant arse's content. Waving the mortgage broker off and out the door, my partner returned to the living room to find me bending over the sofa, trying to release some of the back tension. I turned to him and confessed the utter torture I'd been enduring the whole time, moaning that that man took a *fucking age* to go through the paperwork! My partner was shocked, having no idea of my torment, telling me I hid it well and he suspected nothing. I, however, felt I had turned every shade of purple and red as I sat across from the broker, wishing he would leave, as I widened my eyes in some pale attempt to let the pain exude from my body - preferably into the soul of the nearest male, as this was all the man's fault after all. No good can come from being too close to a man, as I was about to find out.

The Beginning of The End... Of My Perfect Labia

I remember my 'last' meal well. Being a child in adult form, it was some microwaveable *'Louisiana'* potato dish. Basically, cubed potato with cheese and hot sauce, with a few soft and saggy vegetables thrown in for whatever measure (not health that's for sure). And yes, it was as delicious as it sounds. With the pain intensifying after a long day of pretending that my body wasn't actually expanding to let a child vacate my genitals, I thought a nice relaxing bath would give me a few minutes of respite. So, I filled what little space was left in my belly with the much needed microwaved 'nutrition' in order to endure the mammoth task of birthing a child, and filled the bathtub with just 3 inches of water, as my pregnant arse was sure to send even that small amount spilling over the edge.

I'm unsure why we tell heavily pregnant women to have a bath? Sure, the tepid bath water does calm and relax the body, providing some sense of pain relief, but how exactly are you expecting her to haul her sore arse back out of that bath again? With absolutely no form or grace, that's how. I remember calling my partner for assistance as I lay there grunting, unable to pull myself up on the porcelain sides of the tub. Bless, my partner did his best to hook me out, holding onto my arm while I mumbled how stupid this whole pregnancy thing was, rendering me incapable of moving my body in the tub. Meanwhile I was meant to be in there to find a moment of zen. Any peace I found swiftly vanished as my partner pulled me up to my feet as I sidestepped out of the tub, allowing me to groan like a 90-year-old man pushing up from his armchair. In a very narrow tenement flat bathroom (they are far longer than they are wide), it's a one person in, one person out policy, so kudos to my partner for that act of ingenuity and patience, all while I moaned incessantly that this baby cooking nonsense wasn't what I seen advertised and I was so, *so very* over it.

The following hours consisted of being uncomfortable with *everything*. TV and film didn't appeal to me as I couldn't relax or focus on much. Contractions came strong, yet not with enough intensity for a trip to the hospital. We did try various methods of pain relief, including filling my *Tigger* hot water bottle, believing, like the bath, that the heat would provide some respite from the relentless contractions. I **hated** the hot water bottle. No sooner was it filled when I decided it was a hard pass from me. Probably as the water reminded me of the indignity I endured as I groaned my growler out of the bathtub just a few hours previously. We never emptied the water from that hot water bottle. Not for years. We couldn't bring ourselves to pour those memories down the sink. Disgusting, I know. But this hot water bottle, and the water inside that was never used, somehow became an integral part of that night, and thus our memory of it. To be honest, it would have made more sense to keep that shitty microwave meal wrapping than the hot water bottle; at least the meal gave some satisfaction.

With the pregnant lady bathed, fed and ready to saw in half the next male that ever-dared mutter females to be the weaker sex again, my partner took this as a sign to leave and get some rest for the night. To this day, the fact that my partner said he needed to go to bed and get some sleep still brings me laughter. Here was me, about to begin night number two of no sleep, but this poor bugger needed a bit of shut-eye. He will argue he knew the birth would happen the following day and he wanted to be rested enough to be there for me. I will simply ignore this logical fact and tease him till the end of time that he left me labouring, through the night, by myself, while he got some beauty sleep.

The truth is, I wanted to be alone, but I'll let that slide and continue to tease him, especially in company. That's a birthing mother's prerogative, right? Restless, I left him sleeping in our bed and set up camp for the second night on the sofa. With more *Friends* episodes and paracetamol as my aids, I rocked and moaned in my nest the whole night long. As contractions grew in strength, I found I went further within myself, focusing on my breathing, mentally telling myself that the pain would stop in a minute or two and all I had to do was make it to the end of the contraction. Then, I would be able to watch my favourite *Friends* character, Rachel, swish that magnificent hair as my reward. Having no pattern to the surges, between contractions I would doze off. For what length of time, I couldn't tell you. But I did make it through several seasons of *Friends*, season seven being my all-time favourite.

The turning point occurred around 6/7 a.m. Sitting and rocking became painful, something which, for hours, had brought me comfort. As I perched on the edge of our corner sofa, moaning and groaning longer and louder, I wanted my partner with me now. I was reaching my limit and I needed his comfort, which I now understand is a huge sign that things had progressed and the baby would be with us shortly. At the time, however, I thought I was just tired - which I was - and couldn't bear the pain much longer. So I woke up *Sleeping Beauty*, proclaiming that I was in a lot of pain, and I needed him to be with me: a.k.a. make me something to eat and call the hospital as I was at the point of begging for something a little stronger than paracetamol.

Mum And Her Uterus Know Best

We didn't have an app for timing contractions; I'm not sure I really kept track of them at all. My partner did say that he thought the contractions had been coming thick and fast. I think at one point he timed them just to prove that I was deluded in my sleep-deprived state and that maybe we should actually call the hospital. He seemed to be far more in the know than I was. After two nights of no sleep and mind occupying contractions, I didn't know what I was doing other than trying to get through the minutes, just to feel the relief when the contractions stopped before they began again.

For whatever ridiculous reason, I decided I would have a shower before we called the midwife. You think I would have learnt my lesson with the bathtub aggravation the night before. No sooner had I hauled my giant belly into the shower than my waters broke. It wasn't like the tidal wave of water we see in films; mine was more a of a trickle, resembling that of a weak pelvic floor with a very full bladder, hearing a very funny joke. As the water ran down my leg in an even, steady stream - half excited with this new development, half regretting my life choice of having a shower - I shouted to my partner to come help. He gave me much needed support as I struggled to lift my legs over the bath side and out of the shower. I didn't have the strength for lifting my legs and balancing at the same time. As my partner steadied me, waiting for contractions to ease before I could move, my body began to shake uncontrollably. For the first time in my life, I felt as if I wasn't physically in control of my own body. I didn't know if my legs had the strength to keep me standing as the shaking intensified in combination with the contractions. My partner did his best to hide his worry as he dried me off and helped me into my clothes. That shaking, as I would later find out, is a normal and welcomed part of the final stages of labour and he needn't have worried. It meant the baby would be with us very, *very* soon. And something the arsehole of a midwife on the phone could do with reading up on…

Upon calling the maternity unit, we felt belittled and ignored. The midwife on the phone informed us this was our first baby and labour could take some time. Despite my clearly dazed and tired confusion, unable to answer the midwife's questions as the contractions had become so strong and hard, we were told **not** to come to the unit. Sit it out, wait a while longer. We explained that I had been labouring for two days, I had been 2cm dilated the day before, my waters had ruptured, that I was shaking uncontrollably and that I couldn't string a sentence together let alone answer her questions about contraction lengths or how many pads had I soaked with amniotic fluid. But none of it mattered. Being first time parents, *the midwife* knew best, and we had to stay put or else we would just be turned back from the unit when we got there for not being far enough along in my labour.

Defeated and shaking with pain, and really not wanting to listen to the sound of anyone's voice - especially one that wasn't listening to mine - I handed my partner the phone as I returned to my spot on the corner sofa where I had been perched for the previous two nights, rocking back and forth. I couldn't mentally endure trying to speak while my body pulsed in extreme discomfort. I left my partner taking the ill advice from the midwife as I reached my sofa sanctuary. However, this time I did not sit. Instinct took over my body and a few minutes after being told my labour would take a *"lot longer"* …

A primal roar erupted from deep within me as my body instinct-ively moved onto all fours, knees bent up on the sofa, shaking hands holding onto the sturdy sofa back for support. Through the moans I cried *"I want to push! Call an ambulance now!"*. My groaning body and *I knew better* than the midwife and it was time for the baby to arrive. No matter how *"short"* my contractions were, in the opinion of the midwife. No matter how little amniotic fluid had been released, in the opinion of the midwife. I hunkered down on that sofa, mooing and moaning, nature taking over as I felt my body wanting to push the baby out. It kinda felt like I wanted to push a large jobby out, but one I had no control over. A strange feeling really, since we spend our whole life mindfully mastering our sphincters and how to control them.

Running through from the next room on account of the cave woman gripping the sofa, my partner dialled 999 while I continued to hip jive, letting out a whole manner of animalistic groans. The dispatcher on the other end of the phone asked my partner to pre-pare for the birth of his daughter, to go find some towels, and asked that I lie on the bed, in position for him to be verbally guided in his midwifery crash course. Only too willing to oblige (unlike my freaked-out partner), I had already decanted the leggings and knickers, tossing them to the side as I waddled my half naked body into the bedroom. As I lay on the bed, my partner paced the room while listening to the instructions of the dispatcher with great intent. His free hand frantically rubbed across his brow, perplexed by the whole situation, shitting himself as he heard the words: *"I'm going to talk you through delivering a baby".* You've not seen terror until you've seen your somewhat anxious-about-birth-partner receive the news that he would now be playing the role of midwife. Then you've not seen terror like him trying to locate enough clean towels for the task.

Lying on our bed, my legs seemed to pull up onto my feet, bending my knees, allowing my hips to open. Every so often, my partner would place a '*comforting'* hand on my leg, to which I growled ~~hurled venom towards him~~, **"DON'T TOUCH ME!"**. Every time he placed that *annoying as fuck* hand on me, I let rip! He was doing that thing people do on the phone, aimlessly roaming about, not realising that they are dangerously close to death on account of being a pain in my arse. Poor guy, just trying to comfort me. Meanwhile, I'm making him sound like the world's most harassing partner to the dispatcher on the other end of the line. Not knowing what to do with himself as he received instruction about how to help me give birth, my partner continued to put his life in his hands, touching my leg in his absent-minded state.

Much to my partner's **joy**, three medics quickly appeared at our door: two females (one a junior just learning the ropes) and a male. Boy, did the junior get some life experience that day! No sooner had they arrived, placing a large cannister on the bed, did they ask if I wanted gas and air? Um, **yes** fucking please I do! As I inhaled what can only be described as heaven at this point, they turned to my partner and asked if we had any wipes, so they could give my '*necessaries*' a wipe before inspection. There was a whole manner of things throbbing in and out of my vagina, and they needed to see if we had the option of moving to the hospital before the baby would pop out.

Diligently, my partner ran off to find wipes, quickly returning and handing them to one of the female medics. As she removed one from its packet, she turned to my partner and asked, *"Do you have any other wipes?"* before bursting into laughter. My poor, worried, frantic partner had brought them *Dettol* wipes for my fanny. *Dettol.* As in, anti-bacterial kills 99% of viruses and leaves you with a sparkling clean kitchen worktop, *Dettol* wipes. Well, at least I would be 'lemony fresh' for the main event, I guess.

After a quick clean up with *appropriate* wipes, the paramedics had a good look at the scene of the crime below, then quickly posed the question to us: stay in the flat to give birth, with a high probability of ordering a new mattress today (as it was about to be destroyed) or attempt the less than 5-minute drive to the hospital to save a few hundred quid. I think we will take the money-saving option B, please. And with that, we packed up and got ready to make our way to the hospital. And by "packed up", I mean there was no way in hell I was putting knickers on, let alone those leggings, so they best get acquainted with Grizzly Adams down there and hearing the

words, *"I will do it"*, growl from my tongue if anyone dared help
me up. Funnily enough, I didn't mind the paramedics touching my
legs, but maybe that's because they brought the good drugs with
them.

Vagina On Tour

We lived in an old traditional tenement flat in the Govan area of
Glasgow; a notorious area, next to Ibrox Football Stadium. On a
very busy street. On the top floor. Way up large, steep winding
stairs, right at the very top of the block of flats. Deciding it would
be in my best interests - seeing as I couldn't walk the length of
myself by this point - I was strapped to the paramedic's chair so we
could begin the descent down the stairs. Either I got a contraction
on each step, or the movement of lugging my throbbing arse down
the stairs exacerbated them, but whatever it was, the trip down was
brutal.

Contractions seemed to come thick and fast, more intense in nature
than they had been previously. My body taking over once again, I
made it my mission to release the vagina from the 'modesty' blanket the medics had placed over my naked arse and thighs. I wanted
my legs, and my vagina, as wide as possible, not giving one shit
about where I was. Instinct knows no shame. As they hauled me
down the stairs, I groaned, throwing the blanket off, trying to
ensure any neighbours that popped out to see what all the com-
motion was about would need therapy in years to come.

Eventually, we reached the communal doors of the tenement flat,
opening them to be greeted with the bright morning sun, and more
importantly, the ambulance, the place where I could hide my shame
and let the beaver free. We just had to bump down the external
stairs of the flat and open those glorious double doors at the back of
the vehicle, but not before one last contraction. Again, I threw the

blanket from me, widened my legs and let my vagina see the sights of Govan she was so desperately trying to see. In broad daylight, on a sunny Tuesday morning, just as the morning rush was getting well under way, I let my vagina have one final farewell sniff of the Govan air before being rushed off to become a mother.

In the ambulance, one paramedic asked a host of questions as she waited for the other medics to pack up and get this peep show on the road. When did I last eat? What was it? *'I don't give a fuck'*, I thought as I puffed on the gas and air, throwing back answers about times that hadn't even passed, *"I had toast at 10"* I said. *"It's only 9 a.m."* came the reply of the paramedic. Whatever, who gives a toss?! I have a baby *literally* hanging out of me. Get your foot on the gas and let's go, what's the hold-up?! Just as we are set to leave, my partner pipes up: he's forgot his wallet. We now need to wait while he 'runs' back up the stairs to retrieve it. Honestly, as if he wasn't already on thin ice... So, there I wait, in agony, being quizz-ed about my last meal, while Daft Chops climbs the tall winding stairs all the way to the tip of the castle, rummaging around the flat for what seems like an age trying to locate his wallet. *No bother.* I'll just wait down here in the ambulance, showing these poor people my actual insides while you go gather your belongings, take your time.

When Lord Sloth appeared back down the stairs and into the ambulance, we finally set off; wallet in hand, dignity left behind. With sirens wailing, we make it to the hospital in record time. Quickly, I was wheeled down to the birthing suite. I like to think we passed that rude and dismissive midwife as we screeched our way in. If so, I hope my vagina threw her shade and a face of *'told you so'* as she flicked her poorly maintained pubic hair to the side in a boss bitch manner.

We arrived at a brightly lit room and thanked the amazing paramedics for all their help as they wished us good luck while handing us over to the care of the midwife. I demanded that I, **myself**, would get out of the medic's chair and get myself up on the large bed in front of me, with no one touching me, and when I saw fit. Gathering my strength in between a contraction, I 'hopped' up onto the bed, my modesty all but a distant memory as my vagina became acquainted with yet another stranger on this fine day.

Lying on the hospital bed, I ignored my body's want to push with each fresh contraction, something I had no idea you could even do. Each contraction now was more painful than the last, and I was scared. The closer my baby came to birthing, the more intense the pain. And so I puffed on the gas and air, making jokes as I progressively lost my mind. As my eyeballs visited the back of my skull, I turned to my partner and said, *"I'm so fucking high right now"*. Then I complained that I would never be doing this ever again, and how the fuck could my sister-in-law do this twice?! **Twice in the same year**! Crazy. There was none of that screaming and shouting I had so been looking forward to. I didn't grab my partner by the balls and demon-scream that this was all his fault. I wasted my chance by opting to crack out random jokes, amusing no one but myself, all while continuing to ignore my body wanting to push, believing if I just held the baby in, all the pain would somehow stop.

I don't remember the midwife speaking to us, I guess she must have. My memory is of me, lying on the bed, as she, the midwife walked about. My partner was off to my side, neither one of us feeling exactly comfortable in the situation. The one phrase I do remember the midwife saying was, *"I'll need to cut you"*, referring to my lack of pushing. I don't exactly know why she said that, and in truth, six years later I'm still angry and upset that she did. It was unnecessary. It frightened me and prompted me in panic to ask if my baby was okay? She replied that yes, my baby was fine. Seeing this remark as a threat, and knowing in myself I was delaying the inevitable, I pushed my baby out in one go, way after the contraction had stopped (100% do not recommend).

And so, my beautiful, perfect and utterly gorgeous baby girl was born. All within 2 hours of these supposedly 'clueless', first-time parents, calling the midwife asking for her help.

Contractions not intense enough, my arse.

Chapter 3

Pushing The Baby Out Is the Easy Part

Well done to me! I had pushed a human out of my body, fired her out in one swift pelvic floor wrecking push. Phew! That was me, all done. Finished. Good to get up and go, right?

Umm, no…

Women speak so much of birth and the lead up to it, but virtually nothing of the events that occur soon after the baby expulsion. Personally, I found everything after the final push to be far more invasive than the act of birth itself. In the minutes leading up to my daughter 'popping' out, the room seemed to fill with doctors and nurses. All there to ensure a safe and healthy arrival of my baby I presumed. Afterwards it seemed as though the room was just as busy, nurses bustling about cleaning, while the doctor was tasked with damage control south of the border. She pulled a large light from above to illuminate everything below that has rarely seen the light of day, let alone an illumination that would rival the best 'Insta-worthy' ring light. The large light shone up from my vagina, making the doctor behind it almost faceless as she and the nurse mumbled between themselves about stitches, lengths and the best plan of action, only for them to be interrupted by a concerned midwife.

Apparently, I wasn't quite finished getting things out my body just yet. There was an incomplete placenta on the table in front of me and, clearly loving a good old jigsaw puzzle, the doctors demanded that they go inside me to find the missing pieces. This rugged placenta business had some urgency about it. The doctor told me that they like to see a complete placenta on the table; anything else came with the worry of infection that could make me seriously ill. My partner and I, not knowing anything about rugged, partial, or retained placentas, listened to every word of the professionals. For my partner, it made him worried and anxious. His sole concern was for me at this point, worrying profusely for my wellbeing on account of what the doctor had to say. For me, it meant nothing. I knew no better at the time and presumed this was a normal part of the process, just another stage to go through, I supposed. Like having your battered vagina sewn up at an impromptu designer-vagina surgery party that I was to attend straight after they found my missing placenta.

After the brief introduction to the anatomy of the uterus and all it holds, the doctor stood by my legs as she explained how they would remove the placenta from within me. What happened next, I can only describe as my body being used as a giant squishy toy. They created some form of vacuum up in the space that once grew my baby. As the doctor placed one hand on my stomach, the other had a roam around my cervix for the missing placenta. It felt like she was gut-punching it right out of me, akin to that horrible feeling when the wind gets knocked out of you. I lay there holding my baby, thinking, ' *What the absolute fuck is this? Hadn't I done the hard part?'* I thought now was the part when the magical rainbow of love for my newborn would burst from my chest. Instead, I was pretty sure I must have been the first woman in history to receive such treatment as no one had ever warned me of placenta fight club. Of all the internal parties conducted by the many health care professionals over the previous months, this was, by a huge, sad, vagina-dragging mile, <u>the worst</u>.

Once I had completed morphing into a human placenta confetti canon, I learned how I had been torn twice, with several "*grazes*" ("grazes" not the word I would use to describe a tattered fanny), over both labia. The doctor informed me that they would 'numb' the area before they began stitching my poor ragged labia. Apologising in response to my body all but hitting the ceiling after the first injection of lidocaine, the doctor continued to inject my labia as I lay there, trying to keep my body from twitching as much as humanly possible when someone is sticking a needle into your raw and bruised genitals.

Deathly gripping the gas and air, inhaling as much of it as my lungs would allow, I winched through the pain of the lidocaine needle piercing my labia. In my other arm, I held my daughter, rebuffing the plea from my partner that he holds her while I endure the obvious pain I was in. At this point, I had been through so much already; I had so many people examine my insides, had shown the whole of Glasgow my vagina and more, and had willingly allowed internal inspections to anyone who asked, but the aftermath of birth broke me.

Tears streamed down my face as I exhaled all that had happened in the previous hours and days, letting out a pent-up breath of relaxation that we had done it; my baby was here. And yet my body was still being invaded. I had been excavated, quite literally. Now I was being nipped, pulled, prodded and poked during a time I had imagined was supposed to be full of bonding and beaming smiles of *'We did it babe!'*. It all felt too much. Physically too much, as I felt the tugs and pulls as the doctor stitched my labia in several places.

F.Y.I., I could feel every. single. stitch. No amount of gas and air could numb the effect of too low a dose of lidocaine for my body.

Instead of telling them I could feel it, I inhaled as much gas as I could, crying as the doctor set about making me *"good as new"*. *I'll crack the jokes here, pal.*

Bless the doctor, she tried her best. But her sewing skills, as I would see in a few months, were utter bollocks. My once symmetrical labia, which nestled neatly away, tucked in for the night, would now be host to what I can only describe as a whole extra labia; perched on top of another like a lonely hitchhiker who wants to come to the party, poking her head out of the car window to catch some wind beneath her arms. This labia anecdote isn't a metaphor; I could very much use my new 5th labia to catch those butterflies during a game of *Elefun* with my daughter. So, I guess it's an improvement, right?

I Agreed to Childbirth, Not This Peep Show

Maybe I am just a bit of a prude, but up until this point, I had never had this many strangers walking around my bare fanny, having a gander, my legs up in stirrups, creating the best possible viewing pleasure for those of that persuasion. I found the whole experience uncomfortable, to say the least. It seemed like there was always a constant chatter going on, debating how best to repair my mashed potato genitals, rugged placenta and the need for an antibiotic, all while the room seemed to be a flurry of people cleaning in preparation for the next poor woman. Everything was so overwhelming. I felt like I had no time to comprehend what was going on, no time to breathe for myself. There was no time to create headspace, pushing aside the vagina wars below, so I could focus on my baby. At that moment in time, I wanted nothing more than for everyone to stop pulling and tugging at me, to stop speaking amongst themselves while intermittently adding me to the conversation. I needed space and time to understand all that was happening in the room. I wanted a big, reassuring, comforting hug; the type you give to a child when they put on a pity show after stubbing their toe. I wanted the clock to stop, just long enough so I could catch up with it.

As I lay on the bed, my partner stood at my side, stroking my head and smiling in awe at our daughter. He kissed me on the forehead, telling me how proud he was of me, how amazing I had been and what a beautiful baby girl we had. I remember wanting to cry, over and over, but I held it in. I felt stupid for crying, not able to understand why I longed for this release. It's easy to see, now, why the tears wanted to flow; take your pick from any of the above and it's enough to make anyone cry. But I just lay there, holding my daughter, containing my many emotions as best I could. I had already cried and didn't want to be that weepy new mother. I was trying, already at this very early stage, to be like all the other mothers out there who profess this was, and is, the most magical day of their lives. The glorious moment when they know what true love is. When they look at their baby and see the light of God himself shine down upon them. Knowing in this instant life was made, complete, fulfilled.

What a '*pile of shit*' that was I thought.

Hold The Baby While I Wash This Leaking Watermelon

After the body assault was complete, I was told I should have a shower.

A fucking shower.

Had I not been through enough that I was now expected to stand and wash my body in a cold, unfamiliar hospital setting? I remember feeling so weak that I was unsure I would even be able to stand, let alone walk to the shower room. The last thing I wanted to do was move. For one, I had no idea what had happened south of the border. Would my vagina want to stand up? Would she try to make an escape? Secondly, I had just demolished the most tasteless, dry hospital sandwich (which I thought tasted like heaven), chasing it down with two sugar-filled Bourbon biscuits (and not the good cheap ones), but I wanted more. My energy and sugar levels were non-existent. I didn't think I would be able to sit up, let alone get off the bed and wash my new, straight out the back of a van, designer vagina.

My partner held our daughter as I pulled myself up from the bed, gingerly, on account of intense sensitivity thanks to my new vaginal facelift. That first stand after birth needs to have its own Insta handle or something. A surreal experience. You slowly slide your body to the edge of the bed, dropping your leg down with more patience and accuracy than a sniper. Terrified that one swift movement would rip the gates of stitch hell open. One toe touches the ground tentatively, and the sole and heel follow suit. Slowly, *slowly*. If all goes well, you dip your toe of the other foot to the ground, as if this is the first time you have felt the ground beneath your feet, unsure of its solidity. Then comes the test of faith: will you be able to stand up? And will you be able to stand up without your arse falling to the ground? I guess it wouldn't quite reach the ground seeing as your underwear has been stuffed with enough maternity pads that, *should* anything happen to fall, it would land on a comfy bed and cushion, snuggling down for the night.

Cautiously, you lift your arse from the bed, your arm still reaching back and holding on, more for moral support than anything else. At first, you stand, knees bent while you analyse the situation; there are still some trust issues to be overcome with you and those legs before you fully pass over all your weight. Everything seems legit, so you straighten. Knees first, then your back, you stand up tall. You've made it! You've done it! No organs have fallen out your vagina! Although there seems to be a vast amount of *something* falling out there but… best not to think about that too much.

Now all you need to do is move. You can see the room in front of you. All you need to do is navigate that watermelon between your legs, mindful not to tip it. Not to squash or cause any damaging pressure. Just move your body across the room without letting what you can only presume is a lung due to its consistency and sliminess, fall from between your legs.

Making it to the shower room in as much of 'one-piece' a person can be after projectile shooting a baby from their genitals, I asked my partner to leave the shower room. I was embarrassed with my fatigue and how weak I felt. As my legs trembled, I stepped into the shower and for the first time in nine months, I was alone. Under the water, I took a minute to stop and take myself in. I looked down at my now empty body, feeling tattered, as though I had been thrown to the side, told to wash up and rinse off any evidence of one of the greatest acts of the human body. The last thing I wanted to do was be in a shower, alone (although I made that choice), bathing myself after a whirlwind of a morning that I was yet to wrap my head around, let alone rid myself of it. However, I didn't put up a fight. I didn't even second guess the midwife or admit I needed more time to process everything. I went with the 'flow', being assured that going for a shower would be the best time to have a pee for now. Little did I know how very sound that advice was with my twice torn labia and several "grazes".

Blood trickled down my thigh as I tried, with no success, to clean the birth from my body. I wasn't sure how much blood was too much blood, having been warned to report back any large blood clots, but for what reason, I wasn't sure? Something to do with my placenta, I presumed. I wanted desperately to please the nurse and my partner by stopping this blood or at least evidence of it, from running down my body. But the blood wouldn't stop. I'm not sure what I expected. It's logical now to think that a human who has just given birth will, of course, bleed straight after the event. Yet at the time I felt my body was weak, that *I* was weak, failing at birth somehow on account of the blood filling the drain.

As I turned the shower off, my body continued to foil my plans of strolling back out there like nothing had happened, as though I was more than ready to have a go on the trampoline, followed by a quick bout of boxing. Mustering up what little strength I had, I stepped out of the shower, trying to dry myself quickly. I was embarrassed at the mess I had made of the towels, believing that I would be scolded or cause some form of alarm that would require the circus to crawl back into my uterus. I quickly grabbed my pyjamas and added a large maternity pad to my underwear, my saving grace in the fight against the post-birth river. As I pulled my underwear on, I did the dreaded 'feel', tentatively moving my hand down to the lady of the hour. Gasping, my eyes wide in horror, I immediately regretted my life choice.

Huge.

Huge she was. Full-on 'cuppable' and then some. Being unable to bend or manoeuvre my body in any way to get a better viewing (thankfully), all I had was the sensitivity of my hand to mentally draw a picture of the battleground below. Needless to say, my fingers didn't depict the greatest works of art, nor were they kind. Swollen to depths I had no idea a vagina could swell to and fuelled by terror, I quickly shuffled it away into the maternity pads. I mentally stroked my back saying *"There, there, I'm sure it will get better soon"* in my best attempt to pull my jaw back up from the floor (~~along with my vagina~~). Fucking hell… they should crack out the good, strong drugs for that experience alone!

In need of some form of warning on the door, the village clown thought it a good idea to add a full-length mirror into that bathroom. Pulling my dark grey pyjamas bottoms up and scraping my hair into what would be my mum-bun hair style from now until infinity, I caught my reflection in that bastarding mirror. There I stood, in all my post-partum glory: dull, pale, weak and grey. So far removed from who I was just days before. I felt like an empty vessel, second class to the prized possession next door. My stomach full, yet empty. Jelly-like in consistency, full of weight with nothing in it, an odd experience entirely.

Swallowing back tears, I stared at myself as my weak legs continued to shake, struggling to keep me upright. My boobs had begun to leak colostrum and seemed to triple in size from their already enlarged state. I just stared back at myself, so sadly, at this helpless stranger who didn't know what the fuck had just hit them, oblivious to what was to come. My body, gone, now replaced with a machine; my mind not yet making that leap. As I stood there, my boobs bursting out of my vest, my pad already being soaked through, stomach bulging through my pyjamas, glaring back at myself, I was, in that moment, a mother. And it was not the image I'd had in mind at all.

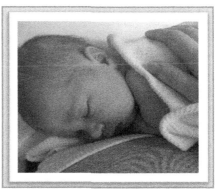

Chapter 4

Congratulations On the Birth of Your Trauma!

The day my daughter was born was not the most magical day of my life. Instead, it was a date stamped into my brain for all the wrong reasons. It took me a long time to come round to the idea that this 'glorious' day was not all that glorious. I felt unheard by the medical staff for the majority of my pregnancy, and thereafter. At 38 weeks pregnant, during a routine midwife appointment, I was told my daughter was breech. I knew she wasn't; I was the one accustomed to her movements, touch and position. Yet the midwife 'knew better'. She told me I would be sent for a scan and if she was breech, I would **NEED** to have a C-section. No questions. No room for sympathy. No want to discuss the matter. I was **told,** there and then, as factual as the day was Monday, that I would have by my baby cut from my stomach and handed to me over a blue protective cloth.

I drove to my parent's house afterwards and retold the story to my mum, bursting into tears at the mention of the words 'C-section'. That should never have happened, but I trusted and respected the midwife. Who was I, really? The first-time mother with no clue, as it had been made out in the whole nine months of my pregnancy.

Every other midwife after this didn't sit well with me either. Not the one on the phone, when I tried to speak through my painful contractions, pleading I had been up for two nights labouring. Not the one who brought my daughter into the world after threatening her mother. None of them treated me like I was human. I felt processed like cattle from all but a few of the medical professionals I encountered. Only one midwife, during the night, when I was breastfeeding my daughter for what felt like the 1000th time, gave me the friendly head tilt and encouraging words of *"you are doing well"*, before she offered me a cup of tea. I was surrounded by people who were there to protect me and my baby. All I felt towards our time there is anger at their words and lack of giving a shit; the lack of recognition that I was a unique individual, new to the whole situation. Rather I felt like a checkbox exercise, a bed dweller to be processed as efficiently as possible in order to make way for another trauma victim.

As a new mother, I kept all the negative thoughts in my head, joining in on the post-birth review with fellow mothers, telling light-hearted jokes about the pain and stitches. All the while, I concealed how I really felt, how draining and foreign it was. How strange I found it to be a first-class passenger for nine months, only to be all but kicked out the aircraft when my contractions began. I left the labour suite traumatised, tired and alone, not knowing what to do with my baby or if I was even allowed to dress her myself.

My instinct was to provide for my daughter straight away. Yet in the same breath, I instantly internalised my pain and feelings around birth, glossing over them with the accepted 'motherly' way to reminisce about the events that unfolded. It would be over a year before I heard about the term **'birth trauma'**, and it would take another three years for me to feel validated enough to prescribe that term to my experience and the triggers it would instil within me.

Let's make it clear: childbirth is invasive. It's intimate, it's unique, it's major, and it poses quite the impact on the mother, child, partner, and anyone who is involved, positively or negatively. Birth isn't to be dismissed purely because centuries of women have been doing it, seemingly making it 'old news'. Nor should it be celebrated and forced upon women as one of the 'greatest' days of their life. It can be empowering, awe-inspiring and beautiful, and with such energy that the sheer love and joy experienced could heal the world if only we left the labour room door open.

As I found out, the hard way, birth can also **be traumatic**. No matter which way it happens, no matter how 'well' it all went, it can, and it does, cause trauma, stress, anxiety, depression, and a whole host of other issues in women and their partners. Yet this is a secret most of us withhold. No mother wants to describe the birth of her child as traumatic. Fuck, we don't want to describe it as anything other than 'the best day of my life'.

The sad fact is, as I learned a year after birthing my daughter, that birth trauma is a real thing, and it is prevalent. A lot of mothers experience some kind of traumatic response towards childbirth, even within birth scenarios that seemed as though everything went well and according to plan. (Well, I didn't quite 'plan' on flashing my arse to the whole of Glasgow in the process). Just like the birth of my daughter went well, trauma can still occur, leaving the mother confused, insecure and believing her thoughts to be wrong in regard to the whole event.

The birth of my daughter really fucked me up. As I lay there afterwards, holding my 'bundle of joy', bewildered by the event and emotions, PND took up residence. Of that I am 100% certain. I was not myself after birth. I birthed my daughter, but also birthed a new version of myself alongside her. My memory after childbirth was of holding my baby on my chest, looking at her and thinking… nothing. I didn't feel like me. I didn't look like me, nor did I feel like a mother, the instinctive beast I presumed I would morph into as soon as the vagina had finished her handiwork. Alas, the only thing that morphed here was my vagina, into a now 5 labia filled flap-fest of lidocaine and stitching, the owner now an empty shell that would be filled with a depressive hermit.

Roll Up! Roll Up! Behold, My Cervix, For All to See

We all need to take a huge leap back and really look at pregnancy and childbirth. Forget about the golden nugget at the end of it, the precious gem that causes a flurry of cooing and oohing. I know, shocking of me, but let's put the baby to the side for five minutes and realise there's another person in the room. Let's talk about the human who housed the baby, who gave up a lot of who they are for that entire time, making a huge sacrifice for their family. The mother. The mother and her journey in pregnancy and birth.

The one factor that is always present within pregnancy is that the birthing body almost becomes the property of everyone else. It is handed over on a plate (well, a somewhat cushioned bed) to anyone who fancies having a gander, whether that be a midwife, a doctor, a doula, or even a very inquisitive partner. At various points in pre-gnancy the mothers' body will be examined, with the amount of times usually increasing in the latter stages to determine if birth is imminent or possible. It can feel as though the pregnant body becomes a free to view, interactive play toy. At the time if it means getting a baby out of you, a hand or five (not all at the same time, though I'm fairly certain at this point in the game it wouldn't be too much of a stretch - pun intended), will be delving in and having a root around. *Hands*, if you are lucky. I swear at one point there was a midwife elbow deep, rummaging around in there, trying to decide the solidity of my cervix. To be honest, I did coax her on a bit by telling her to *"go wild"* and "*get right in there*". I was clearly so over being pregnant.

Meeting strangers and pulling down your knickers after a brief introduction comes as ingrained into pregnancy as the art of making the baby itself. Encouraging them to stick their head up your 'yooha' to have a look in the hope they will tell you baby is coming soon, *maybe* not so run of the mill. But once you have revealed your engorged arse crack to one stranger, then you are kind of 'in for a penny in for a pound', whether you like it or not.

We pregnant folk are expected to open our bodies to be touched and prodded whenever the time calls for it, whether that be at routine midwife appointments, checking the size and position of the baby, or in the latter stages of pregnancy when you are willing, *'oh boy, please be in the right spot!'*, begging for a membrane sweep to kick start the birthing process. All of this can be refused by the mother, however, in most cases, women opt to be touched. There is a real and ever-present fear that something is, or could be, wrong with the baby. And so, we push our dignity far down, further than our expanding knickers, and let everyone enter *The Batcave*. Dropping your knickers for people you have never previously met, nor are likely to meet again (which is a blessing at 40 weeks pregnant, without the want to look at a razor, let alone the ability to use the thing on the unruly mane below).

At the very core of these exchanges is still a human, a vulnerable one at that. One solely charged with growing a child. And by fuck do we know it! Anything goes when it comes to the health of our children. Do what you must to our bodies to ensure a safe and healthy arrival. But that doesn't mean we want to be legs akimbo, midwife and student nurse ahoy, rummaging around our cervix. That doesn't mean we enjoy dropping our drawers, feet together, knees to the side, waiting for the midwife to lube up before her excavation. It is still extremely uncomfortable, mentally, and physically. People are flying around the part many consider to be the most intimate area of our bodies. So, when women are not treated as actual humans - humans in vulnerable, uncomfortable, and for some, embarrassing positions - that's when things can have an impact; that's when trauma can occur. You know, kinda like when a midwife threatens to "cut" you while you are in the middle of birthing your baby...

Pregnancy: An Invitation to Comment

We might be able to get on board with the constant 'hands on' approach to our bodies. Every midwife appointment demands we carry our own urine on our person for evaluation. Arms become pin cushions, checking iron levels, receiving immunisations to protect mum and baby from nasties. These are all part of the duties a mum-to-be will endure. Like I say; anything to keep everyone healthy. But being pregnant also comes with often unwanted, multiple sets of 'well meaning' eyes on the mother. Those are the eyes, mouths, and oh so loud sounds of everyone who feels like popping a com-ment towards the mum. And by "those", I mean the majority of society.

Everyone and their dog will comment on the body of a pregnant woman. The size of her bump - I mean her stomach. The shape of her bump - I mean her stomach. Sometimes I think people forget the bump is an extension of the human, rather than something she chose to carry around, like a handbag. And even at that, most people wouldn't outright comment on the size of a woman's hand-bag as it might cause offense, or be seen as rude.

Next to be commented upon is that age old famous pregnancy *"glow"*. Let's be honest, a pregnant woman glows for about three weeks out the entire pregnancy. The first trimester is often a shit show of hormones, hormonal surges, nausea, food aversions, and not actually knowing you are pregnant for several weeks. The third trimester is kinda like the first trimester, except you are over it and full of fire in telling everyone so. It's been nine months of baby growing and you are seriously over being a human growing pod. The second trimester is the only good months, the only time when one may glow... glowing from the amount of take-away grease covering your face, but glowing nonetheless.

As usual - and we really ought to be used to our bodies being subject to whoever wants to narrate over it - the pregnant body is almost like a huge billboard advert, beckoning objectification from others and seen as a blank canvas for comments, ranging from family members to strangers in public. What's important to remember here, is along with the opinions of others, many pregnant women contend with the insecurities inside their own heads, which sways in perception if others provide it the fuel to do so.

The body changes, rapidly, and without consent, during pregnancy. We have no idea what our body will do, how it will change, and crucially for many, how it will look after we give birth. Many people will contest this notion – yet more policing of women's bodies and our thoughts. Body positivity promoters preach that our bodies do not define us or our worth. We should love our lumps, bumps, marks and scars. And I wholeheartedly agree. But if you think women who have been raised in a modern era of magazines, Photoshop and social media, are not going to have deep, ingrained body views, then you are being naïve. More than naïve; unrealistic, silencing and toxic to her mental wellbeing.

Tigers have Stripes, I have Stretch Marks

There is a tricky and fine line to balance between the female body and her mind. On one hand we want to promote every body type, colour, size, shape, etc. We need to see images that we relate to, seeing more of the untouched, filter-free pictures that expose sagging skin post-childbirth. However, these pictures, no matter the raw sincerity in them, are usually accompanied with a tone of unwavering gratitude that seems to wipe out any body hang ups. With a need to see images we can relate with, we also need to read *words* in which we relate with. For every woman who embraces her scars, enjoying all the marks of motherhood, there are those who hate and fear them. Both women are valid and equal, yet there tends to be a lashing of 'being ungrateful' thrown upon the women who are less than impressed with their 'tiger stripes'.

I find myself to be one such woman, body ravished by pregnancy; my hips, thighs and stomach all baring *rips* - not marks, but large *rips* as it grew to house my daughter. Large finger width tears of skin that was once a taut and firm stomach. Speaking of which, my stomach, a place once familiar to touch, now feels 'not me' as I place my hand in amongst these rips and squishy skin. During pregnancy, stretch marks appeared just under my nipple, visible in the mirror, as I watched my body change over the months. Those marks are now located under my breast, deflated and moved after releasing the gloriously full and ample porn tits of pregnancy. My boobs, a shape I was accustomed to, now gone in what seems a flash. I find no solace in 'tiger stripes'. I find no comfort in the amazing miracle my body has performed. Underneath every sentiment, I am reminded my body is defining me; it is defining me because I am a mother, a mother who should be more grateful for the parenthood lines all over my torso. I should love my body purely because I am a mother now. But I thought our bodies did not define us or our worth?

No matter which way you want to view your body, the fact remains that we *do* scrutinise our bodies in the mirror, even more so when we are experiencing the miracle of pregnancy, or the body deflation that comes postpartum, all of which society just loves to comment upon. I would be hard pressed to find anyone, pregnant or not, who does not have a single worry or niggle about their body, and how the future may morph it. Agreeing to pregnancy doesn't negate these worries. For many, it intensifies them.

The change to my body, seemed to me, to be astronomical after my daughter was born; going from small petite breasts, to ones that could smack on the light switch if I jumped high enough. A previously flat stomach had been stretched, complete with a new mini pouch, surrounded by stretch marks. My belly button is a thing of the past; my naval pierced skin acquired a huge lightning bolt stretch mark through it, a result of being stretched to shiny proportions. Hips became wide, as opposed to my somewhat shapeless pelvis before children. Random thigh stretch marks illustrated that I wasn't being 'harsh' or 'nit-picking', when I say my legs and arse expanded. My entire torso, from my tits down to my knees, changed. Including the gal - how could I forget about my warrior of a vagina? She was ripped and torn, sewn up and left to greet a new neighbour; Ms 5th Labia. For years, I suffered her acclimatisation, this new piece of skin rubbing on underwear, whereas in her natural habitat, she never knew the rough touch of clothing upon her back. Not so much chaffing, more awkward arse-wriggling in the street, trying to kick her back into a safe and unnoticeable place.

The arse-crack didn't get away with it either. Piles are not your friend; a new, unwanted guest, here to shock and surprise you just when you think you are healed. There is **NO** amount of body positivity and tiger stripe loving that is going to make me grateful for a short sharp shit shock, four years down the line, when I thought my arse had finally healed.

Physical Change Means Mental Change

The change to my body should not be construed as negative; no one is implying larger is not better, nor that petite is more appealing. What is being said here is about **change**. The unwelcome, unsolicited, unapproved change. What I'm talking is about **me**, about *my* body and *my* perception of it, *my* internal monologue of concern for my appearance. This change happened to me. I was left with a body that was not *mine*. And I will not, and will never, accept it based on being a 'mother'. For I am still here within it, the Kirsty before children.

Pregnant women don't release their body autonomy (well, what little we have of it anyway) and give up the reigns saying *'Baby, take the wheel'*, giving over all fucks to the Lords of 'what will be', when we see those two little pink lines appear. Many of us accept we will change, yet we still hear the niggle of, 'Don't worry, you will snap back', reiterating, as always, our body is our image.

My body did 'snap back' for the most part. To your eyes, and mine, it's the societal standard of what is 'ideal'. Petite, thin and proportioned. But that has absolutely fuck all to do with my mental health and body image. It gave zero protection against the destructtion of PND, once the Mind Demons (the affectionate term I use to describe the voice of PND within my head) learned they could equate 'lack of perky' tits to 'lack of love'.

What you see when you look at a person gives absolutely no indication of what their mind is telling them. No matter if you say, *'Ugh, that's nothing, look at the size of these stretch marks'*, as you pull out your own battle scars, trying to appease my pain, while belittling it in the process. This is still unauthorised change on *my* body. This is still a change within life that I didn't foresee, and it hurts just as it does within anyone else. There is still a person

underneath all of the 'Mum' on the outside. I'm still under it all
trying to deal with all of the societal stressors placed on wom-
en, and therefore the mental health of women. There is still that
naïve and arrogant 18-year-old in me who thought her body would
never look like that of her peers, and she would stay young and
toned forever. That karmic lesson is a lot to deal with when you
have a screaming baby sucking on your sagging tits, and Mind
Demons only too willing to convince you of how ugly you are and
that you're an unworthy waste of space.

Raise Your Hand If You Feel Victimised
by Your Own Post-Partum Body (and Society)

The change caused by pregnancy and motherhood is something
many women fear, and once we have made it through that change,
society is only too willing to tell us how to feel about it. Whether
you should scream grateful affirmations from the rooftops and post
300 pictures of your tiger stripes on social media, or to become
deathly dedicated to eradicating any signs you carried a child at
all, or resign yourself to the never-ending fight against the dreaded
'mom bod', swallowing calorie deficit diets year upon year.

Nonetheless, whatever path you take, the changes can be
overwhelming and seemingly never-ending. Eating away at self-
worth and esteem, for years, if you let it fester. This can have a
devastating impact on relationships and confidence. Every passing
month of pregnancy adds another notch on the bedpost of concern
and body anxiety. How much more can the body take? What will
you be 'left with'? What will your partner think once the baby is
out and it's just the two of you under the sheets again?

Nothing about this is airing near the vibe of being ungrateful in my
pregnancy or motherhood journey. I've had people tell me
"Imagine a woman who cannot carry children, read your moans?"

She would love those stretch marks". The sentiment I understand; pregnancy and childbirth are certainly a 'know your audience' topic. However, my 'moans' are MY concerns, MY mental health, or lack of. This is about being a valid human, experiencing a rushed and unknown change to my body. Wishing to remove the leftovers of childbearing means little to do with gratitude, nor love, for the path I have walked. What it does mean, that as a person, I, we, have the right to speak our concerns, and feel the empathy of others. Not to have them dismissed because we have been lucky not only to conceive a child, but to grow that child and give birth. I didn't feel so lucky when my 5th labia would irritate me, both physically and emotionally. I didn't feel so lucky when I broke down in tears, embarrassed to tell my partner I thought he saw me as repulsive. I didn't feel so lucky when I was so paralysed under the weight of motherhood that I thought taking my own life seemed like the only way out.

Like cattle, pregnant women are processed; objects of which we all know what they are thinking and what is best for them. Tick-box exercises for many midwives, seen a thousand times over by society as the occupants to a host of *"well, that's what happens"*, when they dare to utter words against their expanding boobs or lack of sphincter control. Pregnancy has happened a billion times over, but **not to that individual**. The monumental act of nature, magnificent in its function, is still as individual as our fingertips, occurring only within that person, at that time. Yet, we treat the woman like she's been here before, like her body is ours and we know her concerns. All of which can build into a silencing and lonely arena, forcing her to act like she 'should'. To accept changes to her body that need not be accepted. I'm eyeballing lack of bladder control here. We tell women to be grateful and love those big purple gouges running the length of her torso, wear them *"with pride - you earned them"*. The mark of a mother - that is who you are now.

Sorry, but if I'm going to *earn* anything after nine months and childbirth - other than the wonderful gift that is a child - before anyone mistakes me for some stark, raving, child hating lunatic (I'm only that on the holidays) - I want something better than an anal sphincter that threatens to open of its own accord if I cough too hard. I would rather something a little better than stretch marks that cause my belly button to concave in ways that defy the laws of physics.

We place women into 'mother' pigeonholes, immediately after they have begun one of the largest changes to their life. We underestimate, or point-blank ignore, her concerns and mental wellbeing. Society has done it all before, therefore we know everything about the mother. What it must be like to expose your genitals when asked. What it must be like to be asked about vaginal discharge, then profess what is normal for you. What it must be like to call the midwife, reluctantly, through tears, asking for comfort that baby is okay and can you have a scan to make sure. What it must be like to hear the words 'C-section' forced upon her, when her mind was set on an intervention-free birth.

We become blind in our assumptions, presuming the history books of pregnancy and birth tell us about the mother and her mental wellbeing. So, we fail to recognise, and give credence to, the accumulation of it all and how these impact the mother. We allow ourselves to stamp trauma into mothers, fathers and families, in our wilful dismissal. As a society, we have deemed pregnancy and childbirth as some form of "normal" in our words, cutting it down to nine months of transformation and a hard few weeks after birth. When in reality, the effects of pregnancy and childbirth, will be life long, the good and the ugly, for any mother (and father) so lucky to walk that path.

Chapter 5

Life As a Family of Three

Other than the horrific mental illness taking root inside my mind, and the worry that my body was still harbouring some left-over placenta, I was good to go; discharged from hospital, the day after giving birth. With my bag rattling with antibiotics, iron tablets, and various leaflets about contraception and what to expect after birth, my partner and I were sent packing. Out into the world, new parents, off to enjoy the 'once in a lifetime moments' everyone preached of so highly.

It was late in the afternoon when we finally got the paperwork completed in order to leave the hospital. There was a slight delay on account of me needing a prescription of antibiotics to stave off any infection that may arise if I did indeed still have leftover placenta flopping around inside of me. *Excellent.* Then off we went! There is nothing like new parents taking the brand new, just out the wrapper, precious newborn baby, into a car for the first time. My partner drove; I was in no fit state to drive on account of having no sleep for 3 days and having just re-enacted a civil war in my genitals the previous day. I sat in the back seat, next to our delicate bundle of 'Fine China' that was sure to smash at the slightest turn in the short drive home. (Well, it should have been a quick drive home, but we were carrying precious, precious cargo.) Crawling at a snail's pace, it must have taken us triple the time to get home than usual, barking out judgement at all the other drivers who seemed to be so reckless, going too fast around junctions, in a rush to get places. While we crawled along the road, trying to avoid the movement of the car shaking the baby, let alone going quick enough to make her feel like she was moving at all.

~~The following year we got home.~~ Pulling the door over, it felt strange to close the front door of the flat behind me, somehow cementing that life was no longer the same. My partner and I looked at each other after we placed the car seat, in which carried our whole life, down on the floor. *"What now?"* Fucked if I knew.

Being a frugal type of tight arse, I refused to buy nursing bras, despite planning to breastfeed our daughter. A foolish error, I'll admit. The ladies had expanded considerably during pregnancy, and I did eventually treat them to new housing units during that time. But after birth, my boobs seemed to double in size again; propelled into action as I nursed my daughter, biology taking over as the once dormant boobs bolstered into feeding machines as my daughter and I began our breastfeeding journey. First came colostrum, and then came the milk - in abundance - as though from factories of an industrial, global scale. Leaving the hospital, I had nothing to contain them other than a grey vest top which I had stuffed with padding to catch the leaking fluid and provide some form of shield from poking out the eyes of anyone I walked past. My tits were **huge** and without restraint. It quickly became apparent my partner and I didn't know what the fuck we were doing, and we didn't have it all thought out.

That same evening, my best friend arrived to meet her new, future best friend. Being at my side pretty much since the day we met, we would sit and gush that our late-night dates of eating McDonald's would soon include a mini human. As we munched our sinful tasties - me with a 'Chicken Legend', my friend with a 'Big Mac' stuffed with extra chicken nuggets - we joked that any children we conceived would be forced to not only like McDonald's, but to like one another too, as our friendship was set to last a lifetime.

After sniffing all the youth from atop our baby's head, my friend could not contain her wonder at the two beasts perching on top of the petite boobs I once owned. *"They are bigger than mine"*, she told me, rather larger chested herself. No shit was she telling the truth. I asked her to come with me to the 24-hour supermarket the following day as I stupidly, and seriously, miscalculated the size these feeding udders would grow into. Of course, she agreed, willingly filling her best friend and aunt duties all at once. She was smitten with our daughter from the very beginning, something that confused me at the time. I felt that was *my* role; I was the mother, *I* should be the one deeply in love with the gorgeous bundle of cute in front of us. But I wasn't. I was like a deer in headlights; fucking blind, and completely overwhelmed by the new person in the room. One that was **MY** responsibility from here on out.

Our First Night as A Family

Shit Show. That's what it was. Our first night as parents was a complete Shit Show. Our daughter started to cry at around 10 or 11p.m. It was late, I remember that, as my friend was with us and she was saying she should really leave as she had to work the following day. As we said our goodbyes, holding back tears as she gushed how proud she was of us and how beautiful our baby girl was, that gorgeous little bundle began to let the room know she was not happy. **Not at all**. Locking the door behind my friend, I returned to the living room to see my partner pacing the floor with our baby. She had fed recently. And recently before that. She fed **a lot**. With her hands bunching up towards her mouth and clearly upset, we presumed she wanted fed again. Pulling the grey, colostrum-strained vest down over my huge, hard, primal breasts, I tried my best to find the perfect latch, as to avoid any pain while she fed. No such luck. The previous night my daughter had fed from the hours of 10 p.m. to 3 a.m. No joke. I have the perplexed text messages to my partner to prove it. All night she was on me. And it looked to be no different tonight either.

However, this time it was different. She didn't want fed. She didn't want my breast. We didn't know what she wanted. Looking at each other in total shock, while our unhappy baby began to expand those lungs that would later scream for hours on end every evening - for weeks - my partner and I didn't know what to do. We changed her. We fed her. We tried our very best to soother her, but nothing worked. Maybe a bottle would work? But we had no formula on account of believing we would exclusively breastfeed our baby. (And I still didn't think to buy bras?!) We had no pacifiers either, having read that they were bad for the baby, leading to dental problems, bad habits or nipple confusion that would hinder our attempts to successfully breastfeed. But fuck that, it was now 3 a.m. and our daughter was still upset. The list of essential items to pick up from the store the following day was growing by the second. Formula. Bras. Pacifiers. Nipple Cream x10. Followed by a quick pit-stop at the book section to find some form of guide on why we are shit* parents who couldn't stop our own baby from crying. *Hint: No such thing as shit parents, crying is just what babies do.

The next morning, two exhausted parents woke to find the baby had only woken once during the night after her screaming fest. Not what we expected. She didn't stir until later that morning, which instilled great concern in her overwrought new parents. I don't think I can stress enough how anxious and overly worried my partner and I were with our daughter, and not just when she was a newborn. It would be the theme throughout her first few years of life; the pair of us being overly analytical, fretting over ways in which things would impact or change her life. We fell into the category of the classic new parents who read and listened too much to the health service issued guidelines and advice. 'Keep sugar to a minimum', meant no sugar or treats at all. 'No salt in food', meant we hand processed everything that passed her lips during the weaning stage. 'Pacifiers damage oral health', meant we discounted them from all of our pre-baby shopping. 'A newborn baby must eat every few hours', meant we became worried when our daughter decided to sleep the majority of her first 24 hours home with us, rather than feed on a schedule we had read about. I remember calling my mother in the first few weeks, asking if I should wake the baby to feed her as she hadn't fed in 4 hours. She quiet on the other end of the phone, sensing the overly worried tone in my voice, pausing before telling me that the baby would wake if she was hungry and that, in her opinion, she would simply let the baby sleep.

We need not have worried that first night; all was well with the baby. All was always well with her. The following few days were filled with visitors and midwives who would confirm that our baby was perfectly healthy. This did little, if anything, to stop us fretting over her. At her first weigh-in, our daughter had actually gained weight, a rare occurrence in breastfed babies, as the midwife told us. The moment brought a tear to my partner and best friend's eyes, as they gushed how proud of me and the baby they were. Rightly so; that baby ate like an eating contestant at an *'all you can eat'* buffet. I deserved a pat on the back for that one.

I remember the first two weeks of being new parents to be hard, overwhelming and very emotional. The 'baby blues' so they say. Being smacked with parenthood, like a sledgehammer to the groin I say. But in that time, we got the hang of it. Into a routine we fell. The times in which she fed (all of the time), the times in which she slept (hardly any of the time), and the times in which we could relax and have some down time (none of the time). We didn't know it, but in the happy 'Newborn Bubble' we smiled as we said it wasn't so bad. Having a baby was actually quite easy - we've got this! What was all the fuss about?

Oh boy, was that bubble about to pop...

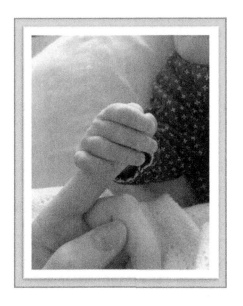

Chapter 6

The Worst Day of My Life

I have this picture of me and my 4-week-old daughter. We are lying in bed, on our side, facing the camera. Her eyes closed, peacefully sleeping. Me behind her, looking young and fresh-faced, not quite smiling, yet looking happy as the last of the summer's sun shines in the window behind us, illuminating the whole image. Each time I look at it, I think, *'Fucking hell K, you look fairly decent there, despite having a 1-month-old baby beside you'.*

Then I look at my daughter sleeping.

Every single time I see this picture, the motions are always the same. I look, hoping the gut-punch won't come, but it does. I look, hoping the tears won't start, but they do. I look at this picture and almost wish it wasn't me, but it is. I look at this picture and my healing heart rips open again. Through my eyes I'm transported back to that day; the day I pushed my baby away from me, and, using every fibre in my body, I screamed. I screamed that I ***hated*** her.

This is, without any hesitation, the most raw and painful day of my life, one that I will never truly heal from; as it is the epitome of postnatal depression and what it does to a mother.

In my memory, for the longest time, I thought my daughter was 6 weeks old on this day. It's only 2 weeks of a difference, although somehow it seems to pack more significance than maybe it should. Four weeks. That is all. Four weeks and already I was lost. It shouldn't be too shocking really, given there are horrific accounts of mothers taking their own life as early as 6 weeks post-birth. That's not really a large time scale for a person and their entire being to be wiped out, mentally or otherwise. Four weeks into my new life and I was already severely ill.

For 2 weeks, my partner and I enjoyed the oasis of the 'newborn bubble', that precious time when everything is new and exciting. We even dared to laugh, *"This is easy"*. But after those blissful weeks, things began to get shaky; shit began to hit the wall and everything else - *literally*. We had a large set of drawers/baby changing station, the type that comes with a removable top section and a place to put the changing mat, nappies and all the other lotions and potions required to keep a baby's arse in tip top condition. It was a lovely piece of furniture, gifted by a grand-parent. Boy did that thing take some amount of shite abuse from our daughter - right down the back and under the cleaning station, with a poo explosion hitting the wall more than once. At one point, my partner and I even witnessed, what I can only describe as a vertical urine show, from our DAUGHTER, that still, 6 years on, baffles me.

Life during the first two weeks seemed to go well, despite the acclimatization to motherhood; the cracked nipples and relentless conveyor belt of visitors and midwifes, forcing me to remove the milk-stained clothing and put on something a bit more people-friendly. It was two weeks of bliss and amazement, mainly at the ferocity in which a tiny human could expel body fluids. But soon we would find that the oasis we had been living in was, in fact, a mirage. This wasn't parenthood. We hadn't struck it lucky. The closer we headed in the direction of parental bliss, the more it slipped through our fingers, being replaced with a dry and barren land of isolation and despair.

My memories of the first few years of becoming a mother are hazy. Yet, *'luckily'*, I remember, almost too vividly, the 'bad' days. Those were the days that would scar and define the rest of my parenthood journey. I don't have memories of the first tooth, the first step, the first word. They are, however, documented in her baby book; I was, and I am, an attentive and proud mother, keeping a record of all these special moments mothers are taught to rejoice over. Her first pyjamas, the outfit she wore leaving the hospital, the tiny little sandals her father picked out in Gap - I kept them all. I tried to fill as much of her *Winnie The Pooh* baby book as I could, longing to be that perfect mother from the beginning. The irony is that I always was. Even in the absolute depths of dark, **real** dark PND, I still cared, raised and nurtured my baby, and documented every little thing my she did. I knew it was important, and maybe I knew I was missing them as I lived in some form of cloud above my actual life. Either way, I'm so glad I did write it all down, or else I fear all I would have left are the memories of these dark and painful days.

After 3 short weeks, my partner had to return to work. Having recently started a new job, he didn't qualify for Statutory Parental Leave, and so he saved and used all of his annual leave to be with me and our daughter after her birth. The first day you are left alone with a baby is daunting to say the least. Just how much, you don't realise until it is midday, and you feel like you have lived a whole week in that time.

Only a week after my partner returning to work and myself being left as the sole parent for the majority of the time, it happened: I broke. In the most horrific way, I broke...

Pictures Don't Tell the Truth

This day, on a sunny September morning, was one of the first days our daughter cooed and looked to be laughing. I recall she was 'chatting' to the white, boring ceiling above. I thought it was funny, what the heck was she smiling at up there? Something was amusing her, so I took out my camera to record one of her firsts, sending it to her dad. Who then, as every doting father does, turned his phone to his colleagues, showing off this beautiful little creation. Our little baby, smiling and chatting to the ceiling, making us proud at such a young age.

Before my partner left for work, I remember him saying *"Stay in bed. Rest. Get some sleep. Have a bed day"*. It had been another long night for me and the baby. My partner woke to find yet another set of our pyjamas on the living room floor, the sofa covered in a towel from my poor attempt to clean up the regurgitated breast milk from it in the early a.m. Most mornings I woke in only my pants, too tired to locate fresh pyjamas for the third time since midnight. Beside my pile of filthy clothes was the sick strewn clothes of the tiny perpetrator after her projectile vomiting, throwing back an entire hour of breastfeeding over the both of us. If I was lucky, it would only be the babygrow needed changing. And, like your chances of winning the lotto, I was never that lucky. She would be stripped back to the bare shit exploding arse apparatus most nights. The stench of part digested milk covering her pyjamas, forcing me to remove everything and start again. By starting again, I mean *everything*. The nappy, the pyjamas and the feed. Straight back to square one. Every night. For hours on end. For weeks. For months.

For whatever insane, idiotic reason, I thought I could achieve having a nice relaxing day in bed with a 4-week-old baby. A baby who didn't nap longer than the time it took me to walk to the bathroom. A baby who, unbeknownst to me, was going to have an epic cluster feed this day and would not sleep a wink longer than 20 minutes from the hours of 6 a.m. until 8 p.m. that evening.

In hindsight, there's so much I would do differently. Hindsight is always a smug bitch. We never let our daughter sleep on my chest in bed - the place she liked to sleep the most, and for the longest. Fuelled by anxiety and fear, we always placed our daughter in her crib to sleep. The 'human mattress' is a real thing, something I didn't know at the time. Babies like to sleep on someone. Cosy and safe on a chest, mimicking the noises and breathing they are so used to hearing inside the body. Makes sense, right? Our daughter loved to sleep on my chest, but neither I, nor my partner, felt it was a good idea. And so, she was always placed back in her crib, taking her off the safety and warmth of her mother, into a cold and unfamiliar bed.

Guess what always happened? She woke. No shit eh?

This day was no different. Before heading to work, my partner removed our daughter from my chest and into her crib, kissing us both goodbye and left for work. No sooner had the flat door been locked behind him, she woke. A bit fucked off with my partner, I picked her up and gave her what she wanted - the breast. All the time. A hungry baby, so I believed. I knew the breast would pacify her and so I always gave it to her, terrified to hear my baby upset, terrified to feel like a poor mother.

It wasn't long before our little lady had gulped enough breast milk and had fallen back asleep. My favourite type of baby: a sleeping one. That's no joke. Whenever she was awake, I was anxious, terrified to hear her cry. As a crying baby signalled that I was failing; I wasn't providing something she needed. It irked me, put me on edge to hear her murmur, the threat of tears imminent. Even as she slept, my ear was always pricked, listening for the slightest sound she was about to wake, forcing me into the mum prison I so longed to be free from. My sole purpose - the anxiety that consumed me - was to keep my baby happy, to make sure she slept enough, as babies need sleep and sleep all the time, right? (*Do they fuck*).

With my little one asleep, I rolled her off my breast, nuzzling her in beside me. I wanted her to sleep but I wanted my freedom. I thought having her right beside me would be enough to fool her into thinking she was on the human mattress. While she was at my side, I took the opportunity for a photo, the beautiful picture previously described. Almost as soon as the picture was taken, the light from the room dissipated and the darkness consumed me.

My baby didn't sleep that day. She wanted on me. **All. The. Time.** She fed and she fed. My nipples were red, cracked and raw - a new, inexperienced mother trying desperately to navigate and establish breastfeeding. With a baby who liked to eat every 3 hours. On the dot. Feeding in excess of an hour, throwing it all back over me, and wanting fed at the next 3-hour mark. My body ached in my recovery from birth. A ragged placenta, low blood iron and birth trauma… it all took a chunk from me. And what was left, the baby seemed determined to have.

Completely drained, I was still adamant I would breastfeed our daughter. I refused all suggestions of formula or letting my partner feed, getting upset at the mere mention of it. How dare he suggest my milk wasn't good enough or that I wasn't handling feeding my own baby? My boobs didn't need a break; they just had to toughen up to their 'buffet' status. I would yelp in the shower, the pressure of the water being painful on my new mummy udders, only able to stand with my back under the shower, gently allowing water to slowly trickle down my torso. It was agony otherwise; my boobs couldn't handle the touch of water, let alone the razor-like towel I used to dry them.

During the early weeks (months), my toes would curl and my fists clenched as she fed, sobbing through the pain some nights. It shouldn't hurt if the latch is correct, so I heard over and over and over. Sure, maybe. Or maybe not. Maybe I had a baby that pro-jectile vomited feeds back at me. Maybe I had a body depleted in nutrients from birth, let alone commenting on the role of hormones. Maybe my latch was a bit shit, but I would straight up choke a MF, with tit strangulation that tells me everything could be sorted with a *"perfect latch"*. Maybe I was a human who, 4 weeks previous, had been through a major life event, leaving me traumatised, now trying to navigate keeping a tiny human alive, along with the life-changing dynamics and her post-partum body. Maybe my body and I were just so, so fucking tired and in need of recovery to withstand the pain and mental strain that comes with establishing breastfeeding. But still, having stubbornness pulse through my veins just as much as blood does, I refused to give up breastfeeding. I was oh-so-adamant to shoulder the responsibility of feeding, alone. I wanted to push through, find that magical latch, and reach the end goal of the time when *'it gets easier'*.

When Mum Screams

At what hour of the day I cracked, I'm unsure. Light or dark outside, I don't know. Cluster feeding comes with cluster shitting. Up and down from the bed we went, taking her into the living room of our tenement flat to the changing station, throwing dirty nappy after dirty nappy straight on the floor. I had given up on taking them to the bin, indicative of my shitty mood. I was growing more and more pissed off with the demands of this baby. In my head we should be having a nice day in bed, relaxing, catching up on all those 4 weeks of missed sleep. Babies do nothing but sleep, everyone said so. But my baby didn't. After another round of arse wiping, I took her back to the bedroom and into the bed with me.

Grumpy again, I offered her my breast. She latched on as usual as I balled my hand in to a fist, enduring the hot pain of my baby latching on to my aching nipples. She fed briefly, using me as a pacifier and fell asleep - and then immediately woke again. She began to cry, for what I don't know. Overtired (like I say, she ate every 3 hours, regardless of the time it took to feed, clean and settle again), most likely worn-out before the day even began. And this was a day of cluster feeding, which, in breastfeeding terms, means you may as well buckle up, get a snack tray and prepare to sit there the whole day with your tits out. Kinda what I did, but without the mental capacity or knowledge as to what was going on.

Sitting on the bed, I held my crying baby in my arms. Her cry grew more and more intense, angrier, as her face turned red, her open mouth taking over the entirety of her face. Her body became rigid with screams, bellowing out seriously pissed off sounds, continuously, like that of a police siren. You wonder how the noise just keeps coming and coming, without a break for air. I looked down at her, shooshing her next to my skin, as panic set in. She didn't need fed. She didn't need cleaned. She wouldn't sleep. What the hell did she want? What the fuck do I do?!

She could be in pain, so I checked her over. Tiny baby fists clenched tight as I pulled open her babygrow, making sure there are no loose threads or missed price tags. Her nappy was strapped on neatly. No obvious marks or irritants on her body. Still, she scream- ed. What must the neighbours be thinking?! I looked down at this tiny ball of infuriated red, her face colour matching that of her gums and tongue which seemed to replace her mouth the more she screamed. Skin to skin, 'baby gold-dust' they say. The smells and hormones released, said to calm both mother and baby. So, I picked her up into my arms. I placed her onto my bare chest, trying my best to soothe her painful screams. She was so red, so angry, so disappointed, in my poor attempts to be her comforting mother.

This skin to skin was a pile of shite; it did nothing to settle her. Movement is meant to work, I read that also. Keeping her on my chest, I hoped that she would hear my heartbeat through the screams, screams that had now turned to some weird, interrupted form of crying. Like turning your key in the car, only to hear that dreaded churn of the engine trying its best to start, but doesn't quite have the energy to get there; it just kind of screeches on and off. My baby's screams were becoming so upsetting and hard for her; she couldn't quite get them out before she needed to take another breath. There is no other noise that a new parent dreads, than A) complete silence, or B) The jittering screams of their red - going on purple - distressed baby.

Sat on the bed, I rocked her in my arms. Still, she screamed, nothing would help. Nothing would soothe her. As I held her head next to my heart, wanting her to hear the familiar sound and know it was her mummy here and to stop crying, I began to rock with my whole body, back and forth, back and forth, back and forth. Her scream continued to fill the room. My eyes filled with tears, silent at first as I rocked. My bottom lip was quivering as my eyes stared at the white blank wall in front of me. She **would not stop** crying. I couldn't control my emotions anymore. With each rock, I let out a sob, a real face-contorting sob. The rocking became more animated, more aggressive, my body trying to soothe me as opposed to the baby the more I rocked and rocked and rocked. I wailed in pain, frustration and confusion and exhaustion. Then the rocking became desperate, soothing neither me nor the baby.

I was squeezing her tighter and tighter against my chest as the rocking grew more futile. She screamed as I tried to contain my upset, but I couldn't. I held my baby up to my face and asked her why she cried, demanded to know *"What the fuck"* she wanted from me?! Why the fuck would she not stop crying?! Of course, this pissed her off even more. Her own mother - her only source of comfort, support and safety - had her held up by the armpits, angrily interrogating her at only 4 weeks of age. In kind, she roarscreamed back at me, changing the pit and tone to let me know I was upsetting her further. Letting me know I was a monster of a mother.

Seeing her become more upset only isolated me further. I felt so alone, such a failure, unable to look after my baby. Not able to stop the screams, instead causing her to scream harder... the exact opposite of what a mother should do. Pulling my baby back into me, my wails turned into deep pain. I couldn't do this anymore, I couldn't be here anymore. I couldn't listen to this baby scream and not be able to help her. I couldn't be a mother anymore. This was too hard. Too hard for me.

I snapped.

I tore my baby from my chest and pushed her away from me, as far as she could go. Still sitting in the bed, I forcefully put her near the foot of it and pushed her away, as I screamed at her:

*"I HATE YOU. **I FUCKING HATE YOU!**"*

"PLEASE LEAVE ME ALONE. PLEASE LEAVE ME ALONE!"

Sobbing, wailing, with everything I had, I screamed at this defenceless, innocent baby.

My baby.

I pulled my head to my knees and rocked as I cried, as loud as I could force. Rivalling the best amateur dramatics of any soap opera.

Through my sobs I uttered over and over that I hated my baby. I pleaded so desperately that she leave me alone. I needed to be left the fuck alone. I don't know why I didn't call someone, reach out to my partner. Instead, I curled up into a ball, rocking like an abandoned child, wanting comfort, confused as to why I couldn't care for my baby. The only mother on the planet who could not care for their own baby. A mother who, at this moment, wondered if she had made a huge mistake in having a baby at all. No one else screams at their adorable, innocent, beautiful baby girl. But I did. Six years later, knowing that yes, mothers *do* scream at their babies, mothers *do* reach a breaking point, knowing that I am so very far from alone, it **still** haunts me and brings those tears back into my eyes.

Every time I read these words. Every time I see that photograph.

I broke my heart that day. It still breaks my heart to think about it now. I have never, and hope to never, experience pain like it again. The complete exhaustion that streamed down my face. The terrifying realisation that there was no love from me to my baby. At least, not the romanticised love people portray on social media.

My baby red screamed in upset pain, while her mother sat away from her, sobbing into her knees. Still rocking back and forth, my arms wrapped around my knees and head, creating a safe space to release the anger, frustration and pain. All the while, opening the door for shame and guilt to come flooding in. What kind of mother screams at their newborn baby? What kind of mother makes her baby cry with their voice? What kind of pathetic mother was I? A fucking failure, that's what kind.

In that bedroom, we wailed. Both hurt, both in desperate need of comfort. The two of us creating a lifelong memory that only one of us would remember and forever hold within their heart. After what felt like an age of bawling my eyes out, I calmed down, my baby still screaming at the bottom of the bed. I raised my head and looked at her, thinking, *'Wasn't it just typical? I can't even have a fucking cry without her needing me'.* And so, I picked her up and brought her back to my chest to feed. I didn't speak to her. I didn't offer her anymore comfort other than a begrudging breast. *'Take it'*, I thought. Just fucking take it. What else am I good for? Fucking feed from me and shut the fuck up.

My tears dried quickly, leaving nothing. That's the only way I can describe it. There was nothing of me there. I felt like a milk machine, a robot. To be used and abused whenever this baby saw fit. Me, my emotions and my needs felt completely irrelevant. I gave her what she needed as I just sat there, completely withdrawn from the significance of what had just happened.

After The Storm Comes... Numbness

I remember looking at the wall clock opposite the bed, watching hours pass as I sat there doing the same thing on repeat, all day. Feeding. Trying to nap the baby. Feeding. Hushing. Feeding. It's funny how hours seem to roll past *and* drag at the same time when you have a baby. I longed for the clock to strike 6 p.m. so my part- ner would come home. Not because I particularly wanted to be with him, nor that he would provide any respite from this baby. By this point I was already wandering the land of resentment and *'I can do this better, on my own'*, with good lashings of *'I need to do this all on my own as this is what mothers do'.* What I watched the clock ticking for was reassurance and comfort, another human in the flat and not the silence of a newborn, whose only chat was demands of feeding or changing. The human equivalent of ringing a service bell, regardless of what I need, let alone want.

I don't recall feeling scared or worried about my behaviour; the screaming and pushing of my baby. I knew I would never hurt her. Everything I felt was so internal, all about me. For, to me, I was the only person interested in my needs. To survive, my mind shut down, it pushed my partner away. I became reclusive to friends and family. Yet from the outside I appeared normal. Only those really close to me - my partner - could see the reality of my life. But he did not know the reality of that day, as I hid it. It was easy to hide my shame and hurt as I barely spoke to him anyway. In the short weeks from when he had returned to work, I had changed significantly. His toes must have been freezing from constantly getting the cold shoulder and walking on ice. Often, he would speak to me, and I would outright ignore him or give him one-word answers, communicating my displeasure at something without using my voice, a trait I still need to work on. My default is to go silent - yet not distant, far from it. I make it known, with my silence that I'm pissed off, only uttering a word when I see a prime stabbing point, usually to the heart. My silence comes with a defensive, cruel sidekick, intent on making others as miserable as I feel.

I wish, on that day, that I could go back and hug myself. Sob into my own shoulder and say *"It's okay"*. I was far beyond breaking point at this early stage of parenthood. A breakdown was inevitable. Through conversations, pictures, the stories of others, I thought mothers shouldered this weight alone, and I thought so must I. To be a good mum was to be motherly, wanting to be with your baby 24/7, knowing exactly how to care for them, loving every aspect of motherhood. Utter bullshit, I know this now.

The pain my daughter and I endured was so unnecessary. Crushed, rocking on that bed, I wish I could go back, take my face into my hands, stare deep into my eyes and say:

"It doesn't need to be this hard. You don't need to do this alone".

I doubt it would have made a difference; I still feel that new mother screaming inside of me, trying so desperately to be heard. The memory of that day alone, drives me to share what parenthood can look like, behind the filtered, perfect images we are bombarded with online. That pain, that anguish; no parent should ever feel this way. But sadly, this would be the tone for my parenthood journey for many years to come. Internalising everything I thought and felt, allowing my mental illness to try and strip my life from me, starting with my partner.

Chapter 7

The Breakdown

I would often wonder why some couples split after they had children. Surely this was an amazing, loving and wonderful bonding experience? Achieving that absolute pinnacle of life; having a child. I never understood why people said they drifted apart, that things changed after the baby, that it became too hard. Not meant to be, I guessed. If a relationship required work, then surely it wasn't the one for you. Like seemingly everything in parenthood, karma was about to teach me a very important life lesson in the most brutal manner.

I was 6 weeks into being a mother when I can first attribute PND to cutting my partner out of my life, within my mind, making him a stranger to me. He hurt me daily, or rather, my mind hurt me daily, convincing me it was all down to him. He had changed since I birthed my daughter. No longer finding me attractive, I was a nag and a bore. This washed up, mess of a human he endured. One he wouldn't look at, let alone run his hand over.

We hadn't had sex in weeks - no shocker there, since I was roughly 6-weeks postpartum. Physically, my body was healing from multiple tears and scratches. Seemingly, our daughter had turned into Wolverine on her exit, taking with her the identity of my vagina. Internally, there was a worry I had retained some placenta, as that didn't fare much better than my poor labia with the tiny X-men wreaking havoc in her birth, ripping everything to shreds on her way out. Torn, swollen and anaemic, my partner wanted to respect my body and mind. Concerned for my health and welfare, he didn't 'approach' me with any indication of a wild night of passion. How I interpreted this, was on a whole other, bat-shit level of insecurity.

During all the turbulence that accompanies adjusting to life as new parents - the fretting, sleepless nights, aching postpartum body, tiredness, worry, savouring precious moments - I became subdued. I was walking along the same path as my partner, the same path most new parents take, yet there was something else consuming my mind. A constant chatter and overthinking. A continued voice that lacked reason, that lacked objection, that lacked anything that did not support the belief that I was a terrible mother, a failure, a worthless piece of space. That voice was the brainchild of PND, spoken by a nasty dementor that I labelled as the 'Mind Demons'.

The change to everything childbirth brought wasn't missed by the Mind Demons - far from it. They used this as a homing missile, finding exactly where my insecurities lay, using it to exacerbate them, or straight up create new ones. One of these seemed to be my self-worth. They told me to equate lack of sex, as lack of attraction. Lack of lust, as lack of trust and intimacy. Ultimately lack of any form of connection with my partner, as lack of *me* in our relationship. As if the very basis of my worth and relationship with my partner was built upon sex and attraction. We met when I was 18; he was 21. So, I mean, to say this was our foundation wouldn't have been far from the truth; a pair of young 'kids', with no commitments or worries. The only stress we had was how to pass college, where we had met, by doing as little work as possible, and drinking as much alcohol as possible.

At 6 weeks postpartum, I didn't recognise myself anymore. My world revolved around the baby, as much as I hated that it did. As if there was a 'me' exorcism the moment she was born, I no longer knew who I was. No funny and witty banter, only sighs and frantic online searches trying to work out if my baby's poo colour was normal. My body had changed and was no longer mine, now prone to midwife inspections as they carefully monitored stitches and a heck of a swollen baby producer. My breasts changed from fun bags (okay, tiny ice bags) to feeding machines. I lost what little body autonomy I had; everything about me was all for the baby. There was nothing sexual about my being anymore. Nothing left that resembled who I was in my relationship just months beforehand.

Instead of practising self-love (a term I didn't know at the time), I filled my mind with disgust, directed towards myself and resent-ment towards my partner. Using a particular brand of self-torture, one that would allow my mind to create a whole other reality, compared to the one I was living, I allowed unfounded suspicion to course through my mind more often than it should in a healthy individual. It fulfilled the Mind Demon's fantasy that my partner didn't love me, nor did he find me as attractive as he once did. More than that, he didn't want to be with me, but wouldn't leave me. Not because he loved me, but because I wasn't worth the time of day to leave; completely worthless. In truth, like a piece of shit that didn't warrant any affection or respect.

Mind Demons Are Not Ideal 'Wing Women'

Most mornings, our daughter would feed at 3 or 4 am, in excess of an hour when you factor in the feed, the projectile vomit and clean up. When she finally fell back asleep, I would lay in the bed, unable to sleep, for hours. My head a constant buzz with anxiety, intrusive thoughts, worry and torment. I would hear my partner wake for work at 6 a.m. Pretending to be asleep, I lay there, frozen, listening as he woke, stretched and headed out the bedroom to start his day. I wanted him to think I was asleep, so I could 'catch' him in his natural habitat, the carefree man who had no worry in the world, other than finding a more attractive mate than the one he left in the bed each morning.

In equal parts, anxiety and resentment ripped through my mind. *What must it be like to be him? There he goes, away to make a cup of tea, drinking it in peace, starting his day how he pleases. With* **whomever** *he pleases. How lucky it must be to walk on the greener grass.* At the time I was aware my thoughts might be wrong, untrue, but therein lies the power of mental illness. With all my heart I knew this man to be the best person I had ever met. I knew he would never willingly hurt me. And yet, as I lay in that bed, I wasn't strong enough to believe it. I didn't possess the ability to allow my eyes to close in the comfort all was well in my relation-ship. I was being fed the lie that something was amiss, with an infinite trail of 'evidence' to support the claims. 'Evidence' as in, he woke at 6 a.m. to have a secret chat with his lover, as opposed the logical and real reason: to get ready for work in ample time. If I tried to stop the internal argument, it only seemed to spur on the opposition, who was much stronger than me and with far better articulation. It physically hurt to oppose my thoughts; my body would twitch and writhe in its discomfort. Almost as if in retalia-tion, a final push, my mind subjected my body to distress, to force me back into the mental arena to be beat. It was an assault on all levels, one at 6 a.m. running on minimal, if any sleep, that I could not defeat.

After listening to my partner make a brief visit to the kitchen to pour his morning cup of tea, I lay in the bed trying to regain control over my body and force myself back to sleep. Closing my eyes, I could hear him walk from the kitchen and into the living room, closing the door tightly behind. The click of the door handle rocketed through my ears and straight into my adrenal gland, adrenaline coursing through my body, springing into 'fight or flight' mode. We aren't ones for closing over doors in this flat. More so, we don't often make a point of shutting the doors closed **tightly** behind us.

Why is the door closed? What is he doing? What is he hiding?

That's when my eyes bolted fully awake. Every sense became heightened. Cold sweat began to surface on the back of my neck. Heart pounding, the overwhelming sound of it, as I tried to keep my breathing and movement to a minimum, desperate to hear exactly what he was doing. I remember lying there, believing I had any choice in the matter. Option one: close those tired little eyes and catch up on whatever sleep there is left on the timer before the baby wakes again - the ideal 'choice'. Or option two (the one being forced upon me): lie there listening to the Mind Demons and become their puppet in this strange, sordid fantasy. I lay there listening to how much my partner hated being with me, tolerated me, disgusted by me. My mind being beaten over and over, to the point of being pulled from my relationship and any trust we had created. Being dragged from the happy couple I enjoyed being a part of, to the now suspicious 'crazy lady' with the decrepit body, who was nothing but a sad pain in the arse.

That morning, the Mind Demons must have been on the protein shakes as they had exceptional strength in their abuse. This wasn't the first morning I had been through the mind hell, but it was the first time I acted upon it. I felt I needed to get up from that bed and see exactly why my partner had closed the door. In no way could it have been something as innocent as closing the door to prevent the sound of the TV from filling a quiet flat at 6 a.m. *No, no.* There was something far more sinister going on and I needed to creep my tired, sleep deprived, deflated self out of bed to find out why.

Silently, navigating the MANY squeaking floorboards, I reached the door of the bedroom. Looking back at my sleeping daughter, making sure she would let me be free to complete my investigations. I had made it, without a sound to the door, so I stepped out into the vast, dark hallway of our flat. The bedroom door was right beside the living room. As I neared it, I heard the voice of a woman. My heart thumped in my chest as I froze, my body pressed against the cold door, listening to the confirmation I had been seeking. I *knew* it. I knew he was speaking to other women. He **DID** think I was disgusting! Mocking me, telling me how beautiful I was, all the while thinking the opposite. There's no way he could go this long without sex; I *knew* he had found someone else, someone he could lust after.

My mind was a confused mess of logic and illness. We had been together for 10 years with absolutely no reason for me to suspect him of anything. But sound reasoning was easily wiped from the board almost immediately. My mind had 20 other ways to refute this simple piece of truth. I was already so convinced he was doing me wrong. I needed to know for sure. I **needed** to see what he was doing. So I pushed the door wide open with force, hoping to catch him in the middle of the surreal love affair my mind had created. My hands were shaking, my stomach doing backflips, my mind all over the place, yet it was all finely attuned. Allowing me the ability to control my body once the door was open. I walked in there with a demeanour that was contrary to my mind and the turmoil I was in. The door swung open and I walked in, calmly, to see the fantasy I had been reliving in my mind, day after day, for weeks.

As you can expect, he shit himself, bolting up in shock from the sofa, not before locking his phone screen. The phone locking didn't go unseen, I noted it; I noted it all. Where he was sitting, the way he was sitting, the teacup on the table in front of him, the darkness of the room, all but the light glaring from the quiet TV which it didn't look like he was watching anyway, with the volume down so low I could barely make out what the presenter was saying.

"What are you doing?!" he *dared* to ask me.

My sentiments exactly. What are *YOU* doing?

I lie, mention nothing about the insanity my mind is playing over and over. Instead, I tell him I couldn't sleep. I told him I wanted to see him before work, to sit with him, spend some time with just the two of us before the baby woke. Utter shite, and he knew it. I had barely spoken to him in recent weeks, let alone rose out from my slumber at 6 a.m. to spend some 'quality time' with him. But still, he seemed to let my behaviour slide. I'm sure he must have thought it strange. Although, considering my behaviour at the time, maybe it was just as offbeat as everything else I was doing.

"What are you doing?" I ask, barely even looking at him, knowing fine well his reply will be a 'lie'.

"Nothing, having a cup of tea before my shower. Are you sure you are alright?" he responds.

Fucking *liar*.

He was on his phone, I heard her. He's chatting to someone, looking at someone, the woman in work that isn't a nag or a chore. The funny woman that makes him smile instead of sighs as he lowers his head in response to my sharp, mean tongue. I wasn't satisfied with his answer, with his 'lie'. My stomach was in knots, almost pulling at my mouth, needing to be satisfied before it could rest. I needed more. I needed to know the truth. I needed him to confirm what I had known for the last 6 weeks; that he no longer found me attractive, loved me, or wanted to be with me. I **needed** to know as much as I needed to breathe. I wanted to ask, to confront him. But, it was a pretty bold and 'out there' conversation to spit out at that time in the morning, when I was supposed to be sleeping, only waking to spend some time with him. I didn't want to let slip that I had been laying day after day stewing, wide awake, riddled with these thoughts, pretending I was asleep, forcing myself to stay in the bed and not get up to follow him around.

Part of me knew how really fucking crazy this all was, yet that part wasn't strong nor loud enough. It was there, like the logical, sober-ish wing woman, warning you **NOT** to drink that last shot. It wasn't a good idea, and for the love of fuck, do **NOT** text that guy when you are pissed. And then she watches, she watches you tank the shot and open your phone, knowing full well there's a major shit-show ahead, yet powerless to intervene. Like the wing woman, the logical side of my brain shook its head in disbelief, pulling its helmet on thinking *'Buckle up, here we go'*, as it watched the Mind Demon take full control over my mind and into my mouth.

"Why is the cup on the table if you are meant to be having a cuppa before the shower?" clutching at straws with that question Kirsty, I thought. I had all but ousted my crazy in the first act.

Before I had finished my ridiculous, not-so-thinly veiled 'you are a liar' suspicion laced accusation, his barricades came up. *Fucked it mate*, I thought. I've shown my true colours now. May as well go full steam ahead here; down two shots and send a tit pic while you're at it.

"What the fuck?" he said, his face full of disgust at my absurd question.

He wasn't daft. He had known for weeks that I had been off. As much as I tried to contain and hide my suspicion, it seeped out of me. Well, enough for the person who knew me best to see it. Following his retaliation, there was nothing else for it but to get in at the deep end. I asked him why he locked his phone so quickly, what was he looking at, who was he speaking to. I stepped over every single boundary in a relationship, smashing any blocks of trusts we had been built upon. I wanted, and I <u>demanded</u>, access to him, his entirely. His thoughts, free time, desires, wants and needs. I wanted it all so I could prove to myself, the thoughts within my head were telling me the truth.

I was so fucking exhausted with it all. The physical toll of thinking. The sweats, racing heart, lack of sleep, feeling on edge, buzzing with ways to catch him out, what I would do when I found out, how we would split up, who would take the kid, where I would live, what I would do for work, why he didn't love me anymore, how I could hurt him in retaliation. Everything. On repeat. Constantly.

As you can imagine, being confronted at 6 a.m. about the proximity of a teacup to your body, when you are drinking tea, as opposed to having wild romantic affairs on your phone, didn't go down too well. He was hurt and confused, also fucking exhausted with the insanity of it all.

"I'm not speaking to anyone! Are you for real?" he exclaimed as he turned to face me.

I stood at the edge of our corner sofa, wearing a yellow baggy t-shirt and pyjama bottoms with cutesy cupcakes in different colours on them. Not looking him in the eye so much, as shifting my gaze all around him, desperately trying to find any evidence that he was a lying, cheating bastard, just like my mind had been telling me.

He **WAS** a liar, I *'knew'* that much. He was speaking to women, I heard him. He's brazen, to sit there and make *me* out to be the fool. Or was he? I didn't know. I didn't know what to think. My mind was going into overdrive, thoughts from all angles pouring in. *Maybe he wasn't a lair? Maybe he was checking football on his phone? Maybe I'm insane? Maybe he's been lying to me for years?* So many 'maybes' to bury at 6 a.m., only to be met with four more in their wake.

No, there *is* something going on. He *is* chatting to other women, I heard him. Maybe this is the woman he likes, the woman he lusts after. The woman who makes him laugh, who makes him happy. The woman with the perfectly slim body, unmarked by mother-hood. After all, he did say his type was a slim frame, small, neat breasts, petite in stature. Every attribute he had ever voiced as attractive all came flooding back, none of it resonating with me and *my* body, and therefore, he can't find me attractive. Plus, he's male; he can't go 6 weeks without sex. There must be someone else. He *is* hiding something.

Three Way Argument

It was too much. I stood in front of him and broke. Grabbing my hair in my hands, I faced the ground and erupted into tears. For weeks I had been taunted in my mind, alone and lost. For weeks I had seen myself in the mirror and wondered where I had gone and how this new woman would fit into our lives, if we even wanted her here. Weeks of constant mental questioning, lack of sleep, feeling nothing like I was 'supposed' to feel, weeks of anxiety - it all presented itself on that morning. I broke down, 6 weeks into motherhood, at 6 a.m., telling my long-term, loving partner - the man I was so willing and wanting to procreate with - that we were through; our relationship was over.

"I can't do this anymore. I can't do it. I don't want to be with you. You need to go. I can't do this. Please. Go. I can't do this."

"I can't do this" I said over and over.

My lips jittered as I tried to subdue my emotions enough to take in air. Perched on the end of the sofa, my heart broke as I cried uncontrollably. My mouth frozen shut, while my heart and mind continued to fight. Not knowing why I felt this way, yet believing I had the solution: to separate and live a life without my partner, thinking I would be better off without him. What did he do for me anyway? There is no love or intimacy. He lies. He goes to work each day, laughing and joking with colleagues. Probably laughing, rubbing shoulders with '*Heather*', his dirty secret, as they enjoy a banter, flirt filled tea break. Heather isn't a chore or burden to him, she never complains, she never cries about dirty nappies and lack of sleep. Her body is perfect, and her vagina probably isn't hanging out of her arse either. It's not weakened after childbirth, and I bet there are 4 nice tucked in labia, not 4 and a 5th guy hanging on, peaking out to see what the weather is like.

Placing my hands over my face, I told him to leave through muffled cries. My distraught pulled him towards me, as he bent down to his knees in front of me, meeting my face with his as I sat on the sofa. I refused to show him my face, shielding my fragility by burying it into my hands even further; I couldn't look at him. My heart was ripping open, and I really had no idea where this tremendous pain was coming from. As his eyes started to redden, he began to plead for me to let him in, let him know what was going on, where this has come from and what he had done wrong.

"Please speak to me?" he begged, his voice trembling, as emotion poured from his eyes.

I could do nothing other than shake my head.

"No, I can't. I'm done" my response to this confused and panicked man in front of me.

Sure, there had been arguments in recent weeks, arguments that he couldn't quite understand, yet he understood that I was not 'right'. There had been a shift, a change, a darkness cast over me that he couldn't quite place yet. Desperate to hold on to us, he apologised, but for what, he wasn't sure. Tears fell from his face as he met the demon of PND; the awe-inspiring destructive force that had removed his partner and replaced her with a hollow shell, intent on self-destruction. He remained knelt in front of me, his hand warm on my leg. I felt the familiar comforting touch that I had wanted for so long, the connection to another human; to *this* human. The one I have, unknowingly, pushed away, accusing him of this horrific, hypothetical situation, of all the situations that the Mind Demons had created within me.

He asked me if I truly, genuinely wanted us to separate, to which I didn't reply. I had thought about this moment for weeks; to be free to live the life in my head without burden or pain. My silence frightened him. For him, there was no question. He wanted to be a couple. My lack of answer is indicative; I do not. Sensing that this isn't the first time I've thought about leaving him, not a rash decision, he pulled back from me. Removing his hand, he kept his eyes on my sullen face, awaiting my decision as he feels that gut punch of pain we all fear. Yet that was exactly the pain I had been living with, almost since the day I gave birth to our daughter.

As we sat in silence, it all hit me; the exhaustion, isolation and vulnerability, the deep hurt that emanates from your heart to your stomach. Everything was so raw and overwhelming. The prospect of losing this man, this family, killed me. The feeling of nausea rose as my body remained on edge, cold sweat pooling on my neck, my stomach knotting with anxiety. I was so confused and utterly distraught with pain. I couldn't speak as I battled to understand what was happening. I didn't want him to go, yet couldn't understand how we could be together. My heart screamed *'No!'*, virtually banging out of my chest in an attempt to save us from the inevitable doom the Mind Demons were orchestrating. But those Demons, they are strong and loud; preventing me from seeing what is in front of me, or hearing my heart screaming inside.

Paralysed in thought, we sat in complete silence as I made my decision. I wanted nothing more than to feel his touch, to be hugged, reassured, loved. Taking a breath, I finally exposed my face from the privacy curtain of hands and hair that I had been hiding behind this whole time. I stared at the love of my life, his heart breaking, watching as his world shattered in front of him. I could see his pain, but I couldn't feel it. All I felt was the swirling within my own head, and how nothing seemed to make sense.

"I'm so lonely", I confessed, unable to contain yet another wave of emotion from spilling out my eyes.

Like gatekeepers, these words threw open the door as others began to flow: the unequal burden of the baby, the feeding and chores, combined with my emotional state and loneliness - it all came out. All the pressures and resentment that had been building up since the baby was born poured from within. Yet, I knew enough to keep back the *real crazy*, the real paranoia. I knew he would try to prove it wrong, tell me how much he loved and adored me, that I was, and always will be, his Goddess, the only women for him; always and forever. But I didn't want to hear it, I knew he would 'lie' to me, and I couldn't endure it right now. I was too upset, too confused, and too lonely to try compute anything to the contrary of what my mind had been telling me for the past 6 weeks.

Seeing the weight of my words and their pull at my already weakened breaking point, my partner began to apologise, over and over.

"I'm so sorry, I can do better. Please let me try. Please. We can work this out", he pleaded.

Terrified that I had the chance to end our relationship and that my hurt may just force me to do it, he professed to change. He would help out more; we would both make an effort in our relationship to work as a team and include each other in our lives. He spoke of how we would make time in our week to be a couple, to reconnect, and the ways he could do more to help around the flat with chores and life with a newborn. Almost frantically, he spoke his immediate thoughts; ways to make me happy again, trying will all his might to convince me our relationship had more mileage in the tank than I thought.

As I sat there, watching my partner in pain, I filled with that familiar feeling I was craving; a connection - a connection to him that I had been longing for. His pain made me feel loved, as though I enjoyed seeing how much I mattered to him. The more pain I saw, the more I knew he loved me. Or rather, the more I enjoyed feeling like an object worthy of love. I enjoyed his heartbreak as it made me *feel*. I enjoyed his pain and wanted more, more of this adoration and love. I hadn't felt anything towards him, nor him to me, for weeks. I didn't intend to hurt him with my words; I could only tell him how I felt when those words found their way to me through the haze within my mind. But even this backwards feeling of love, produced by his pain wasn't enough for my depleted self.

"It's too late", I told him, as I shook my head.

Half wanting to wallow in this weird fucked-up glory of being able to cause hurt, half speaking my truth, I was hurt, extremely so. I couldn't be hurt any longer. Logically, to me, it made sense to end it there and then, cutting out the root of my torture. As I uttered the words, I turned to faced him. No tears. No sobs. Just our faces, eyes locked. *"It's too late"*. The intent of my words, piercing through my gaze, was quickly followed by sorrow. I was serious; there was nothing left in me to give. I was gone. Numb. Lost. Not the woman

I was just a few weeks ago. And I saw nothing for me in this relationship, in this family, other than utter despair and pain.

"I love you, so much. I have never, and I could never, love someone as much as I love you", my partners heart now poured from him in a desperate last bid to keep me by his side.

But his words bounced off my expressionless face; meaning nothing to me. He noticed and quickly tried his best to fill the solemn, empty void facing him.

"Please. I love you both, I can't be without you. I can't not see my daughter every day. Please let me try", giving it one final push in an attempt to keep me.

It was here that it struck me, bypassing the confusion and breaking through the darkness clouding my mind: this was the first time I realised he loved *our daughter*. The first time it dawned on me that *I* was the one breaking down the family, that *I* held the power to tear them apart, to break any bond they had. To hurt two people with my actions. The first time I saw there would be two hearts breaking if I decided to walk away, neither of which would be mine, of that I was sure. Right there and then, I saw in his eyes what I was doing, as if I had been playing *pretend* relationship break-up until this point, not seeing the serious potential consequences of my actions.

The fog of PND cleared for a moment and I saw a glimpse of reality; the real world I was living in, and not the warped reality I had been subject to, over and over again in my mind. I was about to remove my partner from my life, and a father from his daughter. It was almost as if I had a daydream the whole time, not paying attention to anything that had been happening. I couldn't make sense of it all.

What was I doing? Why was I doing this? Why was I punishing him, pushing him away, trying to end everything?

Deep down, in my core, I knew this was wrong. I knew this was the man I wanted to spend my life with. But there was something else within me, something holding me back that I could not understand. Something that enjoyed the hurt I was causing and enjoyed the torment I was under.

Breaking The Spell

For now, staying together seemed like the easier path, less compli- cated. It seemed right, despite everything swirling around in my mind, telling me to leave. Reluctantly, I agreed *"Okay"*, that we should stay together, to work on being a couple and being parents. I spoke the words with my eyes on the floor, as if I had just admitted defeat. Not sure what it is I'm looking for, I agreed we should try work through his rough patch. Much to the relief of my partner - who takes this chance to get close to me, holding me tight, ensuring that I won't push him away further - he held me in silence as we both processed what had just happened that morning. He more confused than I. His body shook from the near miss of losing his entire life in the previous moments.

As he kissed me on the head, reassuring me again how much he loved me, how much he wanted to make this work. I remember feeling nothing. Rationally, I knew he loved me, but I wasn't con- vinced of it. One of PND's many talents is the ability to see an emotion and not be able to feel it. And if you can't feel it, who is to say it's real?

For the first time in our relationship, I felt my mind and body shut down to the person I adored the most, as if all love left me, replaced with suspicion and a seething, **relentless**, need to prove the Mind Demons correct. I no longer felt empathy; in his pain I felt comfort. That deprived feeling I had been craving. This breakdown was the start of two people living two separate lives without even knowing it, as something sinister began to fester at the very core of our relationship, infecting my mental health and self-worth.

Chapter 8

One Couple, One roof, Two lives

Roughly 8 weeks since the birth of our daughter, my partner and I began to settle into our new norm. He left for work early in the morning 5 days out of the week, returning in the evening. While I stayed at home with the baby on maternity leave, creating huge advances into my new full-time role of a severely depressed mother, in denial.

By this point, resentment filled my heart more than love did. My baby was very much an unbearable chore, a catalyst that deepened my unhealthy state of mind, strengthening the torment of my PND. My partner was the *lucky* bastard; he was able to leave behind his parenthood role for hours each day, returning to his life, much like it was before he became a father. He didn't seem to take the huge, life-altering hit that I did. He wasn't glued to this child, suffering a new body and tits that could sink a ship with their weight. He could eat, drink, walk and talk as he liked. No worries, no commitment, no stressing, no fretting over the nap schedule of this chronic sleep avoider. At least, that's how I saw it.

It wouldn't be too far from the truth to say I hated my partner during that time. Edging over the threshold of resentment and into loathing, I didn't want to engage with him, let alone play the part of a smiling and happy lover. Unknowingly, as I pushed him away, it

90

only served to feed the Mind Demons at an alarming rate. My isolation - their favourite meal - allowed my mind to warp my perception even more. Feeding into the warped internal monologue that my partner **WAS** the distant and unloving man I shared a home with. He **WAS** moving further away from this nagging and harsh woman, rattled by childbirth. He saw me as an old washed up, used, bore of a human. One he loved nothing more than to escape from, by heading to work each day where he could chat to other happy humans.

Within these short 8 weeks, we had managed to birth a child, instil anxiety, become fraught with responsibility, avoid at least two attempts of me separating the family, and become so distant with each other that we began to live two vastly different lives. Given that having a child is packaged at one of life's greatest experiences, the dramatic split came as something of a shock to the both of us.

My existence was very much removed from reality, unlike my partner. He could see what was happening to me, the darkness and the change. Still clinging on to our family, desperate to provide the strength and stability I would need to conquer PND, he tried his best to tell me I was ill. Each time I ignored him, thinking him stupid, overly dramatic - an idiot. This was what motherhood looked like, and who was he - the man with the great life - to tell me any different? How *dare* he?!

His kindness and love only reiterated what the Mind Demons wanted me to believe; that I was a poor mother, failing in her role. I misconstrued any of his acts of help as an insult or attack on me and my mothering. If he suggested I take a break from the baby, I became defensive, believing he thought I wasn't up to the task of motherhood. Unable to see the extent of my illness, I reacted to his support by isolating us further, allowing animosity between my mind and him to grow. In my eyes, he no idea who I was or what stress I was under, yet he was the only person on Earth that could see exactly where I was - precariously perched on the edge of suicide.

Anger Leads to Resentment. Resentment Leads To... Suicide?

Each day my partner finished work, he would call to let me know he was on his way home, or so I thought. In truth, he called me multiple times during his day to check in, to see where I was at on any given day, and not in the physical sense. In years to come I would learn he called in concern, worrying about me and the baby, given my poor mental state that was apparent only to him at the time.

Often when answering the phone, I would give short, one-word replies, evidently in a mood and directing it towards the only person I could, treating him as if he was something I would scrape off the bottom of my shoe. Other times I wouldn't answer the phone at all, too pissed off with the baby. The only way I knew how to convey my displeasure was to ignore his calls, arguing with myself as to whether or not I should call him back. *"This fucking baby wouldn't give me peace"*, the distorted tale I gave to his concerned quizzing when I finally called him back after his third attempt to make contact with me. My aggressive greeting, followed by minimal converse, encompassed my grievance with him, the baby and my life. I remember feeling so frustrated and so angry, that he appeared happy and chipper when he called me as he buzzed on about work or the droll of the office gossip. *Lucky him,* I thought. What it must be like to have a life?

As per usual, at 6 p.m. my partner lit up my phone, the call sign-alling he was on his way home from work. Like most days, the call caught me at a bad time. I had been trying to get our daughter to nap, for what seemed like hours, another long day in the flat with the baby who never slept. At best, she would nap for 20 minutes before stirring, becoming upset, demanding I find a way to soothe her back into slumber. Developing what I later learnt to be 'nap anxiety', my life revolved around my baby and her sleep schedule. I was obsessed; controlled by the need to nap my baby, believing it to be integral to her welfare - nae, more than that: integral to life itself. My baby needed to nap and there was nothing that would come in the way of it, else I would go insane trying. I would become so frustrated and angry, perplexed as to why this baby didn't nap. Every time she woke when I deemed it too soon, my irritability grew. The frustration was readily lapped up by the Mind Demons and used as justification for my poor mood and temper, always being projected at my safe space - my partner.

As the phone rang, my partner's name filled the screen. *Fuck's sake*, I thought, quickly silencing the phone, placing it on mute, for he was sure to call again and again, and fucking again. With the blackout curtains drawn, white noise filled our bedroom as I lay on the bed trying to hush our daughter to sleep. Tightly bound in her cream knitted swaddle, her body was pulled in close to my torso. Close enough for her to feel my presence, but not so accustomed to my body on hers so I could make my escape when she fell into that deep sleep I fantasised about. I longed to be free of her, wanting to be me for an hour a day. To do anything I wanted because I wanted to, not because I 'should'. I felt somewhat at peace when she slept. Although, "peace" may a tad strong, for I was never truly at peace with my breath stalling in trepidation, every time I heard even the *slightest* murmur that she was beginning to wake and I was needed, yet again.

The silent phone still demanded attention, as my partner called over and over. The ringing phone light shone over the room threatening to destroy my painstaking work and wake the baby, which pissed me off *immensely*. Quickly, with as little disruption to the baby as possible, using my fingertips I reached for the phone and pushed it far under the duvet, hushing both its vibrating buzz and light show. At no point did the welfare or concern of the caller pass through my mind. His persistence angered me. *Why did he keep calling? Was it not obvious I was busy?* **Selfish arsehole**. He is going to wake this baby. Destroy all the hard work I had grafted in those hours, the sacrifice I had made - lying in this dark bedroom, compulsively watching each move our daughter made, adjusting the ideal sleep situation, being the servant of his child while he was free to roam - and he had the audacity to call me?! Demanding I give him entertainment, comfort? *I don't think so.* I pushed the phone away in a rage, at the same time my partner was beginning to pick up the pace on his walk home, terrified of what he would open the door to greet, or not…

Climbing the three large flights of stairs up to our top floor tenement flat, my partner returned home from work to find the front door as he left it that morning: locked, indicating that no one had been in or out, a telling sign of the mood he was about to receive once he put his key in the lock. Instead of the usual sour face and resentment eyes that normally greeted him, he opened the door to an eerily dark and quiet flat. With no windows in the entrance hallway, its natural light source came from the sun beaming through the windows of the living room, bedroom and bathroom. It was unusual for the flat to be anything other than bright and airy, as it had ample windows to flood the hallway with light. It was a trait we both loved about the space, and always made sure we used the light to its full advantage. However, on this day, my partner walked into the flat to find the living room curtains drawn, the bedroom door closed, and the bathroom door pulled tight, cutting off all the sunlight that normally filled the space.

Surrounded by darkness, no sooner had my partner closed the front door behind him than he began to shout my name.

"Kirsty?"

There was no answer, so he shouted again, and again his call was met with silence. In the quiet, his volume increased in line with his rising panic; in front of him stood a tall, narrow, tightly shut door to the bathroom.

*"**Kirsty**!! Why are you not answering me?! **Kirsty**?!"*

I'm not sure if he knew I was in the flat or if any logical sense of deduction entered his mind. Running on pure instinct, mixed with several weeks' worth of suspicion, he moved closer to the bathroom door, his call becoming more frantic, taking less rest between each shout. He began to thud on the bathroom door as he screamed my name.

"Kirsty! Let me in! What are you doing?! Kirsty?!"

Stopping for only seconds to hear any reply, in my absence he threw his fists against the wood. His banging became so intense, in such a frenzy, as he screamed my name over and over. He was moments away from kicking his way into the bathroom - and that's when he saw me.

"What the fuck? Shut up!" I snarl at him, as I pull the bedroom door closed behind me.

The drama of my partner forcing me to leave the bedroom in a bid to stop the noise - the bangs and shouts - I had finally gotten the baby to sleep, and this idiot comes in the front door shouting like a hooligan at a football game.

Ignoring my partners questions of why I didn't answer the phone, or why I didn't answer to my name, I walked straight past him and into the large kitchen, knowing he would follow me, trying to re-duce the chance of his booming voice waking the baby. Cold in my tone and lacking anything that would even resemble empathy, I gave him one-word answers, as I avoided any eye contract. I was **livid** with him. For calling, relentlessly. For returning from his carefree day, thumping on doors, shouting my name, over and over. For becoming panicked over a closed door. It wasn't even locked for fuck's sake. And why didn't he just try the lock instead of screaming at the door like some sort of crazy, overly dramatic fool?

I had no time for it. No time to listen. And certainly, no time to see the petrified face of a man who had all but ran the entire way home, climbed the three large flights of stairs, taking the deep-set stairs two at a time, shaking as he pulled his keys from his pocket and into the lock, realising his worst nightmare may be on the other side of that door.

What my partner thought would greet him on the other side of that door was silence. In the dark hallway he saw a closed bathroom door which, in his mind, confirmed his fear. Behind it he believed he would find me, in the tub, with his baby. With me dead, at least. He knew I would never hurt our baby, yet in the mist of my darkness, he wasn't confident there would only be one tragedy behind that door. The unanswered calls, in double digits, caused him alarm. For weeks he had envisaged this day, the more I grew away from him, the more his heart crushed in fear. Reading articles and forums online, it was clear many women change after the birth of their baby. Many of them become distant, delusional and dark. Some women head off the rails, patching wounds with addiction. Some mothers run away, never to be seen again. And some mothers do the unspeakable: suicide. Driven to madness, taking their own life and that of their baby.

When Mum Suffers, Dad Suffers

For my partner, I fit the bill. The suicidal mother. Surrounded by darkness. Consumed in delusion. Aggressive in nature, speaking only in snarls and venom. Working tirelessly round the clock in martyr status, dying on the inside while I gave my all to our daughter. Instead of love and happiness, there was fear and distraught within me. So far removed from the mother pictured in the media, from what either of us had imagined. And so very, very far removed from who I am.

To me, I thought he was stupid. Over the top. Not seeing me for who I was, or all that I was doing for our family. Coming home shouting at the top of his lungs, and for what? A closed bathroom door? *Ridiculous.* I was so fed up dealing with the needs of everyone in the flat, including his. This was motherhood and I wasn't enjoying it, but I wasn't unwell, I wasn't suicidal. I lived with a baby who had me whenever she desired, and a partner who had to be treated like a needy child on account of this 'fantasy' that I was under some form of dark, stormy cloud. I remember being so mad with him that evening, so utterly fucked off with his behaviour and the subsequent withdrawal thereafter. I thought he was so dramatic, over the top and a damn needy fool.

We didn't speak about the phantom suicide that night. There's not much to say to a cold-hearted bitch who is very likely to kick off at the slightest mention of her struggling, let alone that she appears suicidal. I let my partner sit at the dining room table, catching his heart from falling out of his arse, as he processed swerving his nightmare. I didn't comfort him in any way; I didn't see his upset as anything other than a fabrication of his mind. I certainly didn't read the situation; that he thought me suicidal. My belief was one of annoyance. So enraged and enthralled with my daughter's lack of napping, I was pissed that he bundled through the door creating a carnival of madness, and loudly so and for what? I felt so unheard and unseen that I couldn't see the pain in the man I had known for all these years. I couldn't see sadness and adrenaline pour out of him as he sat at the table, trying to calm his shattered nerves.

I know I felt alone during this time, but what it must have felt like to think that the person you have invested your future in, the person you chose to have a child with, the person who has your heart, for her to ignore you at a painfully vulnerable time. Dismissing your worry that pushed you to race home after work, to bolt up the stairs and cause you to blindly bang on a closed door. What is must have felt like to envisage your whole life disappearing behind that door, believing wholly that her life had been taken, only to find out she was alive, but really didn't give a fuck about any of that, much less, give a fuck about you.

That's one of the real tragedies of PND; it has the powerful ability to pull happy, deeply in love people apart. Not just apart, but to instil deep emotional trauma and pain. At the time, I couldn't see my partner's concerns, let alone his hurt. In truth, even if I could, I doubt I would have cared. Depression doesn't offer space for sympathy, let alone empathy. I resided in far too selfish a space to care about the needs of others, with the only exception being my daughter. My partner was used as an emotional punch-bag. In my mind he didn't have needs. There was no reason for him to be anything other than happy. He had a job, a warm place to sleep, food, a partner, and a daughter. His life was perfect; a narration I told myself that fuelled the mental removal of him from me.

This couldn't be further from his reality. He watched on as his partner drove further into a hole of depression, unable to heed his warnings of concern, reluctantly closing the door on his family, stepping out to work each day, fraught with worry that neither of us would be there upon his return. There was nothing else he could do at the time. I didn't listen to any of his prompts that maybe I *should* speak with someone, that things didn't seem right. My reality was so warped that I couldn't see the pain in the helpless figure of my partner screaming my name as he banged on that bathroom door, seconds away from kicking it down and being confronted with my pale, lifeless body in the tub, with our baby by my side.

No one would want that scenario for anyone, let alone the person they hold closest to them. The reality of PND is, not only does it make those under its curse, think, feel, and act differently, but it does so under a cloak that makes the victim unaware of their behaviour at times. The phrase *'seeing red'* means becoming so angry we see red and *only* red, unable to control our action in those moments as we lash out. The same can be said for depression. In the thick of it, when the mind is being tormented with relentless lashings, people can become blind to their words and actions. Unable to see or understand their own behaviours while in the middle of depressive fog.

To think now, that I would be so unkind to my partner if he believed I took my own life, let alone be so cruel and dismissive in my belittlement, gives me a tension headache. I just don't get it. What a heartless beast PND made me. In truth, I don't like to think on this day often; suicide seems like the top tier of subjects in mental illness. A place not many recover from, a lonely dark realm in which the survivors are forever scarred in their remembrance. A place I never saw myself, although I did have moments of contemplation in the benefits of suicide, wondering if this would be the best way to rid my family of the toxic beast I had become. In those moments, I related with those who I previously only acknowledged with a tilted head-nod of sympathy. <u>Now I got it</u>. Now I understood the appeal. Now I knew a reason why people took their own life. To end the noise, the constant chatter, the running commentary in the mind that was never kind and that never let up. Suicide was the perfect escape, and one that would protect those around me, from me.

But I would never have thought myself as suicidal. Yet the reality was as my partner saw it. I was severely depressed. I was edging dangerously close to a newspaper headline that stated, *'All the signs were there'*. A new mother taking her own life, leaving behind her 8-week-old baby and broken partner. That's what he saw, what he had sensed for weeks. All the while I pushed him away, finding any means to pain him, laughing at his 'stupidity' of punching an unlocked door.

I had my darkness, yet as I write this now, it becomes apparent I wasn't the only one alone and hurting. I'm sorry he walked that path alone, something he has never, in my mental illness journey forced me to do. I couldn't give him what he so willingly gives me; empathy, support and unconditional love. Words will never describe my partner's strength, his resilience, his ultimate love and devotion to our family. To us. I fear words could never explain how he felt on that day either and for that, I'm somewhat thankful, for I never want to feel an ounce of the pain he endured that day.

Chapter 9

Enough Is Enough

I'm not entirely sure what straw 'broke the camel's back', leading me to visit the GP. At 2 months into parenthood, there was already a hay bale of straw to pick from. I think the time in which the conversation happened was after my partner thought I was attempting suicide in the bathroom. In truth, my memory is fuzzy, but I do recall the pivotal moments, the ones that force me to shake my head as if to throw them out my ears so I can tune into something a bit happier and prevent my eyes from leaking. I do know, and I will always gratefully remember, that my partner was (is) my saviour, pushing me to seek help and possibly the biggest reason that I'm still here today.

I remember sitting at the dining table in the spacious kitchen of our tenement flat, my partner walking around me. The baby wasn't there, fake napping in front of the electronic babysitter (the TV), most likely. The conversation was about me. My partner was trying to make me see the reality of our situation. Me, severally ill. Him, walking on eggshells, trying desperately to show me how ill I was. Not our first conversation on this topic by this point. In the previous days and weeks, he had tried to speak to me about breastfeeding and the link to PND, which obviously I refuted immediately. *Nonsense*, how could something so amazing, wonderful, healthy - 'liquid gold' - contribute to a mother's mental health in such a negative manner? He threw around arguments such as the shift in hormones causing an imbalance, leading the mother to become very ill. The toll of feeding on the body combined with extreme sleep deprivation - but I wouldn't hear any of it. *Complete shite*, I thought.

I always became defensive whenever we spoke about my frame of mind. What I didn't know, nor realise at the time, was my partner had been sinking hours and hours into researching 'why my partner has changed since childbirth'. His internet history was a goldmine of other concerned dads, asking where the fuck their partner went, and who was this new, unapproachable, sad, aggressive, and un-loving person in her place?

When exclusively breastfeeding, and refusing to create a pumped storage of milk, the chances of suffering from sleep deprivation are high. Simply having a baby, the chance of sleep deprivation is high! With sleep deprivation, mental health can take a tumble, right into the abyss. My partner was right in his (well researched) guess that breastfeeding was making me ill; either by the hormonal shift, the sleep deprivation, or the mental and physical toll it can take on the mother. But I was sold the 'all-inclusive package' that breast-feeding was the be all and end all. At no point could it ever make me ill, not in any way, shape, or form. So, I would bite his head off for even suggesting it. For suggesting I was failing. For suggesting I was weak and ill. For suggesting that I was anything other than the strong, put-together mother, just like everyone else. And by fuck, did I 'poo-poo' the notion that breastfeeding was in any way related to my poor mental state.

Outing Post-Natal Depression

At the time, I didn't put two and two together. This man was terrified. He loved me so much, consumed trying to figure out where the hell Kirsty had gone and how could we get her back. He read blogs and articles of men desperately worried about their partner; it seemed to be a 'thing'. A dark cloud that hovered over new mothers, and sometimes the fathers too. The path into parent-hood, taking from them what seemed to be any sense of logic or the ability to communicate. Instead, replacing it with anger, sadness and minimal interactions with people they once enjoyed spending time with.

By this point, a few months in, my partner had had enough. No longer was he willing to watch me crumble, destroying myself and our family in the process. That day I wasn't leaving the dining table without the Mind Demons admitting defeat. My partner sat me down while he all but gave a PowerPoint presentation of the crazy that had been occupying my mind, instead of the light-hearted foolish, humorous crazy, that normally had the reigns. There was no way I was getting away from that kitchen table until I had revealed the truth.

"I'm so sad, I'm so lonely" I uttered as I began to cry, admitting defeat.

My partner had been so adamant something was wrong, maybe he was right. This wasn't the baby blues, not two months into the parenting game. As he pulled my head to his chest, I allowed my-self to release everything I had been trying to hide for weeks. I was *so* lonely. Since the birth of our daughter, I had built up barrier after barrier, trying so desperately to fulfil the image of being the perfect mother. I watched as other mothers truly enjoyed cooing and play-ing with their babies at the playgroup. One mum couldn't even hold conversation as she played with her son, smiling ear to ear with his giggling responses. She loved him so much, you could practically smell it.

I didn't love my baby. Not like that. Most of the time, I thought my baby tolerated me, wishing she had a better mother. Sure, I made her laugh, but so could any jokester. We didn't share the love I saw in that mother and her son. I felt like such a fraud, so ashamed, so unworthy, so different to all the other mothers. They seemed to live and breathe their children, honoured to wear the badge of 'Mum'. I hated my new Mum badge; I wanted my own 'Kirsty' badge back.

I was lost and so alone. Unable to speak out in the mum groups when they spoke of how hard it was. No one said they wanted to climb the walls after another night of no sleep. Being in the 'no sleep club' was almost like a tit swinging contest, the mark of a *real* mum; the one who can function on the least amount as possible. Other mums brought their babies to the group in colour co-ordinating outfits. Bows and tights picked out to compliment the adorable ruffle tutu. I had zero interest in what my daughter wore, other than to make sure it wasn't covered in any bodily fluids. No mother spoke a harsh word about their baby. When I did, the place filled with that awkward laugh. A charity laugh, given out to save face and move on. If no one spoke badly about their baby, then you can bet no one screamed at their baby either. No one pushed their baby away. No one saw their baby as a chore. No one hated their baby. No one was as shit a mother like I was.

Psycho Maw

As I broke down, sobbing into my partner's chest, the armour on my stone walled defences cracked. I remember feeling so sad. More than sad: a *numb* kind of sad. So sad that I had laid back and let life make me sad. As if I deserved all the upset I was feeling. Feeling isolated from everyone, yet wanting nothing more than to be present with others. To want to speak to my friends instead of pulling away in anger. I wanted nothing more than for my partner to hold and comfort me, yet I always pushed him away when he tried. My body image was crippling my self-confidence, reiterating over and over that I was ugly. Especially to my partner, the man who now had an uncontrollable lust for every other female on the planet other than me - or so said my Mind Demons.

With my wet, tear-filled face, I kept my head firmly on my partner's chest so he couldn't see just how distraught I had become in motherhood. Confessing my true feelings for the first time since I gave birth, I opened up to him.

"I feel so sad", the word "sad" seemed to keep spilling from me.

There was no other word I knew to explain the constant feeling in my gut. Seeing my confession as not only one of the few times I had really spoke to my partner in recent months, but also the first time I had truly been honest with him, my partner took a sledgehammer to my defences and said the words I needed to hear:

"I think you are verging on psychotic", as he held me tightly to his body.

Holding me so close that I couldn't escape or run from the truth, he held me there in silence, as I mulled over his words.

Psychotic!

That's the kind of crap you call your mother when she loses her shit on a Sunday as she goes on a mad cleaning rampage. Throwing shoes out the living room, muttering rants under her breath, slamming down the dirty plates left at the arses of me, my 3 brothers and our father. *"Fucking psycho",* we would whisper as we removed ourselves form the vicinity of the woman possessed, ducking under thrown shoes as we scurried out of the living room.

I'm not psychotic. I'm just a sad new mother, who misses her old life, hates her baby, and thinks her partner is having some form of weird affair with an imaginary woman called '*Heather*'.

...*actually*, he might have a point here.

Saying I'm wrong, losing, or admitting defeat, pains me more than a newborn latching onto my inferno nipples. I have absolutely no qualms ignoring you if you beat me at a game, especially when I have tried, really hard to win. There will be zero fucks given regarding the length of time in which I will ignore you. My partner, when he is feeling like he needs to receive a good dose of emotional abuse, likes to remind me he once beat me 4 nil at a card game. This must be going on 10 years ago, but it still irritates the fuck out of me. **IMMENSLY**. We do not speak of that day, if he knows what's good for him.

But maybe my partner was right for a change, much to my displeasure. Breaking down and allowing him in, stopping to listen and agreeing with his words, was difficult. It made me vulnerable. I had to remove those pointless iron cast walls I'd reinforced with impenetrable stone. I needed to eradicate it all, accept 'defeat', allow my head to rest on another human and empty my heart onto his shoulders.

My reluctance to let him in was little to do with shame and more to do with guilt and my ego. For one, I do not ask others for anything if I can help it. I'm a 'one trip' journey kind of gal. Even if that means I break both arms in the process of carrying 5 overly full grocery bags from the car to the house. My ego won't allow anything to the contrary. I would rather I pass out than tap to submission while wrestling or play fighting. Given that I grew up in a household of 3 brothers and a father with a keen interest in Karate, as did I, I learnt to hold my own or die trying. The latter being the more favourable option when faced with saying *"I give up".* Absolutely not!

Yet sometimes, you need to swallow that ludicrous ego, for it doesn't always favour your best interests. Even if that means a large, kale smoothie gulp and swallow, it needs to be done. What I couldn't see or appreciate, while my ego was holding on to the title of 'World's Strongest Mother', was that I had a loving, supportive, and deeply terrified man at my side. If I did not allow him in, he stood to lose everything. In the whole time we had been together, he had always been my cheerleader, even when I made it incredibly difficult for him. He never, and would never, do me wrong; I knew that to be true, despite the best efforts of the Mind Demons telling me otherwise. When he held me, and I allowed myself to feel our connection, I knew he, like always, had my best interests at heart.

Truthfully, I wanted to let him in. I was so tired of being alone, watching my life as an outsider. Not being able to feel moments, despite being there. I wanted my partner back. I wanted to feel love. The weight of carrying such sadness and isolation was exhausting.

Face To Face with The Truth

As my partner released me, he walked round to the other side of the table and sat across from me, taking my hands in his. I heard how worried he was. How much I had changed. How far I had pushed him away. I heard how he was scared to leave me alone with the baby while he went to work. He didn't think I would hurt the baby, but the scenario playing in his head was far worse. He told me what he thought that day he almost kicked the bathroom door down. How he worried every single day if this would be the last time he would see me or his daughter. He spoke of how distant I had become, ignoring his calls or ignoring him on a daily basis in general.

He gripped my hands tightly as he spoke of how frightened it made him when I lost my temper, so easily, with the baby. How I became harsh and unloving with her, and he was too afraid to comment. He never knew which Kirsty he would wake up beside. The funny one who doted on her baby and him, or the cold bitch who would snarl and snap, grunting harsh words at the simplest requests. He spoke of my unfounded suspicion of him and his movements, and my relentless need for information and incessant questions. I heard how he didn't know who I was anymore, how the spark had vanished from my eyes. How he missed the sound of my laugh, and the quick sarcastic wit that he fell in love with 10 years ago.

I wept as I heard how much he loved me; me and the baby. How terrified he was to lose it all. It hurt me to look him in the eyes as he demanded my whole attention.

"Please look at me. Please let me in", he pleaded with me.

I raised my sobbing head to confront the situation. **Fuck.** I was so ill. It was written all over his face, his eyes unable to contain his upset. **Fuckety fuck.** This is serious. There was no playing about here. Nowhere for the Mind Demons to retreat, no place for them to make a snide comment, forcing my partner to recoil in hurt. I was face to face with reality. More than that, the life of two other humans. The hurt of destroying someone's life that I loved so dearly.

PND has an unwavering power of destruction. And it will try its best to exert that power. How many times have we heard of happy couples having children then splitting, for reasons they can't place, other than 'things changed, it was too difficult'? How many times have we read about mothers, imprisoned for doing unspeakable things to their children in a moment of madness? How many times have we read heart-breaking stories of new mothers who have taken their own life, leaving behind a husband and a six-week-old baby? Too many.

My partner was right to pull my face to his, to hold me and demand that I listen to his words and all but force me to speak with the doctor, and to do it tomorrow. For what he saw, for weeks on end, was a new mother being torn apart, ripped to shreds, being rebuilt on the shaky foundations of anxiety, depression and psychosis. But I am stubborn; I hated admitting I needed help, I hated the suggestion of asking for help even more.

"Do it for me, please?" his response to my reluctance of speaking to the doctor.

"I'm not taking medication!" I threw back my rhetoric, trying to grasp some level of control.

I behaved like a child who has been forced to do something they don't want to do, uttering a 'You haven't won' chat back. Stubborn little asshole that I am.

Giving me the stern eyes I deserved, my partner assured me we would do **whatever** it takes in order for the playful Kirsty to reappear. Doctors, medication, couples therapy - anything. Anything at all, he was there by my side. Although, at that moment in time, he was behind me, pushing my big old stubborn mule ass into the doctor's office.

Still, this 'defeat' was nowhere near as painful as the 4-nil card ass whooping of years ago.

I made the call for the doctor's appointment, so *technically* I win.

Chapter 10

The Doctor Visit

With some reluctance, I called the doctor and made an appointment to see her as soon as possible. May as well rip the band aid off in one swift move, I thought. Get this over with. I had been finding motherhood extremely hard, I now knew there was a term to describe how I felt. 'Post-Natal Depression' apparently, according to my partner. I did check off many of the PND symptoms on the online self-diagnosis quiz, but making an appointment to speak to the doctor all seemed a bit *over the top*. Only a week or so ago, I mentioned to the breastfeeding support worker that my partner thought I was showing signs of depression. Which I obviously disagreed with, and the lovely support worker felt the same - yet she did make it clear that I was struggling more than most. Nonetheless, I wasn't in a position to argue, not anymore. Not after my partner broke his heart, making it abundantly clear he believed something was deeply wrong regarding my mental health.

With my partner sat at my side, I told the GP I was finding motherhood hard. Hesitant in my words, my partner looked at me, then to the doctor. Respectful of my vulnerability, he knew more needed to be said. Fearful that I would leave that office with nothing other than the threat of a noose still around my neck, my partner spoke up. He explained how I had been finding the recent weeks more than just hard, having more down days than good, and that my temper seems to flip like a switch. I reluctantly agreed, allowing my partner to speak the words I didn't have the strength to say, yet desperately wanted them to come from me. Deep down I knew my thoughts and actions did not reflect a happy person; at the time I think I just downplayed them, as if it was normal, not that bad, or just something every parent had to endure.

The doctor asked what I wanted from her, and if I would be interested in medication. I could feel my partner's eyes eating into me. We had spoken about medication; I thought it useless, not really helping the root of any problems, merely a plaster to slap on top. In truth, I saw it as a defeat; a physical form of needing help, in order to be a mother. My partner disagreed, imploring with me that they wouldn't be forever, and could provide a much-needed balance to my emotions, allowing me the clarity to seek help if I chose. The nights filled with reading blogs and articles had taught him that for many people, anti-depressants can bring restoration. Stabilising moods. Neither up nor down. Bringing people to a state of balance. Something we both knew I needed.

An uneasy lull filled the room. Both the doctor and my partner uniting against my depression, waited for my ego to step aside and take the much-needed respite and tools I would need to beat my depression. We sat in silence, that heavy weighted silence when you know you are the one who needs to make the decision - one that is so obvious from the faces around you - yet there is some-thing inside wanting you to pull away. My options: to retreat the warmth of the known, no matter how barren and inhospitable the land may be, or take a leap into the *unknown* and hope things are a little greener on the other side.

I took the prescription, *agreeing* to a low dose of anti-depressants. I was still breastfeeding and refused, point blank, to stop. The drugs needed to be low enough for the safety of my baby. At the time, I think I hid behind breastfeeding; it provided a cover, preventing a higher dose of drug which somehow, in my head, meant I wasn't 'on' anti-depressants. I was only on a low dose, akin to nothing, in my eyes. For what a failure I would have been as a mother, the one who needed medication to play the part?

A Hard Pillow to Swallow

On the first 'round' of anti-depressants, I took them for 6 or 9 months. I fucking **hated** them. One: I didn't want to be that 'medicated mother'. And two, three, four, five (the list goes on): I hated the side effects and hated calling the doctor to get a repeat prescription. I hated the word 'Sertraline'. I hated confessing that I needed help to be a mother, to function as any kind of normal human during a time people proclaimed to be the greatest days of their lives.

Never one to lie or hide the truth, being on medication put me in turmoil. I felt as though admitting I took anti-depressants was admitting defeat. Yet I refused to lie or hush-hush their existence within my life. I was caught in some weird, arrogant, ego-driven place of pride, wanting so badly to be the well put together mum; the one who laughed her annoyance away as she underarm carried her wailing child out of the store. I didn't want to be the mother who hated her life so much that she needed to pop a pill each day just to keep the whole ship afloat. It seems so silly now, as I would willingly dress-up as an anti-depressant on the school run if I thought it would help me be the best mother I can be.

The side effects bothered me the most, to which there are many, as the leaflet read. I could have used that patient information leaflet as a scarf, as I unravelled the densely folded leaflet over and over. Taking weeks for my body to acclimatise, I would *literally* buzz some days; I couldn't keep still, I had to move move move. Some days, I would be euphoric, living the dream, so happy, in the clouds, for no reason. Other days, my skin would itch. My knees became uncomfortable, needing steroid cream to stop the itching. A really strange side effect, I know, and what a tit I felt like as I took my itchy knee to the doctor and moaned that I thought it was the anti-depressants giving me a red and inflamed knee. To be fair, in the previous weeks, I had lifted my top as soon as walking into the doctor's office, desperately seeking a resolve to the thrush that wanted to reside in my breasts for longer than it should, according to the mum forums online. So really, what's an itchy and flaky knee in relation to an unprovoked thrush filled titty flash? A mighty upgrade, I'd say!

And here's the biggest reason I hated anti-depressants; they make reaching orgasm nigh on **IMPOSSIBLE**. The finest Pornhub category, subsidised with an overindulgent sex shop haul and fuck - even add in some banging pizza to really get the excitement levels high - still would not release the clit angel from her slumber. Not to say it wasn't enjoyable - it was; more like your clit goes to sleep in the middle of the act, and despite your best efforts, despite a bulk buy of batteries burning out the finest vibrator, nothing, NOTHING would reach the peak of that Everest, and set off a party cannon. I might have a patient and understanding partner, but I'm not sure training for a marathon, in the snow, wearing one of those elastic resistance bands that snap you back to the starting line, is what my poor partner signed up for. There are limits to everyone's stamina. Pleading that we give up for the night; *"It's been an hour, tonight is just not the night",* as my partner downed another electrolyte pack, I thought, *'Aye right, I'll decide'*, cranking the vibrator up to pneumatic drill status, determined not to be beat, yet again, by motherhood. If you are wondering if it's possible to acquire third degree burns on your clit while in the art of 'love making', i.e., 'I will not be beaten', then yes, yes, it is.

Still, I didn't win. I hate losing, especially losing to your own 'may as well be dead' vagina. There's another thing they don't tell you about motherhood.

Crusty knees and lifeless vagina put aside, I persevered with the anti-~~sex~~ depressants for several months, until I thought I was 'healed'. Boy was that a mistake. My partner was correct; they did provide much needed stability, a level playing field in which I could refocus and see things how they really are. However, unlike the pills in *Drop Dead Fred*, it didn't erase *'Heather'* from my mind. This mythical, imaginary woman my partner was supposedly seeing behind my back. Suspicion still festered within me. Distrust was still the foundation of my relationship - with everyone. It was clear, yes, the drugs helped, but for me, they would not be the cure to my illness. They wouldn't stop the intrusive thoughts. They wouldn't stop me watching every move my partner made. They wouldn't magically make me love my baby. They wouldn't remove the Mind Demons. They wouldn't let Kirsty out of the mind cage, berated daily by the demons. They just would not be strong enough to defeat the beast within my head.

Chapter 11

A Year of Intrusive thoughts

Imagine you had amazing news. You're absolutely bursting at the seams to tell your friends. You cannot, and do not want to, keep it in, or else your head will explode. Now imagine that news is intrusive thoughts instead, the Mind Demon's constant chattering that your partner is fantasising about other women. And that's just one example; I have a *whole* bucket of crazy, filled with more of these intrusive thoughts. The more you try to ignore the mental noise, repel it with logic and reason, the more it festers, growing stronger and uglier. A bit like dousing *Gizmo* with water, only for him to spawn real nasty gremlins that terrorise the place. That's how I view the Mind Demons, who were hell-bent on destroying my life, and that wonderful long-term relationship I had going with the love of my life.

The more I tried to 'catch' those thoughts and disprove them, the stronger they became. Trying to hush them only made me infatuated more. As if I was holding in some terrible secret from the rest of the world, mainly from my partner. After all, he was the one having an elaborate affair with *'Heather'*, that fictitious woman from my mind.

What I really wanted to do was scream the thoughts aloud, to confront my partner about 'Heather'. I wanted to know if he really did think my hips had become grotesque, my body 'damaged' by childbearing. I wanted to know if my friends even really wanted to be my friend. I wanted to call them out for everything I perceived they had done to wrong me, like 'ignoring' my texts. What I wanted, was to say these thoughts out loud so I didn't need to keep them in my mind, swirling around, day after day, whipping up into a frenzy that made me hate everyone around me - all these bastards who treated me so badly. I wanted these words out my head, because I didn't know who the fuck to listen to anymore; the Mind Demons, or the reality I had become so far removed from.

This is how people become misunderstood; when their actions are taken way out of context. We often interpret the actions of others through the lens of our own lives, presuming the way they act to be a reflection of what they think of you. This isn't always the case. The majority of the time, how a person behaves, treats or speaks to other people is actually a **reflection of themselves**. How they see and value themselves has far less, if anything, to do with you. Think of the school bully, aggressive and angry, pushing other children around. That bully would terrorise any child they could, not just you, because the issue lies within *them*; it comes from their unhappiness, their trauma or abuse. The same can be said for those fighting mental illness.

A Depressive Mouth Is a Nasty Mouth

In the 12 months since I gave birth to our daughter, I had said and done things that I regret. Hurting my partner with the words *"I'm not in love with you anymore"*, surprisingly isn't the top regret. Screaming at my newborn, however, possibly makes the top three. Sitting in a parked car, outside a shop, in the middle of the day, my face expressionless, I said, *"I want to sleep with other people, just to feel. To feel anything"*, to my long term, understanding but not bulletproof partner - *that* has to take the crown.

For a long time, I held on to my every action and thought. I'm not sure when I told my partner I had screamed at our baby. I kept that deep inside me, completely consumed by shame and guilt, enough to turn my stomach and preventing me from eating. I lost over three stone within two months of giving birth to our daughter, dropping to below my normal weight. Instead of nutrition, my gut was filled with secrets and anxiety, fortified with guilt. I hid everything from the outside world, and from my partner, as best I could. It ate me alive, from the inside out.

Holding on to these 'secrets' only made it worse; it made me mentally and physically ill. When I was faced with the choice to either let my partner stay and be a family, or to let him leave, I also had another choice; to speak up and work as a team, or keep quiet. And well, who really knows what darkness the solitude may have brought? I dare not think about it.

It sounds a simple thing, to speak what's on your mind, but where depression is concerned, it is anything but. Your head might be filled with words, yet somehow, they cannot make the trip to your mouth. They become lost, and you, silent. Or you *do* speak up, and the words become misheard. Depression rarely likes to speak in coherent sentences, at least not ones you want to repeat out loud. At times, trying to speak is what I imagine a deer in headlights to be thinking: *'What the fuck? How the fuck? And where the fuck can I go to be anywhere but here?'.* Huge silences could fill the room in the middle of an argument, prompted by my suspicious mind. *"I'm thinking"*, used as an excuse to buy myself more time when it was my turn to speak, but I didn't know what to say. *"What is wrong?"* Not the easiest question to answer. Not when your mind has been playing a back catalogue of torments and intrusive thoughts.

My intrusive thoughts were a varied bunch. A little bit of *'you are a shit mother'*, here and there, mixed in with *'you are a failure'*, from time to time. But the real gold standard, the real beast my Mind Demons just loved to talk about were always of the genre, *'your partner doesn't love you, thinks you look like shit and just stays here for the comfort'*. A bit niche, I will admit, and completely unfounded. The truth couldn't be further from this. Yet, my mind seemed to think this is our *'let's get it on'* track, cranking up the volume right before the lights get dimmed when my partner and I were are alone.

Literally Can't Hear Myself Think

Sometimes I knew what was wrong, but terrified to admit it. The problem can seem like complete madness to me, far less the human beside me. Even to close friends, I would only hint around the issue; these girls that I had spent 10 years of my life with, crammed into toilet cubicles, sharing far too much drunken detail about boys, bodies and 'sworn never-to-tell' secrets. We have shared everything from bikini waxes to sex positions (not literally, we aren't *those* kind of friends - although, with enough drink in us, we may as well have been). But when it came to saying out loud *"I'm suspicious of my partner",* I could feel how absurd these thoughts were, and I didn't need to see it confirmed on the face of someone else.

Following a short stint with anti-depressants and a quick with-drawal from them, my mind continued to torment me. Sure, time and the drugs had taken the edge off my illness - or at least, that's the image I wanted to portray - but the truth was, on a daily basis, I was still battling a fucked-up perception of my life.

As my maternity leave ended, returning to work only amplified the strain I was under. The hustle and bustle that comes with working a full-time job and trying to chauffeur a toddler about, gave ample opportunity for me to break down, for me to sob uncontrollably once I put my daughter to bed, before my partner made it home for the evening. Each time this happened, which was weekly, my partner and I would sit across from each other in a stalemate situation. He wanted to listen, to help, and I wanted to keep the argument going, not yet reaching the topic of upset; the latest intrusive thought that was warping my point of view. Latest, but not new. An intrusive thought that should have been put to rest easily, months previously after we spoke about it during that particular breakdown. Yet here we are, again. Him completely perplexed, me seemingly going round and round in circles, not quite getting my words out.

The words could be painful, to me and to others. Who wants to say out loud *"I'm toxic to my child"?* What if people agree? What if they don't? Either way, I believed it. It was real and raw to me. Other times, I could only feel the upset, not place it. I didn't have the words to communicate it, as I genuinely did not know why I was having certain thoughts or feelings. All I knew was I wanted to be left alone. The pit deep in my gut pulling me down, the exhausttion of depression leaving me numb, and still after so many months, surpassing the year anniversary of becoming a mother.

As more time passed, the Mind Demons grew stronger, as if they had been working overtime every evening. Some nights they really done me a dirty. Forcing me to shut down. Eyes dead. Ears passive. Body limp. Words aren't going to come freely, not today. I felt like shit, and I didn't know why. Probably because **I AM** a shit human, so say the thoughts, over and over.

Intrusive Thoughts Cleanse - Could Do With a 'Sensitive' Soap

For each time this happened to me, each time I have been forced to speak, it has been **unbearable**. My body becomes covered in cold sweat, hands unable to stay still as my arms itch and I remove all eye contact. I physically squirm, unable to control my discomfort.

That is, until I speak; I speak those words no one wants to hear. I **need** to say them, and I am truly sorry I do. For my partner and for myself. This illness is kind to no one and the only thing I had learnt in the 18 months since becoming a mother was to use my words. **Just say it**. Remove even a slither of the pain. I knew by now these are not *my* thoughts and I did not need to embrace the weight of them. I would say, *"I know I'm bat-shit. I know this sounds crazy, but this is how I feel. This is what my mind is screaming"*, before I verbally spat whatever was circling in there. All the while, I wished the ground would crack open and swallow me whole.

What was circling around my head, were intrusive thoughts. Unwanted thoughts in my own mind, and ones I couldn't stop entering, no matter how hard I tried. Mine originated from some primal, deep, nasty insecurity that I didn't even know I had: being secure and comfortable in my relationship. The shower seemed to be the prime location for the Demons to crank out a chorus of intrusive thoughts. Over and over. If not in the shower, then just as part of the everyday chattering of the mind. Day after day, hour after hour. The more I tried to rebuff the claims that my partner thinks my tits resemble pick & mix sacks that have had a few handfuls taken out, the more the Demons pounded me. I learnt it is best not to bite, to allow them to speak freely and let the thought pass. I know this. But some days I willingly stepped into the ring with the Mind Demons, losing before I had even begun.

These thoughts became more than just notions. In the depths of depression, they became my reality. Genuinely believing I was a poor mum, worthless, an object only kept by my partner, used for sex, should he feel pushed to the point of being horny enough to stomach my body. You have got to hand it to intrusive thoughts; they are smart little buggers, the ultimate masters of manifestation. Making you believe their every word until you change and become them, in your own mind at least. Persistent too. If at first the intrusive thoughts don't succeed, then try, try, try, try and try again, they will. Being sure to hang around long enough, bash the shit out of you hard enough, scream at you loud enough, that you will start to believe them. Major labelling theory, self-fulfilling prophecy vibes going on here.

You are told you are a worthless failure, and therefore you *are* a worthless failure, changing your outlook and behaviour to fulfil that role. For not many people have the strength to stand up against such harsh words, shouting back, *"that's not true, I am worthy!!"* Not at first anyhow, and the Mind Demons know it.

Do (not) repeat after me:

'You are a shit mother'

'Your baby hates you'

'You have no friends'

'Your friends tolerate you'

'Your tits are sad Hacky Sacks that need refilling'

'Yes, your partner can tell the difference'

'Yes, your vagina does look like it's been in the Demolition Derby'

'Other mums don't hate their baby'

'Other mums do it better than you'

'Your partner speaks to women when you aren't there'

'Your partner lies to you'

'Your partner doesn't love you'

'Your partner knows what to say to keep you sweet'

'People think you need to stop talking'

'You have nothing interesting to say'

'You have a 'mum bod' now'

'You should be able to stop your baby from crying'

'Your baby has an undiagnosed disease'

'If your baby doesn't nap, she will die'

'Other mums know you are a shit mum'

'You look like a terrible mother'

...um, no? Surely all of the above aren't true?...

Like some form of twisted, shit affirmation system, these thoughts (and a truck load more) battered me daily. How do you stand up in the face of that barrage? How do you stop yourself believing what you are constantly hearing? Daily. Hourly. When you least expect it. Being a parent is tiresome enough without the added load of a mind focused on dragging you down. At times, it seemed easier to believe the thoughts; why would they be hanging around if there wasn't at least a shred of evidence to support them?

Intrusive Thoughts 2.0

I also learned intrusive thoughts came with 'add-ons' - supporting features, if you will. Detectives and doubters. Like having your very own courtroom drama in your head, although the roles are not defined and can switch with a moment's notice. In a whirlwind of abuse, I stood there, mentally in the middle of it all. Physically, I was in the store, trying to buy fruit, caught off guard by the mother who gave a polite smile. More than likely the smile of, *'kids are little shits, amarite?'*. But I took it as, *'You look so dishevelled. Are those grapes you are buying? There are better fruits. Why is your baby fussing? Do you not look after her properly?'*

As much as I tried to shut down the thoughts there and then, putting forward my evidence to the judge to prove I was right, it was just a friendly mother showing solidarity in the store, my defence was always futile. I had shown the courtroom I cared and so erupted the Mind Demons, wheeling a wide screen TV into the courtroom, ready to play the *'You are so shit'* video to the judge and jury. A video which is quickly catching up with Baby Shark on number of times viewed (8.4 billion, wtf?!).

The only thing I could do was freeze in the store, mentally battling my own mind, arguing how absurd its train of thought was. She was just a friendly mother, nodding her head in solidarity. Not that of a horrible, nasty woman, who judged my very being because my baby liked grapes. *How insane! Now shut up!*

Sometimes I could win, even just a little. I left the store, breathed through the 'event' and tried to shake the thoughts from me as much as possible. But, when the intrusive thought courtroom drama was a little closer to home, a little closer to exposing my deepest and most embarrassing insecurities, shaking them off was a bit more difficult, especially when it was just me (and my Mind Demons) and my partner alone. There are not many places to run and hide from Mind Demons pulling the strings when you are face to face with your partner, in the bedroom...

Chapter 12

Sex and The Mind Demons

For the most part, I looked and acted like the mothers I admired and longed to emulate. The working mother who dropped off the kid before rushing to her job, sipping coffee with co-workers, taking suspiciously long tea breaks while we vented about life with children. My workday seemed to pass in a blur. I hurried about, completing all the duties of the day before heading into rush hour traffic to collect my now toddler, and would then play the part of the doting mother - a tired one at that. With one eye on the clock, I wished away the few short hours I spent with my daughter in the evening, until it was time for the nightly bedtime ritual and finally time I could relax. Obviously not before the back and forth, for hours, in which she would try a whole manner of excuses to stay out of bed, including - and this is my all-time favourite - that one day her father and I would die, and now she was too upset to get any sleep. To say I was taken back by an impromptu discussion of my own mortality and the pain it would cause my daughter is a vast understatement. She wouldn't be the only one not sleeping that night.

I did it all. Working full-time. All the mothering. All the driving around. All the organising childcare. And all the fretting on the days my daughter would fall ill and I would have to call in sick to work to look after her. And I hated 90% of it. I still felt trapped, alone and confused. My mind was still tormenting me daily, 18 months after my first breakdown. I had slipped back into society, back into a form of life that resembled 'me' pre-kid, but I was nothing like 'me'. I felt like a fraudster in my own life. I tried to merge - almost erase - the last 18 months of becoming a parent into the life I once had, as if returning to work would magically turn me back into 'Kirsty' pre-baby. But all it did was add more to the load on my back, giving me less time and space to think, let alone deal with the mental illness that was still heavily influencing my mind.

Around about this time I created an online blog - *HonestK*. This became a place I could honestly share my thoughts, honestly; an outlet for everything swirling within my mind. My grievance at the injustice of society, the unequal load mothers must carry and the mental damage it can inflict. I became hyper aware of the imbalance of pressures placed on mothers, the ones that drove many to dwell in dark places, just like the place I was still shackled to. When the feeling hit me, I wrote about it on my blog; how I was feeling, mentally drained or enraged with life. I shared as much as of my mind as I could, relishing the cathartic release and the validation I found online. I shared so much of my life, so much of the innards many don't wish to acknowledge, let alone share. But there was always one area I couldn't quite find the words to explain, the one area my Mind Demons had a deathly grip over: me and my self-worth behind closed doors.

Scheduled Pump Anyone?

Turns out, children are the ultimate cock-blockers, especially when they begin wailing just as you've decided to pull your best moves - *OK, OK,* "moves" might be extreme; more like, your best moan to your partner that it's been at least 2 weeks since you looked at each other in a manner other than to indicate someone must go buy toilet roll from the store. Seductive lines quickly change to, *"When was the last time we pumped?"* as you peer over the mobile phone, knackered from the two-hour bedtime routine with the kid, mustering up the energy to ~~shag~~ nag your other half, only to be interrupted even looking at each other, as you hear the creeping of tiny feet coming back down the stairs for the third time.

Kids have the tendency to block any hopes of adult entertainment by depleting both parents of all energy or want to engage with one another, let alone 'exercise' together. Obviously, after an evening of wrestling a tired toddler to bed and throwing plates into the sink in a game of 'who will crack and clean tonight', sex will not be on the agenda, despite it being tonight's topic of moan. If the clock is close to 9 p.m. and you haven't even initiated it, let alone worked up the strength to remove those mismatching, oversized and really needing tossed out pyjama bottoms - then *fuck no* - it ain't happening. So, like all great love affairs we see in films, the night of passion will be scheduled for the next available free slot in the week. And, by "scheduled", I mean we swear an oath to each other that we WILL put down our phones for long enough, and we WILL actually spend time looking at each other as opposed to the red 'N', flashing on the screen of our favourite guilty pleasure - the film streaming service.

On the scheduled evening, the mind prep begins. Tonight **IS** going to be a *good* night. We will forgo the usual nightly plan of mindlessly scrolling social media while making bare minimum verbal contact with anyone after the kid has gone to bed. All for a night of adult interaction. ~~Gutted~~. Or maybe at least a solid 30 minutes of adult interaction… I've got needs and all that, but I still have priorities. Not watching that series, the one I paid for, while I stare at my phone all night, ain't about to be put on the back burner just because my loins, or our relationship, need attending to!

A Night of Hot Mental Breakdowns

Rummaging through the freezer, I would acquire the finest beige dinner for the little one. There will be no finely chopped nutrients tonight; mum's got to save her energy for the main event. Squirting ketchup onto the plate, the only thing there remotely the colour of a vegetable, my mind drifts, excited to regain that 'Goddess' title of years gone by. Fuck it, I **WILL** be putting on that bodycon black number! My tits might fall out of it when I do my 'seductive' bend and arse slap, and it might feel like I am flossing my ovaries with the thong, but boy, am I looking forward to this evening - and I **WILL** feel like a sex Goddess tonight! Just the adults. Back in the place the whole love affair started, in our private safe space, shared by only the two of us… and about four other voices in my head.

It's not been just the two of us for a while. The birth of the baby seemed to birth this whole other set of voices that have taken up residency in my head. And for some reason, they pipe up the loudest when it comes to sex. Actually, that's a lie; they pipe up when it comes to viewing myself in any sexual manner, not in the way I view myself as attractive or hot. My arse does look pretty banging in those jeans and I have *"snapped back"* nicely, at least when I have my clothes on. But when I take off the protection of the high-waisted 'hide it all' jeans, when I peel off the fitted t-shirt, when I lay there, bare to the bone, I feel a million miles away from who I was before having a baby. And on the rare occasion I don't, the Mind Demons are only too happy to come out of standby, reminding me so.

My hips are wider. My thighs, ripped. My stomach, wobbly, mark-ed, stretched. My torso, covered in stretch marks large enough to have their own postcode. My tits, *ohhh* my tits... blown up like party balloons and then left to the side (literally), to deflate once the party ended and the buffet closed. My skin, allergic to elasticity,

127

apparently, and in need of a deep, skin quenching hydro mask. My labia, there's a new sister in town. No thanks to the doctor (who my labia could wave at now) given the extent of her poor sewing skills. And the vagina, what do we say about her? I'm sure she could speak for herself after being stretched to epic proportions.

Good pep talk Mind Demons, good job. That's me all primed and ready… for a mental breakdown in the bedroom.

The mental berating of my physical appearance is merely a backup singer to the real, controlling Mind Demon, the overall beast: PND and its relentless pursuit to whip any self-worth from my grasp. The Mind Demons and PND all interlink, like a sewage system, pumping absolute shit throughout my mind. All controlled by PND, the supreme leader. The one constantly figuring out ways to etch away at my core, who I am, my self-worth and how I perceive myself in relation to others. PND uses the Mind Demons to do her evil biddings, to belt out chorus after chorus of what it knows will pain me; the belief that I am an unworthy human being.

There is no better feeding ground to incite hate than when I am bare naked, in the supposedly 'safe and comfortable' space of being with my partner. The space where I cannot hide my vulnerability, for it seems to seep out of my head, infecting my body, taking control and severing all ties with who I really am and what I want. In such a private and exclusive place, PND and the Mind Demons have the scope to push their agenda forward, for where can I hide when I am face to face with one person, in an act so demanding of your whole being, such as sex?

I've been listening to the chatter of these Mind Demons since the birth of my daughter 18 months ago. I know they speak lies; I know they are there to bring me down. By now, I can brush away some of their droning voice. Yeah, my arse is a little wider since childbirth, but I actually kind of like it. The stretch marks around my torso, more of a 'world wonder' than a site of hatred. How the skin didn't completely rip off, given the size of the bump, is a topic you could research for a PhD. As for the vagina? She seems to get the job done. Although the post-partum shrinking clit, I could do without. (There's another secret the mothers before us seem to want to take to the grave! Why didn't anyone warn me of *that?!*)

I can shrug things off, but I'm not immune to the loud team of bullies in my mind. The constant annoying drivel of *'your body has seen better days'* is a little off-putting when you are trying to get your Kim K-esque sex video on. No one needs that kind of dis-couragement. Eventually, when the oven is hot enough, the mental body shaming doesn't matter too much. I can get past it, enjoy the moment, trying not to focus too much on the new tit swinging that amazes me (yet seems to spur on my keen and eager other half), but that's when my trigger gets pulled. No, not *that* kind of trigger - the exact opposite in fact; my partner and my body; my *post-partum* body.

My mind begins to race and the internal fanfare goes a little bit like this:

*"What does he think? What does he **really** think? Surely he can't find me attractive anymore? He must only say he fancies me because there is no one else here to have sex with. He can't really love these new swinging tits, he just knows I won't let him near me if he doesn't butter me up. He's a fucking liar! Mind that time he lied, straight to my face? Such a good liar. What else is he lying about? Oh, fuck, look at my belly hanging down. There's no way he doesn't see that and give it a double take. **Liar**. I bet he's thinking of someone else while we are together. He doesn't love me. I'm such a mess. He must think I'm so ugly. But men are men, right? They will pump anything, even 'mum bods'. Needs must. I'm such an idiot, an ugly idiot…"*

I'm no sex or porn expert, but I'm going to hazard a guess that this kind of dialogue wouldn't make it into the script of the world's best foreplay or pillow talk. If you want to snap up a vagina, closing her doors in an almighty parched slam, then may I suggest using the above as a sexual affirmation.

When the Mind Demons found a crack in my defences, like wondering what my partner thinks about my postpartum body, then they tend to go rapid fire. And when the Mind Demons unload their full arsenal, right in the middle of love making, there is no chance of me being able to focus on the duo act, not when my mind is intent on bringing the third wheel into the bedroom.

Intrusive Thoughts Make for Poor Foreplay

Women are perceived as being some kind of 'masters at multi-tasking', however; I think we draw the line at trying to have sex when our mind is so focused on destroying us. Trying to have any form of enjoyable or meaningful intimacy isn't going to happen once I've 'lost my mind'. Entirely unable to stay in the moment, participating instead as batter, mentally hitting away negative thought after negative thought. The longer I stayed in the realm of self-hate, the less I wanted my partner to touch me, and given that we are in the middle of the *act*, that is less than ideal.

Like a tidal wave, the mental abuse washed away any of the structures I had placed to keep the thoughts at bay. As they began to spiral, it was evident to me that the Mind Demons were winning. I soon started to analyse every move of my partner and feed it to the Demons. His facial expression means he doesn't like me. His tone implies I'm not good enough. In the mental chaos, old memories and conversations are pulled into this obscene sex-narrative. I remember he once told me petite women are his type. I don't fit that bill, not anymore. Sure, I'm short, but those hips aren't so small anymore. As best I could, I tried to bring my mind back to the current event, but it was not safe there either. *Careful!* Don't move to the side too much or you'll squash that pliable tit under your elbow. Look at them, what the fuck happened to them during pregnancy?! *Sad sacks.*

On and on my mind bullied me. Soon enough, I was completely out of the moment. Too far gone down a horrid rabbit hole of self-sabotage mixed with high doses of nasty comments that would inflict emotional abuse if directed towards another human.

As much as I tried to settle my mind, focus on the here and now and the wonderful man I have to myself, it was no good. Whatever he said, my mind had another view of it. If he told me he loves my curves, I would remember he once lied to me before (having a cigarette on the sly and telling me he wasn't smoking again), and so he *must* be lying to me now. My mind told me I am a means to an end, that he's a man and would say anything, to any curve, on any woman, to get his end away. In my confused state, my mind be-came activated in all the wrong areas; quickly accruing pieces in some form of dark, weird, spiteful jigsaw puzzle, depicting utter distrust in another person. Everyday acts, I saw as malice, full of ill motives. My partner hasn't spoken to me all week (but he had), so did I really think he is here in this bed with me for the 'connec-tion'? *Not a chance.* He's only here with me because he can be, because he has needs. Even if those needs must be filled by touching my horrendous body.

To add a little *more* flavour to the events - as if the mental circus wasn't enough of a distraction while trying to be with my partner - I was reminded that **I am with** my partner. In a private space. A reserved space that only the two of us share with each other. And here I was, wasting it all. If I loved him, then shouldn't I enjoy it more? Shouldn't he be my sole focus? If my love was so strong, why would I even listen to, let alone second guess, the thoughts I was having? And that's when the tone changed. My focus was completely lost. I felt like a failure, yet again. First in motherhood, and now as a partner. I scold myself for lacking the ability to be present in the moment, a moment that I wanted. I scold myself for not loving my body. I scold myself for saying I have beaten PND, when it is quite clear that I have not. I scold myself for the hurt I have brought into our bedroom, yet again. I hate myself for the pain I bring to my partner, for the love I feel I lack for him. As the mental character assassination of two people, combined with deep rooted insecurities, snowballed into anxiety, it's safe to assume that no one is having their end away tonight.

Naked Therapy Sessions - 1/10 Do Not Recommend

Ultimately, I get busted - and not in 'that' way. There are limits to my multi-tasking abilities, and having a full-blown, internal debate, while trying to focus in the bedroom is well out of my remit. My body lets me down first, pulling away, becoming uncomfortable with my partner's touch. I can't have someone touching me who I believe doesn't lust after me, let alone doesn't love me. Unconsciously, my hands come up to cover my body, mainly my breasts. My body screams *'leave me alone'*, while my mind watches on. Confused. Alone. Upset. The demons have twisted the cogs on full steam tonight and my body language shows it. I lie to my partner when he asks if I'm okay; I tell him everything is fine, as I deathly defend my body from his touch.

Pulling my face away from his kiss, the air quickly spoils from the anguish. This time, *he* pulls away, angry, upset and confused; the place *I* always seem to be when I'm meant to be in the moment. I lay there, accosted - and rightly so - by my partner, asking me what is wrong. I have the answer, but I don't want to share it. I don't know *how* to share it. It's been almost two years since we first heard the words "post-natal depression". How can it still be infecting our life, and in such a private and intimate place? Plus, this is **awkward AF**. I mean, I may have done the classic birth-poop in front of him, been at my absolute worst after childbirth, but that's a walk in the park compared to a weird, naked, half argument, half therapy session, MID-SEX. Take a bow Mind Demons, *take a bow*.

There was absolutely no getting out of this one. We had been here before; this isn't the first naked conquer for the demons. Usually, I can skirt around the issue. Say, *"I'm having thoughts again"*, then reluctantly share a palatable variation of what is really going on in my head, then hopefully get back to business. Sometimes they cannot be shared, as I don't know exactly what they are or how to convey them. I know the thoughts are lies, horrible, nasty talk from my mind, that they aren't real. But once they have grown so strong, so loud, there is nothing I can do to stop them dwelling in my gut, making me feel physically sick. All the reassurance in the world won't quash them, no loving words, no amount of body praising, no matter how much he looks me right in the eyes, with everything he has and tells me *"You are the most beautiful woman I've ever seen".* Nothing will dampen the power of these thoughts. Once they take hold, I may as well call it quits for the night, before they **force** me to call it quits.

For some reason, that night was a little different. Something had been on my mind a while. And although sharing exactly what was on my mind to my partner often helped, there's was still a deep doubt, eating away at me inside.

When PND took up residency, it did so by removing certain parts of who I am. One of which was who I am as a partner. I am a failure as a mother, and I may as well be a failure as a partner. To get to this place, PND had broken down the very fabric of our relationship: trust. And I broke it, with the help of the Mind

Demons. Pillar after pillar, they destroyed the foundation of our bond. Instead of reassurance, there was deceit. Instead of lust, there was suspicion. Instead of me, there was someone else. The constant every single day chatter in my head had whittled away the core of our relationship, one in excess of 10 years. With absolutely no cause or basis for these mind accusations, it was crumbling - in my head at least. The reason I could not stand his touch, was because I felt I did not know him. The reason I imagined he envisions other women, was because I was so suspicious. The reason I could not connect with him, was because I 'believed' I was not in love with him.

And there is it, the issue eating up my mind: I'm not in love with him anymore.

I wanted to scream the words and hold them in all at once. I didn't know what to do, or if my thoughts were real. I could not understand the confusion within me, but I knew the emotion. My partner asked what was wrong, his appetite unmet with my pleas of everything being 'fine', so he pushed harder for the real reason. As my heart pounded and the familiar cold sweat covered my body, lying in the least favourite sex position - 'Therapy Session Within the Sheets' - we lay side by side. Me trying to place space between us, my partner, doing the opposite, knowing, given a chance, I'll pull that duvet over my head like the invisibility cloak of *Harry Potter* to escape this awful situation.

He placed his hands on me, pulling my body to his. In return I became rigid, wanting him to leave me alone. Wanting to be anywhere but in this forced confessional booth.

"I don't think I am in love with you anymore." There. I said it.

I **had** to say it. The words blurted out from my mouth. I gasped, just as much as my partner was shocked. Not quite believing what I had just said.

The words brought an immense hurt, silencing the room. I couldn't bear to look at him. He reacted in kind, by removing his comforting hand off my shoulder. He has been nothing but supportive in all these years, despite the words and vile my PND had thrown at him, abhorrent at times. He is a strong person, the strongest, most admiral person I have ever met, or will likely ever meet. My cheer-leader always. The absolute love of my life, and I, his. Always. But even he cannot rebuff those words; everyone has their limit, a kink in their armour. Hearing that I was no longer in love with him - that was sure to leave a mark.

Pulling the duvet up, to somewhat cover my vulnerability, I sobbed uncontrollably, as my mind went **fucking crazy**.

"What the fuck have I done now? Am I really not in love with this man? Why am I here then? What am I doing, stringing him along? What a fucking monster I am. I will never find a person who loves me, truly and unconditionally - as I've sure tested these last few years - more than this amazing human next to me. I am about to seriously fuck up, I better get this under control. But how can I? I don't even know who is speaking, who do I believe? If my mind is so set for ending this relationship, then why do I feel like I could vomit if he stood up and walked out? Why won't I let myself be happy? Why do I listen to these Mind Demons so much?"

Wiping the snot from my seriously contorted, ugly cry face (hey maybe I am channelling my inner Kim K after all!), I pulled the duvet up a little higher to my chin, as I turned to see the damage my mouth had inflicted this time. I saw the exhaustion on his face as he wiped his eye, removing the tear before I could see it. I knew he was upset. I didn't need to see the wet on his face; I could feel his pain. It was the force keeping us on our own side of the bed, for once.

As we lay there, both with our eyes forward, looking at those large doors of the sliding wardrobe we both hate so much, I snuck a peek at him like a scolded child. Too scared to catch his view, but also desperately wanting his attention. I took a large breath in knowing what was about to happen next would be a turning point in our relationship. No more pissing around the subject. No more giving brief, filtered, snippets of the mind. I've just killed this man, and I'm not even sure I wanted to.

I could feel it rising, the verbal diarrhoea I felt on the morning I threatened to end our relationship, just weeks after giving birth. It was coming out; I couldn't hold back all the things racing round my mind anymore. A literal a 'mind dump', in all the metaphorical senses one can pull from that statement. My body was rejecting whatever poison was inside of me. It needed to come out, long ago. And it was about to come out now, at 1 a.m. after a failed night of passion. *The best time to clear your chest.*

I didn't say I was sorry for confessing I'm not in love. I would never apologise for my truth. But was it the truth? I was so torn. Unable to think, let alone make a balanced decision. I knew I loved him. The thought of being without him tore my heart. So, I couldn't understand why I wasn't **in** love with him, or if that was even true.

I told him I felt like an unfit mother, toxic to our child. Terrified of passing down this mental illness, or worse, raising a child who lives in fear of their mother. I felt like a selfish partner, incapable of giving love when I felt nothing. Dead inside, numb. Resentful too. Giving anything to be in the relationship he was in; loving, comfortable, stable, safe, and madly, deeply in love. I wanted to be in love so badly. To be taken in his arms and believe him when he tells me he loves and adores me. Those words just roll off me like ketchup on that 'washable' paint we used in the living room. (Praise be to us, for that stroke of genius.) Gone without a trace, as if it was never there, much like anything nice he said to me. I ached from missing him, missing our connection, yet I rarely granted myself to be relaxed in his embrace. Everything about this situation hurt. The turmoil was too strong. The thoughts in my mind are not my own, but I couldn't decipher what was reality or the words of PND. So, I told them all. Everything. I knew it was painful to hear, but it was no picnic to feel or express them either. I just remember crying, so much. Being so alone in a room with the person I idolise, the person who would never let me feel alone or hurt me. But I *was* so alone, from everything and everyone. Continuing to carry this illness as a core character trait, wiping out any happiness I felt in the process.

"I'm so broken."

"I don't know how to fix this. I don't know what's wrong with me"

"I'm so broken. Please leave me. You deserve better"

"I'm sorry. I'm sorry I've done this to us."

"You should go. You and the baby. You can't be around me. Find someone better, someone who can love you."

"I'm broken"

"I'm so broken…"

The words **"I'm broken"**, on repeat, poured from my soul as I rocked back and forth on the bed. Now sitting up, my head buried into my hands, pleading: *"Take the baby, get away from me. I'm so fucked up and I have no idea how to fix it".* I make it clear. This is exactly how I'm feeling. This is exactly the narrative I have day in, day out.

Listening to my words, my partner stood at the edge of the bed, witnessing yet another breakdown. As I tried to gain some composure, stop the flood from my eyes, the room became awkwardly silent, again. Both confused and upset, subdued from my exorcism, wondering where we go from here. It is clear PND is not quite the ghost we hoped for; rather it's a powerful poltergeist, swirling the room around us, angrily pulling at our hearts in her exposure, as she has been caught and ousted from her destructive domain once again.

Who You Gonna Call? Anyone At This Point!

Where did all this insecurity and disconnect come from? How could it be fixed? Neither of us had the answers. Hours passed as we lay beside each other. Single words seemed to take minutes to vocalise, much longer to be understood. I knew I loved him; it brought some comfort, no less to the man who had been threatened, again, with losing his whole world. Not seeing his baby each day, the thought bringing tears to his eyes. But this relationship, it was hurting me. It was hurting us. Again, the inevitable ultimatum was brought to the, already so unbelievably awkward evening: Stay or go?

This intimacy madness was becoming thin for us both. Unfair to everyone involved. There was a pause in emotions as I thought about the choice, not knowing what to do. Genuinely feeling as though there were two little relationship advisors on my shoulders. One wants me out the door; I could make a run for it and leave these two to live a happy and fulfilled life without me in it. Sound, logical advice really, given I seemed to be absolutely bat-shit and don't know my own mind, far less how to control it. On the other side, she was sad. Asking me *what the fuck I am doing* and why I am ignoring my gut so much. She reminded me of the pain a sep-aration would cause; the baby with no mother and her father dis-traught, his heart broken. She reminds me of the 10 years previous, the look in his eyes as we dance on nights out. The cheeky glint that only I know. The power of his hold that makes me feel safe. She reminds me of my heart and how we got here in the first place.

But man, that other side, she does make some valid points. And hey, it's like big Tina said, *"What's love got to do with it?".*

As my partner sat on the edge of the bed, moving every so often to shake off the unease of the room, he waited to hear my response. He had made his side of the story very clear: he didn't want to give up on us - he never has. He only wants the best for me, whatever that may take. Whatever it is that will make me happy again. And if that meant we needed to split and no longer be a couple, then he is prepared to do it. No matter how much it will devastate him or how much he believes it to be the wrong choice. The choice is still mine to make.

Of course, I wanted him to stay, to be with me. I wanted nothing more than to be with him, to be happy and feel loved. That's what this whole breakdown was about. It's what it has always been about. I just didn't know how to do that. To be happy. To feel loved. To allow myself to feel joy and peace. The contentment that comes with knowing everything is okay. The only reason I wanted him to go was for his own sake, not mine. Or so I believed. PND was trying to hoodwink me into a cave of loneliness as I was so very, clearly confused.

During the wait, in my mental back and forth, my partner made a good point: *"Will anyone else change how you feel? Will you be happier with someone else?".* The answer was no. I knew this beast was mine, within me. But this fact did nothing to stop the aching of my heart, orchestrated by the confusion I was in. The tone of the room was far more serious than it had been during previous break-downs. This was the final ultimatum, and it needed a concrete answer, *now*.

As I bowed my head, I knew what my heart was saying, I felt it all the time, hence the anger and frustration. I told him to stay, as I welcomed another round of ugly crying. I wanted to be that carefree couple we had once been. I wanted to be 'us' again.

"I don't want you to go. I just don't know what to do, how to fix this?!" my heart spoke loudly for once.

Apologising profusely, the breakdown continued, the weight of the mental fight finally starting to lift. The Mind Demons were not happy. For once, I had **fully** and honestly spoken the truth. All those nasty intrusive thoughts many of us have, but simply don't allow them to fester, pushing them away, replacing them with love. The thoughts similar to getting cold-feet before any major life event, the doubts, worries and what ifs. Only I had let them in to settle, and in the process, I had chilled my feet, legs, torso, arms and mind. And almost my heart.

As I pulled my hands out of my hair, they brought the lies into the light. The problem was I felt no connection. Not to my partner or anyone. At least not in the way I once did. Disconnected, at best, seeing the world from behind a pane of glass. Being able to see everything, yet unable to feel it. Any of it. Even within our relationship. He and I both knew we loved each other, just as I knew I loved my friends and family. But that was the problem. I didn't **feel** in love with my partner. I couldn't describe what to feel 'in love' was like. It was gone. Just like I felt tied to my child through instinct or the right thing to do, I felt bound to my partner. Yet ached the whole time, unable to place the 'where' and 'why' of this shift, until I broke down that night and said everything out loud. Literally baring my arse and soul at the same time - and I'm not sure which one was more awkward.

Seeing my torment, the exudence of raw pain pulsing out of me, my partner pulled me to his chest. The place I wanted to be the most.

My haven. We joked at the naked absurdity of the night as he affectionately called me a '*numpty*' as I continued to sob onto his body. He reassured me there was no need to be sorry. We had been in a hard place before and got through it; this time was no different. Plus, I had nothing to say sorry for. I was ill. All this pain, hurt, confusion and torment was the work of PND.

My partner held me, reassuring me everything would be okay. But it would only be "okay" if I got help, again. *Really* got help. Without looking at him, I nodded my head in agreement as I repeated over and over how broken I was. How fucked up I had become. How scared I felt. How I had no idea where to start or what was broken within me. But something was broken, so awfully broken. Although it was frightening to say it all out loud, it was also liberating. Being the stubborn cow that I am, if something is broken, there is *ALWAYS* a way to fix it. I just maybe needed to use something stronger than sticky tape this time.

Chapter 13

Back To the Doctor

This time, after the whole naked-breakdown debacle, I wasn't so reluctant in my admittance of needing help. I agreed that I wasn't yet mentally heathy and that I needed to dig deeper. I needed to get into my mind and seriously rewire the place, to find a way to wrestle those Mind Demons into a cage once and for all.

I remember weeping on the bed, crying *"I'm so broken"*, knowing only I held the power to make myself better. A scary thought, yet one that also brought me relief. A weight I could take from my partner, as he had carried the brunt of my baggage since our daughter was born, offering unwavering support and logical, kind words. He was, and always will be, my rock, my moral guidance and my soulmate. For him, for myself, and for our relationship, I knew I had to find a way to beat my PND.

On the back of the previous night's naked therapy session, with a swollen, red-raw face from all the crying, I called the doctor and made an appointment - for as soon as possible. Again, my partner accompanied me, holding my hand through the entire process. I was quizzed as to why I stopped the anti-depressants without consulting the GP. As much as I am an over-sharer, especially when nervous and put in the spotlight, I thought it best to spare the blushes of my partner, and not inform the GP that they may as well rename the drugs as 'Orgasm Be Gone' pills. Like a naughty little schoolgirl, I hung my head in shame and pulled some - not made up, yet not quite the truth - excuse, that I didn't like the side-effects.

I felt reassured by my partner sitting to my left, with my genuinely concerned GP in front of me. She had told me in the weeks after my daughter's birth to slow down, which was advice I didn't understand at the time. I hadn't said anything of truth about how I felt. I would, in jest, make comments about parenthood, something I had done in the many, *many* visits to the GP with my daughter in the months following her birth. Therein lies the clue as to why the doc was urging me to slow down. I don't think it necessarily takes a genius to spot the tell-tale signs of mental illness, when that illness is presenting itself in your surgery every few weeks, frantically looking for cures to a variety of phantom baby aliments. Nor would it be hard to read it on the pale, sunken, grey face of my exterior.

Here's Your Suicidal Mental Illness, Now Off You Go and Sort It Out

As I left the GP's office, clutching my low dose Sertraline prescription (once again), I also walked out with the phone number for a local mental health charity. The doctor handed me the number, almost apologetically, as this was the best our health service could offer. A *charity*, to deal with the - and let's be frank here – life threatening illness, that is postnatal depression. By this point, fast approaching 2 years since giving birth and still threatening to end my relationship at the drop of a hat, I was game for anything that could help. Fuck, if you had told me there was a magical cure for depression, but it meant you had to endure sitting on a cactus after a haemorrhoids flare-up, then I would have been fair game, finding the prickliest seat amongst the bunch.

It might have seemed as though I was being referred to the charity for treatment, however, *I* would be the one charged with doing the referral administrative work. It was abundantly clear *I* was the one charged with improving my own life-threatening mental illness. *I* would be the one to call the number, explain my situation, make the appointments and push myself to attend them. All of it. All on my own shoulders.

At the time, I was so preoccupied in beating my Mind Demons that I didn't see the injustice of it all. A new mother - the responsible parent of a tiny human, tasked on her own, with no previous experience of illness - told to go ahead and battle an illness that is the **leading cause of death** in new mothers: suicide (Reference on p274). It takes a whole lot of strength to even admit to yourself how you are truly feeling, let alone to a partner or a doctor. But there I was, returning to the doctor, asking for help, leaving with a number in which I could seek help, *if I* called it. And if I hadn't, that would have been the end of my treatment. No one ever checked up on me after that. No one ever called a young, new mother, to ask about her mental health, despite attending the doctor twice, desperate for help.

That's more than just a bit fucked up.

It is absolutely, **fucking diabolical**.

Chapter 14

Therapy Is Brutal

Luckily, the charity was a familiar place; a well-established corner of the community where I grew up. I knew of the place from family members, yet never knowing exactly what happened behind the heavily bolted, 'buzzer entry only' large door. I was keen to find out what secret the door would reveal. I knew medication alone would not 'fix' the fuck-up my life had become, so I willingly called the number as soon as I could.

As I dialled the number, I felt a little scared. Maybe I was being dramatic; maybe I wasn't *that* ill after all. People only call these numbers when they are suicidal or have reached some form of wall that is preventing them from living life. What if they thought I was just a shit mother who needed a break and not therapy? What if I wasn't ill 'enough' for treatment?

I began to feel like a fraud, my hands clammy as I waited for the call to be received. I didn't know what I was going to say to them. Just the same as I told the doctor, I imagined. But surely you need to be more than 'struggling' with life to take up the time of a mental health charity? I remember doubting my own mind while I waited for the call-ring to stop, wanting desperately to hang up and not to be a nuisance. But I waited the call tone out. I wasn't sure my partner would be convinced all I needed was a spa weekend to massage all my troubles away. Plus, on account of his pleading tears, I was certain he was convinced I warranted the expertise of a therapist. And who was I to question his logic? I couldn't even hold a conversation these days on account of my brain fog, never mind put forward a rational reason as to why I thought it best I should *not* call the charity.

After what felt like a year (when it was in fact 30 seconds at best), a lovely, warm, kind woman answered the phone. After taking all my details and asking why I had contacted the charity, she had a genuine tone of concern. As I spoke about the doctor appointments and being directed to the charity by my GP, she asked if I had been suicidal. Immediately I said *"No! Oh no"*, thinking, *I'm not that level of ill*, when in fact, I had been fantasising of suicide since my daughter was born…

To be suicidal doesn't necessarily mean you have the razor ready or pill-bottle to hand. It can also mean you have spent a little too long down that thought-path than the average 'happy person' would have. At times, I had felt my head to be in the vice of parenthood and I would dream of my best means of escape. The bathtub a likely destination, as I consumed enough alcohol to settle me into a deep sleep while the pills took effect. Or would that just make me sick? Would it be better to cut myself while drunk? Would that numb the pain and allow me to carry through with it? Did I want to do this in my own house, traumatising my partner in the process? Or should I just run away? But then, would I be found and begged to come home? Would I be able to deal with never seeing my daughter grow up? Maybe suicide was the best method to escape all the pain. But then, what of my daughter, that would surely cause her unimaginable pain, growing up without her mother?

Round and round I went. Spending far too much energy on a 'hypothetical' scenario. But who would entertain such a scenario if they weren't to be considered suicidal?

Lying through my teeth about my suicidal ideals, the kind lady on the end of the phone asked if I would be able to wait until the appointment, or did I feel like I needed immediate help? I, of course, replied that I would wait until the appointment. I was just a *bit depressed*, not actually 'mentally ill'. No, not at all. Just your average struggling new mother, who thinks about suicide as much as she thinks her partner is off having some sordid affair with an imaginary woman. *Perfectly fine and healthy…*

The PND is Out the Bag

Without a doubt therapy is the hardest thing I have ever done. It went deep; right into my psyche deep. I cried a lot. I called in sick to work a lot. I felt every emotion a person could feel on a weekly basis, for months, often being in an emotional deficit for days after the particularly brutal sessions. I felt like I was dragged through Hell itself some weeks. Sitting in a strange chair, telling a stranger all my deepest darkest innards, wasn't something I read in the parenting books, nor is it something I hope to do again, yet it is the best thing I have ever done. Without therapy, I wouldn't be in the place I stand today.

Attending therapy coincided with one of my first 'big reveals' surrounding my mental illness; telling my boss about my mental health situation. My first appointment was scheduled for a Monday or Tuesday morning, and on this particular morning at work, we had visitors coming - the kind that demanded we all be present. There was no way I could miss the meeting, but there was also no way I wanted to miss or rearrange my first appointment. So, I made the decision that I would stick to my appointment and tell my boss what was going on and ask if it was okay to be slightly late for the meeting. I was adamant that I seek help sooner rather than later. Asking for help was a huge step. It was nerve racking and consumed my mind for days.

Should I be going? Was I wasting their time? Would they think me
stupid? Would they judge me? Would they send me packing as
soon as I arrived? What would it entail? When do I tell people? Do
I tell people? How would I hide it? Do I want to hide it? What does
my partner think of me? Am I weak? Am I broken?

All of this, all the time. On repeat. There was no way I would
prolong the torture. Plus, it's in my nature to be impatient; I wanted
to make it to that first appointment, sooner rather than later.

I was extremely lucky throughout my PND journey. Anyone I
spoke to about my illness was nothing short of understanding,
supportive, and often opening their own heart to share their
experience with me. My boss was no different. As I stood in his
office, out of the blue, spilling words such as *"anxiety"*, *"depres-*
sion" and *"therapy"*, his first response was one of shock. He told
me I hid it well, that he would never have suspected I was ill at
all, and that I wore a brave face as I turned up for work every single
day. This was the first time I had told someone other than my family and friends. The first time standing in front of someone, not
quite against my will, yet not entirely on my own schedule either. I
didn't find speaking out difficult - it was the opposite. When I'm
nervous, I tend to have the ability to speak for days and in great
personal detail. A bit of an over-sharer, I say things as they are, as if
everything is a fact, with no emotion attached. I felt no shame in
telling my boss I had been finding life hard, that I was struggling to
fit into my motherhood role, and that I now required time off to
attend therapy sessions, of which there may be many, for months.

Just as my boss was taken aback with my impromptu 'depression
confession', I was startled by his words: *"Don't be so hard on*
yourself". His reply caught me off guard; I knew I had the ability to
zone out a lot, but at this time I was intently focussed in the somewhat awkward conversation. I wondered what I had said for him to

say those words. I don't think I actually said anything. He knew from my body language - and my ridiculous need for perfection and self-berating - that I don't settle for 'half-jobs', nor do I settle for being the cause of 'poor-quality jobs' either. In truth, his words upset me - in the nicest possible way. I was so very hard on myself, for years. I wanted to be the best mother, to provide the best environment for my child to thrive in and to be the best person to my partner, all of which I felt I was failing at.

My boss made me feel understood: there was no more explanation needed between us. I was free to attend therapy, to take as much time as I needed, and have the space required to rebuild myself back up from the hellhole I was dwelling in. His words released me from any worry that I would need to juggle work and therapy, or that I would be penalised in some way. All of which was running through my head, as I wondered how I would explain needing time off each week so I could cry on a therapist's chair.

The Essential Oil Obsession Begins

Arriving far too early for my first therapy session, I sat in the car nervously as I waited for the clock to catch up on my anticipation, and allow me to knock on that the big, bolted door. I had seen the door and charity sign for years. In true working-class fashion, the charity was located behind a pub. A bar and restaurant, to be cor-rect. Next to which was a chip-shop and an Indian Takeaway. I say "Indian", although I'm fairly certain the establishment sold a whole host of goods, such as pizza, kebab, curry, cow's milk, and a fine selection of confectionery. Just your typical Scottish-Indian takeaway then.

The car park for the charity was located at the rear, looking over a railway station - the one I would walk across with friends, pre-teens when I told my parents I wasn't going far, when in reality I was walking miles from home to hang about in the street, being an obnoxious A-hole by playing 'Chappie'. (Chappie: A hilarious game of knocking (chapping) on people's front door and running away, like your life depended on it - which it did after you had "chapped" the same door 4 times in *very* quick succession)

As I sat in the car (in the middle of young carefree memories), I began to feel nervous. Yes, I was about to find out what was behind that large secure entry door, but I was also about to become a person, out in the open, who *needed* to knock on that door, sealing my diagnosis as I stood in front of the camera, waiting to be buzzed into the building. I would now be known as both 'mother' and 'mental illness patient'. *Great.*

Standing in front of the great bolted door, I pressed the intercom. After confirming my name and appointment, the large metal door was unlocked with a mechanical buzzing sound. Pushing it open, I was greeted with large signs on the walls, informing me to pull the door closed behind before walking up the stairs to the office. As much as the signs and doors suggested some form of secure facility, the atmosphere was welcoming, not intimidating at all.

I climbed a set of small stairs and pulled the door to the 'office' open. To my right sat the lovely lady who had taken my first phone call and booked me in for the session. Her desk was filled with books, leaflets and her computer, amongst various other items - a few plants I'm sure. I remember the area being busy, warmly so. Like visiting my friend's house, her living room filled with knick-knacks, full of happy memories and comfort.

Being a hater of all new environments, I stood nervously as the receptionist asked if this was my first-time attending therapy. I replied *"yes"*, to which she handed me a few forms to fill out with my details, but not before I had signed the book of attendance. It was a diary, I think, filled with everyone who was present in the building, a large book in which everyone filled in the date and time of arrival and departure, next to which we wrote our name and the name of our therapist. Would you believe, I wrote that woman's name **wrong** for the *entire* time I attended therapy! That's one of those thoughts you have while in the shower that still makes me cringe, and will until death!

Across from the reception desk was an expansive room. I remember it being so large and open. A nice seating area with sofas, a coffee table, magazines and newspapers, waiting to receive patients until the therapist came to greet them. Next to the sofas was a tea and coffee station, free of charge, often with a variety of herbal teas and a few biscuits to nibble on. Surrounding the large room were doors, I'm not sure how many. Of the three doors I went behind, I was met with a private office space, if that is what you could call them. They were more like tiny living rooms; cosy, comfortable, dimly lit and inviting.

The best thing about the entire place was the sound and smell. Given that it was such a large space, they must have used a bottle of essential oil a day, because the scent floated up my nostrils and straight into my relaxation camp as soon as I opened the door. Clearly working well, I loved the comfort of the smell and space. Soft meditation/relaxation music played throughout the office, coupled with the essential oils and free tea that I was able to drink without a child hanging off me - well, I was in heaven!

Now For the Hard Bit

As I sat in the communal seating area, shortly after filling out the forms, my therapist walked over to introduce herself, asking if it would be okay to talk further in the privacy of one of the offices. She would be the same therapist I would meet each time I attended my sessions. A genuine, compassionate woman, she put me at ease instantly. She spoke firmly and to the point, yet with a soft conviction that my illness was treatable if I was open and honest during the sessions. '*Please, I'm the master of "open-talking"*', I thought. And in a private setting, secure in confidentiality and mixed with my nervous disposition of over-sharing, this woman was in danger of a post-partum body presentation, if I felt it prudent to my explanation as to why I felt so shit.

Speaking in a small private room next to the reception area, I remember the therapist filling out forms on her lap, creating a file with my name on it. Notes and diagnosis, I presume. She already knew my story on account of the receptionist taking my details a week or so before. I was then handed a questionnaire - a depression questionnaire - which would be used to evaluate the level of low I felt, giving it a numerical value. In front of me was a similar form I had been asked to fill out in the weeks after the birth of my daughter. Questions to be answered in the form of multiple choice: 'Are you positive about the future?', to be answered as honestly as possible, from a list of answers ranging from 'yes, I'm positive', 'somewhat positive' to 'not positive', each with their own numerical values, to give a score of how depressed I really was. In for a penny, in for a pound, I thought, and so I answered the questions as brutally honest as I could, for my own sake, for what did I have to hide or fear, now that I was sat in an actual mental illness treatment facility?

Unsure of my exact score, I do recall the therapist saying it was within the *"moderately depressed"* category. My recollection of this is mainly due to repeating this survey at the end of my stint in therapy and receiving such a low score that it caused my therapist to hug me, pride beaming from my face, after all our hard work. *'Moderately depressed'*. **Fuck**. How does one go about that diagnosis? I *was* ill - who knew?! Ill enough to take up place in the therapist's office for the following few months, a long time considering that during my first visit, she told me that on average, people only attend sessions for 6 weeks. I blame *'Heather'* for my lengthy time in therapy. Or maybe I blame the free biscuits and tea, not to mention a whole hour of 'me-time' out with work or being a mother. Not really sure why I left to be honest.

Have A Word with Yourself - Literally

What followed in the months after was nothing short of ripping my heart and soul out, piece by piece, rewiring them and placing them back. Adding extra stability and love in the process.

I gained the ability and strength to remove barriers while creating boundaries. I learnt where my pain originated, why it manifested as depression, and what I could do to combat it. On several occasions I sat across from my therapist and spoke to her, words I have never, and will never, share again. She was a space of no judgment, no gas-lighting, no quips of *'you are too sensitive'* or *'it's not that bad'.* In my own words, she could recognise, and told me, what I had never been able to see before. After she spoke back my experiences to me, she gave them labels, terms I had never associated myself with previously.

Click, went another light-bulb as a sack of weight fell from my shoulders that I had been carrying for the majority of my life. This wasn't my trauma to carry. I had been hurt by those who themselves were hurting. It all made sense. I understood where part of me, part of these Mind Demons had been created.

I began to develop a keen sense of self-awareness. This was half the battle in defeating mental illness, I was assured. There was nothing taboo in that room, nothing too far or too insane to be spoken out loud. No eyebrow-raising when I said my partner was having an affair, that I knew was more than likely fictitious, but it still bothered me all the same. No shock or horror when I spoke of breakdowns, or my inability to let my partner touch me in bed. There wasn't so much as a flicker of emotion from my therapist when I spilled the buckets of poison the Mind Demons had filled my head with. The only time I felt anything from her was when she congratulated me in my honesty, praising me for opening my soul, and told me I should be extremely proud of facing my demons *"head-on"* with a *"can-do"* attitude.

She was exactly what I needed: a person to question every self-doubting, hatred-filled word about myself. Forcing me to answer the warped point of view I held, as if *I* was the therapist. During one session, she had me pull two chairs to face each other; I sat on one as I faced the other, empty chair. In one seat I spoke, letting out my thoughts in great detail; why I was a shit mother, an unfit partner, a monster, a beast. Then I stood up and took my place in the opposing seat. In this chair, I was to fight back at the words I had just said and heard, trying to imagine as though they had come from a friend. What would I say? Well, of course I would say it was all shit, untrue. And here are 300 reasons why. Up and down, I went, changing seat each time I felt a counter argument coming. It felt as uncomfortable as it sounds; arguing with myself, in great personal detail, while - let's be honest - a *stranger* watches on. But I'm a game lass, up for anything, no matter how weird it may be. I was here to save my relationship, my family, and most importantly, I was here to save *me*.

I fought with myself for the entire session, gradually feeling more relatable to the logical and sensible Kirsty in the opposing chair. 'Mind Demon Kirsty' didn't have a leg to stand on. Her argument was weak, pulling at any thread in a poor attempt to convince me I neither loved, nor worthy of love. By the end of it, I all but had myself in a headlock, beating the shit out of the lies the Mind Demons had me believe. Like some form of mental illness rap battle, opposing Kirsty did a mic-drop, walking out of there with her head held high. Logic won over fantasy. So simple, and so effective. If not really, really strange.

Each week, the therapist and I dug a little deeper, my words revealing the next course of action. Why do you feel like that? When was the first time you felt like that? Tell me how you feel when you argue with your partner? The questions from the therapist bounced back that I was the one who held all the pain, emotion, weakness, and strength, within me. The answer to finding the way out of the darkness was hidden in my chest somewhere; I just needed to pull it out and onto the warm, blanket-filled therapist chair, giving it nowhere to go other than into a healing light.

My Own Worst Enemy

The human mind really is an amazing machine, a powerful one. Boy did I know that. It has the ability to create new realities and cruel lies, which it then uses to self-destruct. It also filters out memories or events; things that you lived, yet the mind saw fit to remove for your own benefit, and safety. It also conditions itself into seeing only what relates to you, labelling anything to the contrary 'strange' or 'abnormal'. How you react and behave in response to your emotions, being one such example.

I considered myself to be a moody person; sensitive and quick to defend myself, even when a threat isn't a threat. I take things *very* personally, and in doing so, I can become mean. I'll hurt you with my words, before I let you anywhere near impaling me. Many people praise this quality as *'feisty'*, myself a small human with a big, cheeky, aggressive, *'I'll find your weak spot and go for it,'* kinda attitude. What I was learning in that chair was this quality isn't as fun as it sounds. It's mean, it's hurtful, and it's malicious - which my partner knew only too well. This feisty attitude I harboured was killing my relationship, as well as dragging me into a hole of despair. Doesn't seem so cute now, eh?

I lacked any form of emotional intelligence when it came to my frustration and how I treated others. If someone pissed me off, intentionally or not, I reacted the only way I knew how; by hurting them. All part of that cute, feisty attitude I had presumed. After dissecting my behaviours and where I had been taught them, the therapist dropped a bomb: *"Emotional abuse"*, she said, matter of fact, as if it was so obvious. My thought process, my defensiveness, my reactions, my recollections of events, all synonymous with someone who has experienced emotional abuse. Like a dying man in a film, the screen flickering with flashbacks of his entire life, it hit me all at once. Fucking hell! Of course it was!

How I speak to people **isn't** normal. How I react to people **isn't** normal. How I interpret the actions of others **isn't** normal. How I perceive everything as a threat **isn't** normal. My constant state of defence **isn't** normal. My heightened awareness **isn't** normal. All of these traits had been created within me via various methods, forcing me to behave, think, and now act, in abnormal ways.

The way I treated people was comparable to emotional abuse, but I couldn't see it, for it was my norm, my reality, how I expected things to be. Anything, bar pushing people away was alien to me. People giving out hugs was bizarre to me. People not losing their shit when an accident happened, was downright the 8th Wonder of The World to my mind.

I'm Pretty Fucked Up, Where Now?

You might think it pretty taxing to realise the entire way you function is abnormal. In fact, I found it to be the opposite. As soon as I understood a reason for something, I observed the thought-pathway being changed, corrected, almost out with its own will. A piece of pottery is what you make it, not what it has chosen to be. You can't blame the vase for not holding your soup if it was never intended to be a bowl. I can't relish in self-hate if I've never developed the correct way to manage my emotions, in a positive manner. As though being pulled from the cleansing water of a baptism, now understanding that I lashed out of anger due to my inability to deal with emotions, washed me of all shame. Like my heart had been telling me, I truly didn't mean or want to act the way I did. I just didn't possess the ability to act on or understand my actions in any other way.

Throughout therapy and talking, I gained an understanding of myself and the *whys* and *hows* of my inner workings. A pretty brutal process really. I went from believing that I knew myself, to being told that my very thought pattern is in need of major reconstruction. The only way to do that was to challenge myself and become uber aware of my thoughts and actions. All of which stemmed from carving my soul open to this no-nonsense therapist sitting across from me.

For days after some sessions, I grieved. What I was grieving, I wasn't sure. A loss of self? Confusion? Anger? Who am I? And all with a big dose of *'What the fuck?'*. It felt like I was having an out of body experience, my soul realigning with the truth. The conflict and frustration I had been feeling was set in believing I was that person who was quick to anger, yet hated it. Knowing it to be wrong, but not understanding that if it was so wrong, why did I continue to act in that way? **I couldn't help it**, is the simple answer. My hardwiring was set that way, as I sure as shit didn't 'check-box' that in my creation. There was a bit of a wiring issue. We had discovered the problem. Now all we needed to do was fix it.

Chapter 15

Things Get *Really* Shit Before They Get Better

I wasn't an angry cow after all. Well, that's not *technically* true... I was still charging about like a raging bull on the days where I didn't get enough sleep, felt stressed, overwhelmed, entertained my intrusive thoughts for 2 seconds too long, hadn't spent any quality time with my partner, or didn't get an instant reply from my friends. So basically, it was just my average day - still being a moody, on edge, grumpy bitch. The only difference was, I knew the cause of my frustration: parenthood. Coupled with a serious lack of ability to communicate my emotions and handle them efficiently. It's one thing to sit opposite a therapist and be told you have piss-poor emotional management skills, although, through no fault of your own (mainly), but what do you do with this information? How was I meant to apply this to my life outside of that cosy, essential oil-filled heaven?

A Day in The Life: Therapy Aftermath

Following a particularly gruelling therapy session, I placed my phone on the bedside drawers as I pulled the duvet over my head, creating only a small hole for my eyes and face to peek out. I had pulled the curtains closed again before returning to the sanctity of my bed, where I would call my boss and let him know I wasn't feeling myself. I didn't need to say anything more. This wasn't the first time I had felt depleted, numb and unable to function. Lying in complete silence, I would stare out of the window, and just *be*. Not feeling emotions as such - empty and lethargic, yes - but not sad, nor happy. Just there. I just stared out the window from the warmth of my bed; a place I have always retreated to for comfort. It was a quiet, safe spot to be still, away from the demands of others. I didn't feel like being around people. Pulling on my fake smile, pretending I gave a shit about anyone and their happy life. Everyone was so busy, full of bustle, full of inane small talk about work, children, hobbies and the latest gossip. I couldn't give a shit about any of it. I didn't even want to say *"hello"* to other parents as I dropped my daughter off at nursery. I found everyone and everything intrusive, unkind, and insensitive to my needs - an internal monologue, reflecting my empty, broken frame of mind. I knew by this point in my journey, that feeling so beaten, as if I had been in battle with humanity that the best thing I could do was to retreat to the safety of my house where I could lick my wounds and regroup.

Replaying therapy sessions - the words I had said, memories only known to me, the absurd fucked-up point of view I held, in which I was hateful towards everyone else - I lay in the bed trying to make sense of it all, now as the observer rather than the perpetrator. Sure, I understood that I didn't want to act this way. I didn't want to reply to the messages from friends with rude, dismissive responses or straight up attacks (shielded by humour of course). I didn't want to be this person, so intent on bringing others down, purely because I was the one hurting and miserable. I knew I was ill, with demons in need of exorcism, but living with this amount of thought, reflection, and anticipation, was exhausting. It took tremendous energy to get those self-awareness clogs to click into place, as if I were a psychology student studying the family history of a serial killer, understanding exactly why past events encouraged or defined future behaviours. I was a mess; a tired, salvageable one - I'd bet my life on it - yet a mess all the same. An overwhelmed one, in need of clarity in the form of space.

Prior to therapy, when I became too overwhelmed, I would allow that stress to manipulate me in a negative manner. Making dinner was a task far too much most nights. Returning from work, rushing to pick up my daughter and bring her home, getting her ready for bed - teeth brushed, book read, 300 glasses of water later - I often stood in the kitchen and sighed. The sigh interrupted by the tiny patter of feet, sneaking down the stairs, to ask me weird questions or profess how much she missed me, and wanted to sleep in my bed. Making dinner isn't a simple, thoughtless act - not now anyway. As two full-time working parents, still adapting to parenthood, it wasn't a rare occasion that we stood in the kitchen, hopelessly opening the cupboards and asking what was for dinner. We didn't meal plan - we barely food shopped on the regular. Our daughter had her evening meal at either one of our parent's houses - lunch also. So, all we had to do was cook for ourselves, and even that seemed like too much.

Being the first parent home from work, I was the one most likely to provide the evening's meal. My partner wouldn't be home for several more hours. Not that it was my 'job' to make dinner, it was logical that I make a start on cooking once I got *'Ms thousand-and-one questions'* settled in bed. The problem was - well, there are many problems here… Firstly, cooking requires foresight and planning, which is a mental load in itself. I hated going to the store with my daughter after work; it was always stressful. Me tyring to think what was easy, healthy, and quick to make. My daughter, full in narration of her whole day, complete with a verbal questionnaire, as I tried to navigate the busy store. Secondly, I was exhausted by 8 p.m. Feeling overworked, underappreciated and generally fucked-off with my life, the tiredness meant an abusive text would be sent to my partner. *Why the fuck hadn't the dishwasher been emptied? Why was I the only fucker to put clothes away? And I am absolutely sick of not having food in the house!* All legit reasons to be mad, yet completely unfair most times. Nevertheless, I was angry and needed an outlet, and so I pressed 'send' many a time on messages that had no other purpose than to project anger and hate towards my unsuspecting partner.

Stop Crying Over Mouldy Potatoes

Instead of curling up into a ball and rocking on the kitchen floor - wiped out by the prospect of cooking a meal, while my daughter increased my irritation levels with each illegal out-of-bed visit she made - I should have stood up, stopped sobbing in overwhelm and seen that I held the choice not to feel that way. My choices were; ask my partner to bring home an easy-cook ready meal, or we could order food in. Simple. We could afford the luxury to do as such. But my mind would tell me it was a waste of money, which it is, in terms of the cost of buying premade dinners, or take out, is financially true. Yet the cost to my mental health is priceless. At the time, I didn't see it that way. I never saw a choice. Upon my shoulders, my so tired shoulders, I wanted the 'best' at all times. The best home cooked meal, for the best price giving us the best nutritional value in our best little family.

I have far too many memories of breaking down between the hours of 7 p.m. and 9 p.m. Far too many times I yelled at my daughter to *"get to bed and stay in it"*, while I balanced pots and pans, trying to find a healthy meal for myself and my partner. If something is beginning to bend, threatening to snap in the quest for "best", then we should really release that tension and re-evaluate what "best" actually means.

When it came to my own breaking point, I allowed myself to snap, continuously. Under the weight of responsibility, eating healthy, providing, and filling my role as the 'mother and partner'. I broke down over mouldy potatoes. Seriously! Crying in frustration that I would need to come up with something *else* for dinner, when all I wanted was to catch my breath, sit on the sofa and have someone look after **me** for a change. There was no need for this weight on my shoulders, especially not over a fucking meal. Therapy told me so. I needed to do something to ease the tension, long enough so that I could get to grips with motherhood and life, this wasn't forever. Who cares if we ate 5 beige meals in a week? Who cares if we ate the same amount of takeaways in 3 months as we did in the whole year previous? Who cares? I did. Overly so. *Waaay* overly so.

When I spoke to my therapist about my breakdowns, whether at dinner, in the bedroom, being with my daughter or my frustrations at everyday life, the dialogue after was always the same:

Why?

How can I prevent it next time?

And did I understand what made me act that way?

She didn't convey meal planning to be the way forward if my frustrations peaked at meal preparation. Sure, it would help, but ultimately, my reaction was always going to be there. It couldn't be avoided by having 5-days-worth of meals in the cupboard. The bending point and frustration would occur with something else. How I could prevent it was by simmering my tits, and not allowing the event to stress me out in the first place. I was to see myself in the reality I was part of: a stressed mother, working full time, trying her best to provide from the moment she opened her eyes in the morning - mentally planning the lives of 2 other people - while trying to 'fix' her own mental health. I was to look upon my situation with as much love as I could. Take a step back, forgive myself for my behaviour, reach out for help, and go and have a moment of solitude if I could. (A pity party if you will.) A time to sit with your emotions with no judgment or hate, only empathy and understanding.

Sitting with my emotions after one of my usual temper flips - often in the bath, in an attempt to tease out the neck tension - my partner would return home to find me stewing. My body language would be defensive, replying all he needed to know in response to his question of *"What's for dinner?"*. After, we spoke about why this question pissed me off so much. The mental toll of it. The unfair burden. My exhaustion.

Thereafter, the question would be *"What shall **we** make for dinner?"* and if I gave so much as a pause in response, my partner would reply *"No pressure, I can get something on the way home"*. There was never a bad or pressuring word uttered from him when I told him I wanted take-out, again, for the third time that week. He got it. The task of making a meal and my mind-blank over it all was symbolic of the pressure I was feeling; the vice around my head on a daily basis, twisted tighter and tighter by seemingly simple, everyday tasks, making everything feel far too much for me to handle. I couldn't find the headspace to think of a meal, let alone enjoy cooking it. Many evenings, when life seemed too heavy to carry, I would lay in my bed after getting our daughter to sleep, waiting for my partner to come save me, to feed me, to make me feel as if I wasn't failing, to hug me and let me know my "best" was enough.

The more I attended therapy, the more I had these moments of *'Nope, I'm not doing that'*. I began to feel justified in my refusal to do anything I thought would stress me out. The words of my therapist merged with my internal monologue, reminding me nothing terrible was going to happen if I decided not to cook.

Nothing terrible would happen if I didn't read a book to my daughter each night. Nothing terrible was going to happen if I crawled into bed and let someone else look after *me* for a change. I wasn't a failure. I wasn't a shit mother. I was not, and did not need to be, in control of everyone and everything. It was more beneficial to me and to my family, if I called 'time' on life for that day, and took the opportunity to recharge, blankly staring out of the window from my bed, even if it was dark outside.

Chapter 16

Rewiring The Mind

While therapy was helping to dissect and illuminate my depression at its root, it was clear the path to getting better was going to be a long and winding road, often feeling like the journey took 2 steps forward, 3 steps back.

I regularly attended therapy and took my daily dose of Sertraline in the evening. I worked out that taking it in the evening would help me sleep off some of the worst side effects, such as feeling nauseous or buzzing for life. With my mental healing in full swing, I still worked full-time, chauffeured my daughter to and from wherever she needed to be, rushing so I could make it to work on time. I still cooked, cleaned and chore-managed as equally with my partner as I could. I continued to laugh and joke in work meetings, offering my best humour where I saw fit. I pushed myself to message my friends and worm my way back into their lives - in my own head at least. On the outside, I was a mother doing it all; carrying life comfortably on her back as she sheared the branches of PND from her mind. And yes, that was all true, yet it was far uglier than I made it look.

The mental breakdowns still occurred regularly. Attending therapy was a beating force, knocking the wind out of me on a weekly basis. The frustration and effort that comes with managing therapy and work is breakdown inducing within itself. I would often call in sick, pleading that I needed a day to myself, advising that I would be in the following day, even when I knew this wasn't a 24-hour bug that I could shake off. My boss was never a 'knuckles to the bone' driver; he understood and offered nothing but kindness. For me, with my crux and fear of letting people down, or feeling like a pest, I felt awkward each time I rang that number. There was work to be done, and if I wasn't there, who would do it? I fretted over wasted material, wasted time, asking too much of others to pick up my slack while I buried my head in the sanctity of my bed for the day. I pushed myself to return to work the next day, whether I felt better or not.

At home, the pressure wasn't much different. Although I was learning about self-love, expectations, and letting go, I was still immensely hard on myself. I was yet to fully develop the thick skin of not giving a shit and making my boundaries clear. I tried to be the mother and partner my family deserved, therein lies the error: they already had it. I was impatient in my therapy, wrongly pre-suming that if I went down a deep and painful rabbit hole on the Monday, that I would have healed all my issues by the Wednesday.

During therapy, we had spoken about my recurring nightmare on a few occasions. Me, with my partner, who then decides to leave me behind, alone, often disregarding my feelings, belittling me in front of his friends, or sometimes his new love interest. The nightmare always woke me, causing that uncomfortable toss and turn for what seemed like hours during the middle of the night. In the morning, I would believe the dream to be my reality; I would feel hurt by my partner for the whole day. Even in my slumber I couldn't escape the Mind Demon's horrid games.

At therapy I learnt that the nightmare was a product of my own insecurities; of being forgotten, laughed at, left behind, and feeling like a pest. The latter being the most significant issue, as it is the place in which my defensive 'nature' originates; the factory in which I produce my best insults, dismissive facial expressions, and lengthy silent treatment if I deem anyone to be too close to upsetting me.

As I exposed the Mind Demons and the areas in which they exploited - using them to control my thoughts and actions - things grew even tenser at home. I had muddled through PND for almost two years by this point, casually snapping, crying, and wondering why the fuck I couldn't be a great mother like everyone else. The breakdowns and warped perceptions of the previous years were by no means a picnic compared to the healing path I was on, yet at least it was a *comfortable* reality. One at least I knew. Comfortable in the knowledge that I was just a 'grumpy' person, one that would let her tongue run rampage around her partner and toddler, when she was pushed too far. Comfortable, but not right; I wasn't blind to how unhappy this made me, how unhealthy it was for myself and anyone around me. However, this attending therapy thing was brutal. The toll of navigating unknown, uncharted territory, creating new mental pathways on the back of exposing my unhealthy ways of thinking. It all added more onto my buckling back, making things far worse before they would get any better. I hoped.

Talking

Each week as I drove away from my therapist appointment, I called my partner to spill the gossip on what fuckery we had been dealing with during the session. I was extremely open with the therapist and my partner, although at times I wouldn't be able to speak to my partner the way I could to the therapist. As I nattered on about this week's findings, the phone would become silent. Confused, or trying to fit things into place, my partner didn't understand why I was saying what I said. He did wonder what I discussed, about him, about us. He never asked for more information than I offered, and I always gave him the abridged version anyway. He would reply with an *"okay..."*, meaning the start of a silent spell, as I tried my best to divulge my demons, without actually divulging my demon to him. I was embarrassed. Even to the man who had seen the pre-birth poop and watched me have naked breakdowns, I was embarrassed. Let's not forget that my nightmare is steeped in embarrassment, being laughed at and mocked by this man. Something I knew he would never do in real life. As open as I am, it appeared I had a limit as to how much I would let the person I wanted to speak with the most, into my mind. There was never a time in which my partner inter-rogated me about what I was saying in therapy, he respected my privacy, despite it being largely intertwined with his. Whatever I was saying needed to be said, and he encouraged me to do so. It didn't matter what he or I thought about it; if those were the words and feelings that came from my mouth, then those were the words that needed to be said.

From an outside perspective, you may wonder, if I was in such a supposedly loving and happy relationship, then why did I believe in a fictitious woman, suspecting my partner of having an illicit affair with? Why did regular nightmares haunt me, in which he walked away from me, laughing, leaving me behind, while he went off to party with his friends? The truth is, years later, I still don't have the answer. Not entirely. I'd hang the feeling in the region of self-worth; of feeling unworthy or underserving of love and kindness - somewhere in that area, I'm sure. What I *am* 100% sure of is that this desire to push people away and feel underserving is entirely down to me, never on the back of his or anyone else's behaviour. I'd push great friends away when I felt like it; when I had mis-interpreted a text, or when they failed the latest 'true friends' test I had set them. This beast was created within me, I knew that much. All of the outside factors anyone saw were the manifestation of an insecure creature that resided within me. I just had to decipher its behaviour to find the root cause of the issue, the pain that needed love and healing.

The best tool therapy taught me is **communication**. I held all the answers to all of my own issues. All I had to do was speak them. Simple enough. Life should be a bed of roses for everyone then, right? But there's a reason therapy exists. Many reasons.

What I have learnt, is we act from our emotions in the most backwards of ways, completely contrary to how we want to feel. I was insecure. I desperately wanted my partner to hold me, but what did I do instead? Tried to kick him out - various times; literally kicking him out of the bedroom when he got too close to me. With my daughter, I roared and screamed at her when I felt maxed out, frustrated and in need of peace. I created turbulent, uncomfortable situations when what I needed was the space to breathe and catch my thoughts.

The mind and body seemed to be in serious disconnect when I edged too far across the boundary of my own needs. This a trait I see in many parents; often mistaking their own screaming fits for lack of willpower, instead of recognising the mountainous tension brought on by the role of being a parent in this fast-paced society. Whether this fault comes naturally, or is a product of poor emotional management, or a combination of factors, the result is the same. We mistake our behaviours, struggle to effectively convey our needs, and in most cases, we don't even know what they are.

Say What You See

In the privacy of the therapist's office, secure in confidentiality, it was safe to speak my truth. Albeit, I am speaking to a stranger, one who may judge me or feel that my story is worthy enough to joke about with their friends down the pub. Doubting thoughts still pushed around my head, despite sitting in that safe setting.

Voicing my most vulnerable thoughts was excruciating, causing me to blush in the process. Focusing my eyes down to a hang-nail on my index finger, that needed fixing that <u>very</u> instant, I confessed how I thought my partner found me unattractive. Worse, that he finds other women far more hilarious, fun and sexy than he has ever found me. The bowing head symbolised I knew those beliefs to be utter shit, yet I couldn't say the same for the gut punching feeling they were giving me, or the cold sweat beginning to wash over my body. I relived and confessed to the therapist that I thought my partner had some love affair in work. All because I watched him leave the building, as I sat nervously in the car nearby - me, and the Mind Demons, that is - waiting to take him home, I noticed him speaking to another woman just yards ahead, and it was enough to set my mind off. To be honest, I don't even think he knew her. But anyway, that kind of logic need not apply here.

Revealing why I thought my partner was having an affair or that he saw my body as hideous, when the bow of the head and the mini manicure session began, my therapist reached into that portal and asked a simple question: *"How did that make you feel?".* Similar to the question my partner asked when I had a breakdown: *"Why?"* followed by, *"Speak to me"* or *"Let me in".* Whether I was in the therapist chair or at home, all I had to do was speak honestly to be free; to let another person know how I was feeling, so they could help me, so that I could help myself. The problem is I was never sure of my words. Not that I didn't have any; my mind always **SCREAMED** how I was feeling, almost as though it was throwing words to my frontal lobe in the hopes they would smash out of my forehead and be seen. I desperately wanted to speak and feel heard, but it's not that easy. *"Just say how you feel"* - so simple. Yet it paralysed me, leaving it up to my body to communicate how I was feeling; picking at my nails in an attempt to hide my face and hold the tears back, showing that this was too much for me.

The therapist used her expertise to tease out the issue. Her questions demanded self-reflection, often handing me the answer to work backwards into the event. I screamed because I was frustrated. She got it, and she let me in on the secret. With my partner, however, it was a whole different ball-game; neither one of us specialised in drawing traumatised blood from a stone. We both had to learn, quickly, how to communicate with each other, without destroying our relationship in the process.

Chapter 17

Soulmates But with The Phone Lines Down

During the time I attended therapy, it seemed like all my partner and I did was argue. While I was defensive and quick to fill with resentment, my partner was somewhat alone in our parenthood journey. He had become worn down and tired, dealing with the trauma on his own while keeping the family together as a unit. He was the glue that held us together, the wall in which I bounced my vitriol off, regularly. Through writing this book, I learned that the first year I suffered with PND was among the hardest times of his life, whereas I see the years following that time - the months of therapy and recalibration - to have been the toughest.

In my illness I wasn't there for him: I couldn't possibly be. He took my horrible mouth, silent treatment (which could last for 4 days), acts of hate, and several stabs to the heart. (Not physically; he has his limits.) He withstood it all, largely on his own, often battling his own personal concerns with employment or mental health, all while trying to accommodate my needs first. Through everything, we stood by one another, solidifying our dedication to our souls with whispered vows as we hugged tightly after each breakdown. But no matter what we promised to each other, no matter the strength of our bond, it was apparent it would take more than commitment to keep us as one.

In time, the resentment and tension built up on each side; the arguments became heated, more in depth, and with more resistance towards each other. These arguments could last all evening, right into the small hours of the morning. More than a handful of times, we slept on these frustrations, me being the one to drag them out over several days using huffy behaviour to display my displeasure at whatever was grinding my ass that week. We knew we loved each other, we knew we wanted to be with each other, but it took us a while to find the source of our tension. What it all boiled down to, was *piss poor* communication - on both parts - and an intense amount of frustration gathering as a result.

Men Really Are from Mars. Women? A Whole Other Universe

Chances are, if your partner pisses you off, you can send a one-line description to the friends group chat and get digital head-nods back in solidarity. The same goes for the partner. Your circle of friends just *'get it'*, most likely because that gripe is a returning topic, or one they face themselves.

I'm not about to get all *sexist* here… *buuut* if I send a message saying *"his socks are still on the floor at his side of the bed"*, I know fine well I will get 3 *"tell me about it"* replies. Make of that what you will. **Some** men leave their socks at their side of the bed. Or women moan about the most trivial ~~annoying AF~~ shit and share it in the group chat. But the fact remains: those girlfriends just *"get it"*.

When I talk about my altered boobs, they get it. When I say I can't sleep from anxiety when my partner goes on a night out, they get it. When I say I believe my partner thinks about other women when we have sex, they just get it. Maybe I gravitate to fellow 'crazy' women, or maybe most women just ***get it***.

Naturally, I presumed my partner should just *"get it"*. Surely, he should know why the dirty plate left on the counter of the kitchen I had just cleaned, would piss me off? Surely, he could see how hurtful and disrespectful this act was? The answer is no. Why would he see it that way when in his eyes, he only left it there as he was rushing to finish his meal after a long day at work and wanted to join me in bed to watch a movie together, seeing a dirty plate as something he could get to later. I saw the plate as lazy, rude, and another thing left for me to pick up. My partner saw it as nothing more than something he would get later, after he had spent the night holding me, like I had asked, as we watch a movie. Indeed, he did not 'get it'. It was becoming apparent neither one of us 'got' each other.

I was shocked to learn that never did any malice or ill intent cross his mind when it came to chores and leaving stuff at his backside. In fact, his mind was preoccupied by thoughts of quickly joining me in bed instead. He never meant anything bad by leaving the plate; it wasn't an act of being lazy or thinking, *"I'll leave that for her to get"*. Actually, what he had done was kind of sweet, only to be met by a raging fucking bull the next morning, slamming cupboards and throwing plates in the sink, muttering how someone was a lazy fuck in this house, and it wasn't me.

Like many couples, the daily grind of chores drove a wedge between us. We bickered at the list of things either one of us neglected, misinterpreting each other's words as personal attacks. We presumed we could read each other's mind, growing more and more frustrated when the other appeared to throw logic out of the window and start to fulfil tasks that weren't at the top of the other's 'needs done' list.

Whether it was chores, delegating childcare duties, or mental breakdowns - all of which intertwine anyway - the path of communication became muddied. Reacting first, blowing up second, and rarely listening as a third (if at all), our lines of communication soon became battle a ground; seeded by the adjustment to parenthood, and bloodied with a warped and defensive civil-war of mental illness on the side.

In truth, I *wanted* to argue and fight. I wanted to be heard, I wanted to say how really fucked-up the balance was in our life. How I bore the brunt of chores as my partner worked later hours, often too tired, nor wanting to start deep cleaning the bathroom at 9 p.m. after a long day. I was so fucked off with everything: society, motherhood, depression, my life. So much so, that yes, I wanted to argue, but I *didn't* want to listen. So, the inevitable happened: we argued until one of us broke, then we continued to argue until we needed to sleep, made up, and then had the argument all over again, in 6-months' time.

Resentment Is a Mask of Poor Communication

Chores, and the mundane workings of family life, can combine to stoke the fire of the *"I'm fine!"* lies many of us are prone to reluctantly forcing out, failing to mask the grievance bubbling under the surface. But when it comes to combining family life into the web of mental illness, the spindles get mixed, confusing the true frustration at the core, with the smaller frustrations on the surface.

The dirty cup on the side becomes the catalyst to a tirade of abuse, all because I was cowering under the weight of intrusive thoughts; struggling to stand tall under their load, unable to straighten my back in an attempt to reduce the perch on which they sat. Nights in which I returned home from work to deal with a tired toddler would send me over the edge. Becoming increasingly angry once my daughter was in bed, I would continue to create more tension by sending aggressive text messages to my partner. Once my frustration had been heightened (courtesy of my daughter behaving like most toddlers do in the run up to bedtime), anything out of place while I was on the war path enraged me. I'd flip out at empty toilet paper holders, muttering under my breath, begrudgingly taking it to the recycling only to find an overflowing bin. I became mad at everything I had ever been mad about, voicing it in the most unproductive way possible: aggressively, wrongly, and contrary to what was really pissing me off.

We all presume we know why we behave in a certain way or what is really pissing us off, but when you push past all the snide text messages sent to your partner in a fit of rage, the real reason is usually buried there within the subtext. Therapy helped me see this by teaching me to question my motives, to ask myself if it was really an empty loo roll that upset me, or if there was something else festering underneath.

Flying off the handle was getting us nowhere. My partner, calling me in frustration after a long day at work, having opened his phone to yet another nasty message from yours truly, was getting us nowhere. Luckily, he was level-headed, seeing my behaviour as a window to my frustration. Having a calm (albeit pissed off) partner, voicing words of reason was like having a live-in therapist. He asked me why I felt the need to send a message like this? What did I hope to achieve and did I think it fair? As much as I would have loved to deliver a first-class presentation on why I was right to relay my 'displeasure' that no one had carried the clean laundry up the stair, far less made any attempt to put it away, my partner was not here to entertain that frustration. And annoyingly, he was correct in his debate that there was a logical reason the laundry hadn't been moved, and I wasn't innocent in all of this either. Plus, I instantly became the bad guy when I decided to send an angry, accusing, and rude text message. Add into this, that the messages often contained 'random' points of frustration; my partner knew fine well I was mad at something I wasn't saying and taking it out on him.

I was mad because I was stressed. Because I wasn't the one coming home to a cooked meal after work. Because I wasn't the Dad who got to enjoy a quiet train ride with no rushing to pick up the kid. Because I was the one going up and down the stairs trying to get the kid to sleep when I wanted to run myself a bath. Because I was so sick and tired of picking up clothes, plates, toys and any other shit lying around, just for the kid to cause twice as much mess in my wake. I was **fucking livid** with my partner having the *easier* role in parenthood, only for him then to phone me, angry on account of my text, quizzing me as to why I was so angry all the time.

I can't express enough how lucky I am to have the man beside me that I do. I know it would have been easier for him to label me the 'village crazy lady' and dismiss me - like society does to all women who aren't being heard. The *"nag"*, the overly dramatic *"ball and chain"*, who yells profanities down the phone when told her partner is going for a pint after work.

This was a two-way street though. Matched to his ears keen to listen, I settled my voice, keen to be heard, and I told him all of those thoughts we so often keep inside. I resented him and his life. I hated being the 'Mum', house-bound each evening, while he had the freedom to roam the world; his kid always looked after without much effort on his part. I stood back and questioned my frustrations and motives as I voiced them aloud, sharing what was really pissing me off, as opposed to the rant-filled text message I sent that blamed the unhung washing as the source of all my anger. In reality, my frustration was at the inequality of motherhood, mixed intensely with my fight against PND.

The worst thing about my frustration and resentment was that it allowed the Mind Demons the ability to rub their little hands in glee. I was pissed at my partner, and now was the perfect time for them to get the band back together and start the same old chorus of *'you can do this better without him, he doesn't love you, he doesn't care'*, and *'you are just a high maintenance pain in the ass'*. Not only was I having an argument with my partner, but an internal one also, with the ever present mental third wheel in our relationship.

I began to notice when I was being pushed too far, ignoring my own needs of rest, relaxation or time off from adult life. Having an empty cup to pour from seemed to ignite the energy source of the Mind Demons. Instantly they would fill my mind with quick counter-quips to everything my partner said. More importantly, they could refute even my own logic, replacing it with the 'woe is me' attitude that would aid in my self-destructive behaviours. The Mind Demons pulled at the thread of making my partner the villain, and therefore someone to be angry at. Someone who I should remove from my life. They wanted me to believe my partner was lazy. They wanted me to believe he was leaving me to do it all. They wanted me to see him as unkind, unloving, and uncaring that I was crumbling. My mind tried its best to keep me quiet, feeding the same bullshit lies as it had done since the birth of our daughter. That I was stupid, over the top, just a nag, and should really be getting on with life without pulling my partner down in the process. And in regard to the latter, they were right.

12 Years of Relationship: Only 2 Years of Knowing Each Other

It was clear by this point - 2 years into parenthood, two GP visits, two rounds of anti-depressants, and therapy booked for the fore-seeable future (and that was just *my* story) - that neither one of us was going to give this relationship up lightly. I did try, still at this point, to end it. As much as therapy was helping, I was doing little in the way of homework. I would gladly confess my innards in the comfort of the therapist's chair, but when it came to speaking at home, it didn't flow quite as easily. For one, the therapist isn't going to yell back at my screams, telling me how unfair and unjust my behaviour is. She wasn't about to meet my rage with a defensive bellow, telling me to rethink my mean comments. Plus, this person before me has heard far worse than what I brought into her room. I'm not sure the same could be said about my partner.

My partner and I were dedicated to being with each other, but in the chaos of trying to deal with my mental health, we clashed. *A lot.* It was a new experience to both of us. In our novice status, we butt heads more than we listened to each other. But we were beginning to realise that you can't fight fire with fire. If we wanted to work through this depression, we needed to do so together, and on the same page. We needed to get to know each other, *really* get to know each other. The thought-pathways we each took and why we went that way. For a couple that had been together so long, it turned out we didn't actually understand each other all that well. Often, we just presumed we knew what the other was thinking or feeling, making no effort to check if our perception was true, or if it was causing unnecessary stress in an already stressful situation.

We needed to communicate at a better level. To figure out a way of leaving our ego at the door when the other had a complaint. Take it on the chin, then figure out a way to improve it. Or to improve the thought process behind it, which was the case for me. I perceived things the wrong way, controlled by 'my way or the highway' approach to pretty much everything in parenthood. I held so much anxiety surrounding my daughter, my partner and my life, that I found it all but impossible to let my partner be part of the equation. When I did, his effort was almost never good enough.

I came to realise - and I hope you are sitting down for this - that I, and possibly you, are… not… always… right.

Breathe deep. Breathe deep.

Martyr Mum

We all have notions in our head how something should be, or the ways it should be done. The correct way to drive *(apparently)*, isn't to use 'blind luck' to judge whether or not you should move at a junction. Similarly, I believe you should close a cupboard door straight after using it, and not leave it open (and all the other cupboard doors), as if we live in a fucking horror movie. Left unchecked, these notions of what we think are right, can become controlling issues. Not only will they force you to control the behaviours of others - resulting in narky comments and under the breath belittlement - but believing your way is always correct, will start to control you.

People do things differently, and *shock*, shit still gets done. ~~Mostly~~. I had to let go of my control, my need for perfection, my eagle-eyes that picked up on every single chore my partner 'missed', and just let him be. I made comments, even in public, about him, and how he should do this or do that, in relation to our daughter. *"Give me her, I'll do it"* - a verbal reprimand, and disapproval all in one. Horribly embarrassing for my partner too. All of my behaviour was horribly embarrassing and deeply uncomfortable for those in our company. If my face does nothing to hide my displeasure, my words sure as shit makes it abundantly clear.

Like some form of perfect queen, I threw out insults, passive aggressive or filled with resentment remarks, when my partner didn't live up to my never-achievable, high expectations. I was never shy on showing him up; feeling it was my 'right' to squash him, for I felt like I was drowning in this life and he did nothing to help. Even if he did try to save me, he would probably have *asked* where we kept the life jacket anyway.

My partner began to question why everything had to be done my way: What did I fear would happen? It forced me to really think, and then confess the truth: he would make my life more hellish than it already was, adding more shit for me to do, or to clean. Rightly, upset with my lack of confidence in him, he asked me to tell him when that was ever the case. What had he ever done that wasn't good enough? I couldn't give him an answer, not a serious one at least. He had every right to parent our daughter how he saw fit, to tidy how he wanted, when he wanted, and to do things on his terms and time schedule.

I never saw myself as thinking of him as incapable; I think I saw myself more as the one to do everything, so I didn't need to bother anyone else. And if I did it, everything would be just right, just the way I like it, and therefore less likely to bring those tension shoulders up to my neck. Placing myself as 'House Manager' - enabled by my partner to a point - I almost let the power go to my head; driven by anxiety, needing things to be done my way, or else my head would explode. All of which could be sparked by a dirty glass not put in the dishwasher, signifying that the world would end and my partner treated me like a maid.

It's easy to see why defences on both sides would be high. Me, feeling like I do it all: a robot running on empty, and an invisible one at that. Him, the second-class parent, berated for not doing enough, and scolded when he tries. He also, feeling just as invisible; the strong hand holding us all together, kicked to the curb when my mind fancied a game of nasty football. Running through the heart of it all were two people, on the same team, with their own ideas and viewpoints; both trying to make everything work while depression tried its best to pour venom in any exposed cracks.

In time we learned to allow the other person to speak, without comment or interruption, until they were finished. To take a minute after the chatter to think upon what had been expressed, especially from their point of view. A lot of tension in our relationship came from miscommunication, if not **all** tension. Instead of letting things fester - the perfect breeding ground for intrusive thoughts - we had to address it, there and then, if something pissed us off. For me, I needed this check on a daily basis when my PND was going through healing. I was an angry beast, one quick to huff and exaggerate problems. My partner reprimanded me for my tone more than once, as did my daughter. As if assigned a safety code word, if the other deemed a behaviour, word or action too harsh, they can call the other out without fear of meeting a sparring partner, and the other must listen.

We worked incredibly hard at bettering our communication. If it took a 10-hour discussion to reach the bottom of why one of us was so upset on that given day, then that is what we did. We had created a safe space in which we understood each other, where we felt comfortable to share the darkest contents of our minds; the thoughts that are hardest to say; the ones that swirl around your mind constantly, yet fail to make sense when we want to release them. We allowed those words to become as much of our language as *"I love you"*, for they are just as important, if not more so. Nothing was off limits, no matter how stupid, crazy or wrong it was. Everything needed to be aired, understood and then packaged off into the appropriate box, instead of always being wrapped up *'nicely'* into the box of resentment.

Chapter 18

Falling in Love Again

All the therapy in the world could try to teach me how to garnish self-worth, self-love and acceptance, but it was never going to fill the void. The void I created when I refused to let down my barriers, preventing my partner entering into the same space as I did the therapist. But, given that as time passed, and I was still struggling to feel any connection to my partner - unless that that connection was resentment - it was *essential* I learn to let him in. Otherwise, we would tire of going round in these circles and no longer be a couple.

My Mind Demons made bonding and connecting with my partner **extremely** difficult. Rather, it made the authenticity of that bond tricky. For every moment I felt at peace with him, there would be 3 examples of why he didn't love me being worked on behind my eyes, courtesy of the Mind Demons. Like acting out over missed chores, I pushed my partner away when I felt alienated, finding reasons to be mad with him. Seeking the *'evidence'* I needed to unload my frustration, directed straight at him; wanting to hurt him just to feel that he loved me, seeing his upset face symbolic of love, more so than any of the warm, affectionate reassurances he could ever offer.

The only way I knew how to free myself from this mental game show was to speak, to release the gnawing inside my head. Fuck, by this point, I had confessed a dirty plate equated to my partner taking on a new lover as I was a 'nag'. What else could I say that was actually insane now?

I wanted to tell him everything I thought, no matter how strange, how bizarre, how seemingly unrelated to anything the thoughts were. I wanted to tell him how he hurt me in my nightmare, and how I woke feeling the same way; unable to speak to him, for I thought on some level, he *did* want to leave me and saw me as a pest. *"I know, I know it's stupid, but I can't help how it makes me feel"*, became my new slogan. Emphasis on the *"feel"*.

With each therapy session attended, I felt more validated. With a little bit of embarrassment chipped away each time I left the office, making it easier, yet not at all easy, to say those words again to my partner, if I felt it was necessary. Given that much of my mental illness revelled in how much my partner didn't love me, there was much I **needed** to say to him.

In this turbulent time of frustration - working, parenting, adjusting to a kid and a mental illness, the chaos and the need for calm - our arguments could become heated, with one of us daring the other to *"JUST SAY IT!!"*, knowing a full cleanse couldn't be established with nothing other than complete honesty. There was no space for little niggles, no room for words unsaid that could be cast up in 3 months' time, when they could have been put to bed there and then. Therapy was teaching us both to *just fucking say your peace* and get it over with. If something was bothering me so much, causing my behaviour to change, causing me to act like a colossal bitch, then I had to just *fucking say it*, and get it over with. For when I released a thought, its power was out. Good or evil, it's out. Like ripping a band aid off in one swipe, I said it, whatever I needed to say in order to move on, and not to hurt my partner or cause friction. The no ill intent had to be made clear before starting to spill the nastiness of my mind. A warning of *"I don't want to upset you, but...*"followed with the most upsetting words: *"You feel like a stranger to me". "I don't like you touching me". "I don't know you". "I want to hurt you (mentally)". "I just want to be happy again".*

These words were usually followed by silence, but now with great respect. Yes, it hurt to hear them, but it hurt to say them. No one wants to admit this to anyone they admire. I said them to release their authority over me, to let them be part of our relationship, as for me, they defined our relationship. I knew from therapy that these issues did not belong to me, nor should I keep them close to my controlling chest. It was okay to reach out; in fact, reaching out was advised. If I was lucky enough to have a partner who wanted to listen, and who could do so with no recoil, then I should make use of it. Just as we made it clear getting mad at a pile of dirty laundry was a response to poor teamwork and not a personal attack, we both worked through the destruction of depression as a solid unit. No matter how ugly it got.

Stop! Reflection Time

Through our bickering, we understood we fought for the same team. We had nothing but respect for each other. Granted, we could mask it in how we spoke or treated each other at times. Taking a reflective step back during therapy granted us access to the tool of thinking outside our own head. I applied the calm demeanour of my therapist when things got heated at home, urging us both to stop and hear what the other was saying before we came to a *wrong* conclusion.

It's really simple when you think about it. Just stop. Think, *really think,* before you reply. Get your head out of your own arse and see things from someone else's point of view. A dose of reality I had to swallow, as my depression lacked empathy at times, or completely removed it altogether. My partner, learned that words spoken by someone suffering mental illness are not always true. Words spoken by someone trying to heal from mental illness need to be approached with heavy-duty protective gear at times. Yet at the middle of it all is the core of someone else, sharing with you their vulnerability, placing all their faith and truth within you - a huge burden to bear I know. But I deserved the same space and safety to try and describe my mind and why I felt like that, just as he deserved the same space to justify why it's acceptable to leave 3 cups on the worktop, and not put them in the empty dishwasher. I don't pretend to understand my own workings, let alone the logic of my partner, but I am grateful we have been granted the ability to listen to one another, no matter how utterly bat-shit we may appear to each other at times. My partner - his ability to see past my anger, rage and spite, combined with my refusal to 'settle' for the above being me - pushed us through PND. Our openness towards each other has been, and will continue to be, the weighted safety blanket that we know we can rely on when we don't even know ourselves.

Chapter 19

PND and The Rage

You don't need to look far to find the symptoms of PND. A quick online search will return a list of the top 5 (top 10, if you dig a little deeper) defining characteristics of the illness: feeling sad, lack of enjoyment, fatigue, lack of bond with your baby, intrusive thoughts, withdrawing from people, having no interest in the things you once enjoyed. They are all listed and all completely accurate. If you check-box a fair few of them, you might even discover that you are suffering from mental illness. However, what the lists do not contain, are the *actualities* of these symptoms, failing to put them into real-life environments, and what other symptoms may manifest as a result of PND. You might say that the lists online - even the lists used in actual diagnosis - do not encompass all the symptoms, at least not the major ones, that most people tend to shy away from admitting.

During my healing process, I stumbled upon a goldmine of support online in relation to my PND. The first time I had one of those **'Wooohaa!'** moments was during a browse through Pinterest. I discovered diagrams and graphs, all listing certain emotions and behaviours, that are also symptoms of PND.

One diagram depicted a circle. In its centre was the line *'Rage and Post-Natal Depression'*. Other words synonymous with rage floated on the circle outskirts: frustration, hot-headed, uncontrollable, temper, quick to snap. The words drew me in, as if I was reading my horoscope for the day or for the whole time since I had given birth. I had figured my quick temper was a learned trait, something I grew up with, fundamentally something that was a part of me, and nothing could be done about it. Worse, I felt it *was* me, to the point that I became ashamed of it, believing that only *I* grew hot-headed over seemingly nothing. These thoughts helped kick me firmly into the dark den of isolation; a freak, compared to the other level-headed mothers.

When I saw that post, everything seemed to fit. Of course, my temper was short; I was mentally ill! Mentally struggling, being choked with the reigns of my own mind, while I tried to find my way in the new world of motherhood. Time after time, I would say, *"Happy people don't act in unhappy ways."* Yet, at the time, that simple piece of perspective, never flashed before my red-filled, rage-eyes. And I certainly never noticed it when I would act out on account of my rage.

Rage Against the Toddler

One evening after work, I collected my daughter from my parent's house and went to the store to pick up something for dinner. My daughter behaved like any over tired 3-year-old would; she wouldn't listen to a word I said as she ran rings around shoppers, while I tried to pick up food for the evening's meal. At the checkout I asked her to stop jiggling about and she obliged - for all of 3 seconds. I became increasingly flustered; annoyed this child wouldn't stop moving around, pulling at me, unintentionally kicking me, as she danced at my side, crawling beneath the conveyer belt, knocking over bags and packets of nuts as she continued her expedition.

At one point I asked her again to stop, using the classic muffled 'mum growl' with piercing eyes to show I was laying down the law.

Beside us stood a man, holding the contents of his shopping in his arms as he narrowly avoided my daughter's flying arm and leg dance. He watched on as my daughter disregarded the mum stare, using it only as a source of energy in her relentless path to be annoying as fuck. I was absolutely seething with embarrassment. Seething my child couldn't be controlled. Seething she wasn't listening to a word I was saying, not stopping her shit that was giving me anxiety and making me feel over stimulated by the whole situation.

No Simmering

As soon as we got outside, I let rip, scolding her for not listening to me, raising my voice to match my temper. Quickly she apologised, as we rushed our way into the car, trying to avoid the stare of strangers as I walked 2 paces in front of my child, harping back my displeasure with her behaviour.

Our daughter is a well-behaved child, she really is. She does the usual kid crap, like being over excited, cheeky, wanting to show you 3 hours' worth of 'shows', in which she is the star, right before bedtime. She never got up to any of that kid nonsense that I was warned about. Only once did she have a major tantrum in the store, to which I walked away and told her it was no skin off my nose if she wanted to live in the hardware store for the rest of her life. Our kid doesn't generally 'act up', no less because she thinks her mother will, at any chance she gets, leave her behind and make a bolt for the Bahamas.

People always comment how polite and thoughtful she is. She's been horrified a few times at the behaviour of other children, watching as they drew on walls or smashed plates in front of her. Her eyes glancing to me, then to the child, as if to say, *'what is his problem?!'*. From a young age, she has always had an old head on her shoulders, knowing more than most adults about what is right and what is wrong. Not that the behaviour of my child matters, as there is little, if any, behaviour that warrants any form of attack from anyone. Yet it is crucial to note, just like I tell my daughter, none of my actions are a result of something she has done: sure, she can tease at my sanity thread, but ultimately, I'm the one in control. Or not, as it would seem, when I was in the depths of PND.

In the confines of the car, I strapped my daughter into her seat, and in utter rage, I told her I would speak to her once we got home. Before pulling the car out of the parking space, I turned the volume of the music up to max, cutting off her apology in the process. She knew I was at my limit, that her shop antics had been too much for me to shake off that day. This wasn't the first time I had given her the silent treatment, forcing her to act likewise, as we drove home. Sat strapped up in her toddler seat, completely silent and solemn as we made our way home, not another word did we speak.

Livid, I relived her behaviour over and over on the drive, shaking my head in exacerbation that she wouldn't let up and let me shop in peace. That I was so fucking tired of picking her up after a full day of work, sitting in excess of an hour and a half in traffic - passing our house on the way to pick her up from my parent's house - only to return to the chaos of traffic on our way home at 6 p.m. Then I had to get the kid home, get her ready for bed, read a book and hope she settled for the night so I could begin cooking. I hated how I had no time for her, no time for me. As I drove home from the store, I racked up everything I had done for other people, and here was me, in the store, tired, humiliated by a three-year-old who thinks I'm good for nothing, other than for her to treat as a piece of dirt.

My victim spiral continued until we pulled up outside our house. Usually, my daughter and I joke as I unclip her seat belt. She enjoys the 10 seconds it takes for me to walk round the car and open her door, with her usually climbing into the front seat and demanding I let her out the passenger side. This day, she didn't so much as move when I unbuckled her seat. She stood only when I opened the door and walked in silence to the house. I made no attempt to soften her upset; instead I made it worse by using cruel one-word commands. I might be tiny in stature, but I have always held the ability to bring any room I'm in down with my facial expressions. If I want to make a point - a point that I'm pissed off - my face seems to have an uncanny ability of showing exactly that, while forcing an air of discomfort around anyone sorry enough to witness it. My daughter was no exception. Whether or not it's some form of bond we share, she always knows exactly what mood I'm in; the good, and the ugly. With her tail between her legs and her head bowed looking at the ground, she walked straight to the front door, waiting for me to unlock it. There was no hide and seek in the bush that day, no doorway dances, or playful pulling of the door handle. She stood in shame, like a pup who had been busted for ripping apart the brand-new pillows.

As if I had to make my upset any clearer to my daughter, I let my rage run its mouth. At the foot of the stairs inside our house, my daughter stood on the first step as she took off her shoes. I bent down to her face as I helped untie her trainers, seeing this as an opportunity to continue chastising her for the unacceptable store performance. *"I'm sorry"* she cried, but for my anger it wasn't enough. I stood up, towering over her, and screamed with every-thing I had, that never again would she be allowed to conduct herself in that manner. There are rules in society, reasons why hyper little girls cannot run around the store, hiding behind fruit carts, while their mother called for her to return. I screamed so hard, and so loud, that my voice felt as if it would break during my tirade. As my innocent 3-year-old stood there, with her wide eyes looking up at me, her comfort, her security, her mother, I yelled her into terror. Her body froze as her face changed from upset into being terrified. Every movement she made I noted, I saw it all, and I didn't care. Rage poured from me; my words were far more powerful than any touch could ever be, and I knew it. I know the face of a displeased mother fills a child with dread, an intimidating force that means nothing other than utter disappointment from those we wish to please the most.

I used my power against my daughter, my tiny daughter, who had already felt my force outside the store, in the car, and here again, in the privacy of our home. I knew I was going too far, yet I couldn't stop it. I screamed at the top of my lungs for her to go up the stairs, to stay away from me. To her credit, she stamped up those stairs and shouted, *"OKAY THEN!!"*, as I warned her not to come out of that room until she had thought about her behaviour. She is a force in herself, a quality I'm extremely thankful for, and will never encourage her to lose (even if it does drive me up the wall sometimes).

After The Rage Comes the Fall

I told my daughter to get away from me, that I didn't want to see or speak to her. She was to keep away from me until I decided I wanted to speak with her. I knew fine well I was being malicious. A child always wants to be with their parent, my child especially so. We often played in the evenings, or a more accurate description: she danced around and sang, while I was the lucky solo audience member with a front row seat. I knew cutting this off would upset her, and in truth, I wanted to upset her. I wanted to continue acting out my anger. I would never go so far as to lift a hand to her skin, so I used the next, and possibly just as traumatising, action I could by removing her mother from her. More fool me though; my daughter simply closed her bedroom door - supposedly over the moment - and saw this as a perfect opportunity to get a quick play of the toys in before bed. Meanwhile, I sat in the living room, allowing the rage to leave my body. It had been satisfied; it had verbally abused another human, feeling justified in its attack.

Sitting on the sofa, I couldn't get the image of my daughter's terrified face out of my head. *What the fuck had I done? And for what?* She was so scared - petrified - of her own mother. I imagined myself in her shoes, cowering under a human 3 times my size and one that I adored, one I hung onto every word they said. I imaged that human towering over me, screaming from their gut, their face laced with pure hatred and venom, all of it directed at me.

I took my face into my hands and began to cry. I couldn't believe what I had done. I felt torn between feeling like I had no choice in the matter and knowing that I should never let my behaviour be justified by the actions of someone else. I was tired and she was misbehaving. We are human, I know. But she wasn't misbehaving really, her behaviour was logical. She's a 3-year-old in a store, bored, forced to be there against her will, trying to make the best of it. *I* was the one with the out-of-control behaviour; I screamed at her as if she had committed the worst crime imaginable.

What scared me most was that I had hurt my daughter, created trauma in her that I was sure to see in years to come. All while I didn't want to do it, feeling powerless to my own mind. I couldn't understand where the screaming match had come from, why I couldn't calm myself down on the drive home, or why I got so enraged in the first place.

Curling up into a ball, I rocked on the sofa, hiding my face into my knees. I sobbed like I had done many times before; broken, confused, and so utterly in despair of who I had become. A direct opposite of what I felt my true nature was, and all that I wished to have avoided doing to children of my own. I swore I would never make them feel as if they were the cause of any emotional upset, as if they should know better, as if they are the ones who should watch their behaviour to avoid making *me* upset. I swore I would never cut my child off or use my parent authority to silence them in any way, never using the words *"because I said so"* or *"this is your fault"*. My heart ached from the pain, the abuse I directed at my daughter, a tiny developing human who knows only what she sees. And what a role model I was turning out to be.

The amount of guilt and shame pouring over me was suffocating. I worried what my daughter would think of me. What my partner would think of me when he found out. I worried what I thought about myself. The keeper of a terrifying beast that was able to roar out its cage when it saw fit, but only roaring the loudest behind closed doors, in the shadows, away from retribution, just like any other coward.

This wasn't the first time the beast had ruled my mouth, but it was the first time it had gone to this extreme. The first time I couldn't stop its attack or put down the verbal branding iron, preventing myself from inflicting pain my daughter would never be able to remove. I really hated myself for what I had done. I knew better than to treat anyone like that, let alone my own daughter. At times like this, after my outbursts, I would feel so beaten by my own mind, unable to stop it, not knowing how I would ever stop something that was 'me'. My temper felt as instinctive as catching a falling glass. It just happened. My only glimmer of hope was I knew my rampage was wrong, and I felt so deeply sorry for my actions. My daughter needed to know that, no matter how young she may have been.

Sorry Is Stronger Than Rage. So Is Forgiveness.

When I finally managed to compose myself and wipe the tears dry, I header up the stairs to greet - what I envisaged would be - the traumatised child, cowering under her bed away from her beast of a mother. To my surprise, when I got to her bedroom door, there were no tears. Instead I was met by the muffled mutterings of my daughter happily playing with her Playmobil set. I opened her bedroom door and asked if I could speak to her, telling her we needed to chat about what had just happened. She agreed that it was best for us to talk; we had been through these conversations before. My quick temper, often erupting with no warning, had forced me to sit my daughter down and apologise, and explain my behaviour on many occasions by now.

We both sat at the top of the stairs, I'm not sure the reason why; a neutral, informal and easy spot for us both to sit. Reducing any need to prolong the discomfort that often follows being told *"we need to talk"*, the stairs seemed like a quick and mutual area for us both to be open and honest. I deliberately sat on a step below my daughter so I could look straight into her face, my equal. The person who needed to hear my apology, and me, hopefully the person she could forgive.

We spoke through what had happened in the store and why I grew more and more irritated with her. The logic of a child is intelligent in its simplicity; she was bored and didn't want to be in the shop, and she certainly didn't want to stand still while we waited in the long queue to pay for our food. Simple. I agreed with her that the store was boring, that, in fact I didn't want to be there either. That's *why* I got so mad. I was tired too. I was grumpy. I was one hundred things other than actually mad at my daughter, and for that I was sorry. *So sorry*.

My heart began to break again as I sat there, asking my child for forgiveness, a child of 3-years-old, who had shared the brunt of my illness just as much as her father had done. It seemed unfair of me to add such a burden to her, being the one to pacify the parent.

There were times she would comfort me, patting me on the back, telling me everything was okay, after I had snapped at her, making *her* cry. She would rub my back and tell me I was tired and asked if I would like breakfast in bed the next day, so I could rest. With each kind hand she offered me, I felt as though I was an unfit mother, asking too much of a child, which only made me cry even more.

Wiping tears from my eyes, I apologised to my daughter. For the screaming, for the yells, for demanding she sit up in her room while she was clearly very upset. I made sure she understood my actions were just that, **mine**, and nothing to do with her or her behaviour. Never did I want her to think I hated her, or that she caused any-thing she witnessed from me, other than love. Yes, she could be annoying and in need of discipline - this, I explained. Yet scream-ing at someone **was not** discipline; *that* was rage. That was me fulfilling my own needs, while dismissing hers. That was me being a dictator, a harsh parent, the exact parent type I wanted to avoid. My child is my equal, she needed to know that, always. I thanked her for screaming *"OKAY THEN!!"* at me from the stairs. I told her that screaming at people wasn't right, but it is *always* right to stand up for yourself, especially to your mother who is off on one.

Her little lip began to quiver as she saw my remorse, like her mother, tears filled her eyes as she apologised profusely.

"Sorry I made you mad", she spoke through her tears, causing my heart to sink.

"You didn't make me mad. I shouldn't have got so angry! It wasn't your fault!!". It killed me to upset my daughter; it positively tore out my heart and burnt it in front of my face to feel that she thought it was her fault.

I was failing her, again. First, I screamed her into panic; next, I muddled my words enough that she felt she was to blame for my outrageous behaviour. I couldn't have that for my daughter. I was never going to rule through fear; I didn't want to rule at all. I wanted her to know her worth, to stand up for herself and never be silenced, and certainly not because someone is older or bigger than she is. I didn't want my daughter to be passive towards me. I needed her authority to pull back my ego when it fancied a verbal trip out of my mind. I needed it from my partner too. Both of them, pulling me back into line when my judgement got cloudy and my mouth nasty. *"Don't speak to me like that"* and *"I'll tell you why"* - my saving grace in the battle against the Mind Demons, almost as if I had my very own cognitive behavioural therapy in-house, pushing me to question and rewire my mind on a daily basis.

I couldn't hold my upset from showing across my face, nor did I want to. She had to know how painful this was for me, for us both. She needed to know just how awful I felt in my abhorrent error, screaming at a child, guilty only of being just that - a ***child***.

Several times, when she added in that she was naught at the store, I explained why the outburst was all on me, all my fault. And yes, she was correct; her behaviour in the store was unacceptable. However, my reaction to her misbehaviour was far more unacceptable, not warranted, **ever**. What I should have done was scold and ignore her, dish out a calm punishment once we got home. But like that of a toddler mid-tantrum, my mind became unable to focus on logic and reason. As if my brain had switched off, guided only by adrenaline and rage.

In the hours after our argument, my daughter couldn't have been nicer to me. Snuggling in close as we watched TV, asking me to colour-in as we relaxed. Praising me for my excellent effort as I kept my pen between the lines. She complimented the colours I used and told me how much she enjoyed colouring with her mum. The whole experience pained me. I didn't deserve this beautiful human. So kind, so forgiving, so readily available to be fucked-up on the back of me being her mother. I did my best not to burst into tears as she smiled from ear to ear, dropping her face down into the colouring book, gazing up at me, making sure she knew I heard her compliments. I did hear them, I just couldn't respond without my heart bulging out my body via my tear ducts.

After I got her down for the night, I sat on the sofa and bawled my eyes out again. Where did this magnificent little human come from? Why did she love such a beast so much? Maybe it's because she had to - I am her mother.

I didn't deserve her, I told myself over and over again. *I'm failing her. She's terrified of me. She is being so kind, so sweet, in an attempt to keep me sweet: to keep me from roaring her face off the next time I felt like it.* I threw my head back onto the cushion of the sofa and I roared. This time in a different pain, as my mental straight jacket tightened around my body. I **hated** what I had done. I hated that there was nothing I could do about it. I hated that this event would now be more fuel in my mind to tear me down, a video on constant repeat. Another one I would need to endure, while hearing the words ***"You are a shit mother"*** in my head. I hated that my daughter was a pure and brilliant soul, and I would wreck her.

Soon after she was asleep, my partner called en route home after finishing work. No sooner had I answered the phone than I confessed my rage-sins. Unable to finish the whole story, I held the phone at my ear as I cried. *"It's okay"*, came the reassuring words of my partner. By this point in our parenthood journey, he was no stranger to silence-filled phone calls, hearing only the laboured exhaling and snot filled sniffs, as I tried to settle myself enough to converse.

He and I both knew my actions were wrong. However, like our daughter, he was also extremely empathetic and forgiving. He could tell in my silence that I was hurting deeply, that I knew in myself a mark was not only over-stepped, but obliterated in the process. He granted me the space and security to confess without reprimand. Still, even with his unwavering support and reassurance that these things happen, and I shouldn't be so hard on myself, it hurt. Sure, sharing my horrible secret made me feel less alone, but it did nothing for the internal lashings I was forcing upon myself, minute after minute.

Reliving the event on the phone, speaking the words, *"She gets it, she forgave me"*, was too much. I couldn't handle the maturity of our daughter, a trait she shouldn't need at such a young age. A trait I didn't feel I deserved from anyone, least of all the person I'm on this planet to protect and nurture. Over and over, I worried I was breaking our daughter, that she would learn to feel powerless and afraid of her own mother. That she would be the victim of other people screaming at her or become the heartless screamer herself.

My partner did his best to reassure me that my outburst was natural, expected, a result of a long day and being tired - just the same as I tell our kid when she becomes hyper-emotional after a late night. But this wasn't enough to pacify me; I was a beast. Nothing could justify that.

I Was Never a Beast. PND Is the Real Beast.

When I retold the event to friends, even sharing a post on social media, I spoke in a logical fashion of *why* it happened; the mother tired and stressed, overwhelmed, feeling pushed - a mother still fighting her way through PND. What I failed to share was that despite the logic, the rage being an accumulation of various factors, I still took it as who I was, still defined by it. When in reality, it was a product of environment, poor emotional skill on my part, and a very large dollop of PND.

At the time, I didn't realise rage was a symptom of PND; I mistook it as a part of *me*. Something I carried with me just as I do my relentless sarcasm and dry humour. I would overreact to simple things, like a glass of water being kicked over. An accident, yet my response was as if the person had done it with intention and the glass was filled with lava. My daughter started to change her behaviour, going to her father if she had an accident of any kind, often whispering for him to come to the next room so she could tell him what she had done. Each time, I was reminded that I was a monster, a beast that my daughter would rather avoid, than ask for help if she spilled her drink.

My partner would ask why I reacted to accidents in an aggressive, moody manner. The truth is I had no idea. My reactions happened so quickly that I would be in the middle of a scolding about how cups shouldn't be on the edge of the table, before I realised the cup was in the safest place it could be, and not perched on the edge. The constant quizzing made me feel even more worthless, even more strange, compared to people who just pick up a cloth and wipe up the water with nothing other than an *'accidents happen, no problem'*, state of mind.

I felt powerless to myself, to the rage and temper I harboured. When I saw that rage is a common symptom of PND, my eyes pricked. Scrolling deep into Pinterest, I somehow ended up on Instagram, a place filled with perfectly filtered parents *'living their best life'*. When I pushed that bullshit to the side, I scrolled upon accounts dedicated to mothers and their mental health. Burnout, overstimulation, rage, resentment, anxiety, trauma, depression, and mental load, everything people don't say about parenthood - it was all there. I read one post about rage that detailed exactly how it made a mother feel. Not in control, ashamed, scared of herself, struggling to communicate her needs. It was me. I saw myself in that post, I saw myself in every post thereafter. Other mums commented under each post that they felt the same, some even admitting their actions; what they are most ashamed of, and how they worry that their child will be traumatised as a result or grow up to hate them.

In the familiarity of the posts, I began to question why I didn't know rage was linked to PND, or why I didn't suspect it to be part of PND in the first place. Not many children are encouraged to feel and/or act upon their emotions, certainly not the 'bad' ones, such as anger. We are told to silence these emotions, stamp them out, and not to act on account of them; to pretty much pretend they aren't as integral to being human as it is to feel happy. The likely outcome for anything to the contrary is that we will be scolded for feeling or acting upon any form of '*negative*' emotion. This, in turn, pushes that emotion firmly into the list of unacceptable behaviour, and one we fail to properly understand.

To admit, seemingly without warrant, that you feel rage, angry or frustrated, and especially around children… well, that is a big **no no**. It's almost as if anything remotely swaying too close to rage or frustration is a repressed emotion that none of us want to feel, never mind admit being unable to control. Therefore, its presence is shrouded in shame and guilt, more so when we experience it during the 'wonderful' glory that is parenthood.

I didn't know rage was part of PND, part of parenthood. I could see snippets of people speaking about it online, yet it was never one of the trending parenting hashtags. Rage wasn't up there with *#motherhood* and *#blessed.* It led me to believe that rage, and therefore myself, to be in the minority within the parenthood realm.

It's logical, and seemingly natural, for people to favour posting happy - sun beaming in the sky, smiles all round, beautiful family days out at the beach - kind of pictures. We don't often have a burning anger session and then feel the need to vent online with a rage-filled picture beside an angry caption. Like myself, many people are quick to presume the *'bad'* emotions aren't part of parenthood for everyone. Far less then would anyone, especially those new to mental illness, make the direct link between PND and most other actions and emotions they are feeling at the time. Given that I didn't even know childbirth could lead to depression, it was naïve of me to think that I knew all about PND after a quick online search. What I hadn't realised was that I had been living the symptoms of PND in real time, mistakenly beating myself up when I experienced them. Once I discovered that my neck tension and door slams might be the result of something tangible, something I could begin to manage, I suddenly realised I was a victim of illness, and **not** the grand source of it all.

Chapter 20

The Many Faces of Postnatal Depression

There's a notion in motherhood that you should find your *'Mum Tribe'* and stick with them. The team that has your back, with no judgement. The people you can rely on for moral support and a comforting ear. A network that will remind you there is no point in running away, for the baby can sniff you out in a 100-mile radius. Plus, your tribe needs you too. And they sure as shit won't be doing this alone, so you need to stick it out too, for them.

I found my tribe online. Many of these people may not know I count them as my tribe, as creepy as that may seem. Whereas with others, I have made lifelong friends who have guided me through hard times, offering support when I feel like I'm failing. Or those who give me a boot up the arse, kicking me out of my pity party if I have been spending a little too long at the buffet.

I follow various social media accounts, all of whom speak openly and honestly about parenthood - a high proportion of them knowing the confines of PND very well. Six years in, I'm still learning and working through the remnants of PND, having *"Aha!"'* moments. Reading posts created almost as if they have been sent directly to me. Words reading off the screen, playing out scenes that I'm sure are mine, but are the words of another mother. Parents are now finding their strength and validation in the digital world. We share posts that may be harsh and revealing, yet in the comments there is a welcoming community of camaraderie.

Our words aren't exclusive to illness either; many people can tick the rage-box who have never suffered with mental illness. The frustrations of parenthood seem to be universal, yet for many, if combined with other factors; it may be symbolic of an unnecessary pain they are carrying, one that may just lead to a diagnosis and a route to freedom from that pain.

No longer do mothers settle for the symptoms of PND being seen as excessive crying and feeling sad. Whole accounts are created online to discuss the **many**, deep, intertwined symptoms of the illness, in all their smashing-the-stigma glory.

Depression doesn't always look like being confined to a darkened room, unable to leave your bed for days on end. Depression can be much more subtle, often manifesting in ways we don't auto-matically associate with the illness. Creating a high functioning human, one who can go about their day - smile at work, laugh at jokes - only to return home and be confused as to why the want to lie in a darkened room, feeling empty.

The many faces of depression can look like:

Feeling unmotivated, yet unable to sit still.

Being unable to concentrate on a film.

Being triggered by mess.

Cleaning up said mess, or else you will never be at peace.

Obsessive cleaning - As in, it was the only thing I felt any form of joy in. I would rather scrub the bathroom than spend time watching a film.

Never being at peace anyway, as your mind is constantly running.

Having absolutely zero faith that the future is anything to look forward to.

Feeling alone in a room full of people - Or like me, pushing through attending a wedding. Only to need a week to recuperate and having very little memory of the event as I was on edge the whole time.

Experiencing anxiety when you have never felt it before - I once almost freaked out while getting the train into town. The whole time I sat with confusion, never having felt anxious or sweaty on the train before. Wondering why I was beginning to panic when I was excited 2 minutes previously.

Waking up more tired than when you went to sleep.

Zoning out when people speak with you, yet you can still hold the conversation. Only to leave and have little recollection of what was being said.

*Despite being tired, you cannot sleep. **At all*** - My personal *'**favourite**'* trait of PND. I've never felt so tired, yet wired to the moon at the same time.

Not giving a shit for the emotions of others. In fact, you might want to inflict pain on others, to make yourself feel better.

Being extremely forgetful, entirely unable to remember why you walked into a room.

On the flip side, having a photographic memory about something that you wish you could forget.

Being hypervigilant - I joke I'm like a Terminator, seeing **everything**. Half curse, half useful. Wholly depletive of energy.

Intrusive thoughts which then become reality - for you at least.

Having recurring nightmares that wake you in a panic.

Mindless scrolling through social media to avoid living your life.

Living behind a pane of glass. Being able to see everyone, yet unable to <u>feel</u> them at all.

*Being on edge. All the time. **All. The. Time*** - This made me unable to sleep, as I was always listening for the baby - which feeds nicely into sleep deprivation.

Neglecting habits that you once enjoyed - I used to love painting my nails. After my daughter was born, I didn't have the energy, or desire to decorate my nails. What was the point?

Entertaining suicidal thoughts. Detailing when and where you would take your life. Seeing it as the best option to stop the pain or to cleanse your family of your toxicity.

Daydreaming about running away from your family. To protect them or to get away from the madness.

*Noise stimulation. This is a **big** one* - The noise of the TV while my daughter danced about, and my partner spoke, made (still does) the hair on my neck stand up. I wanted to scream while I turned everything off. Far too much stimulation for an already cramped mind.

The list goes on and on, and on and *on…*

Anger and rage seemed to be the hot topics online, the ones drawing me in the most. And it's easy to see why. Those '*bad*' emotions we have been taught never to feel, let alone share with others. Under these *taboo* feelings, comes an even longer list of reasons why we may experience them. All linked to PND in some form, yet not all indicative that you are suffering from the illness. At the base of them all is neglecting who you are. You as a human.

You and your needs and wants, coupled with any unresolved trauma that helps to create tension, upset and frustration in our everyday lives.

Parents spend so much of their time giving to other people that they become burnt out, exhausted, touched and sounded out. We get angry we have no time for the serenity of yoga, the laughter in coffee dates or quietness of reading a book. Combined with no time to dwell on, let alone be active in our aspirations and dreams, it's a bit of a 'take your pick', as to the reason why a mum flipped her shit at the store.

My Tribe Took Away My PND

My tribe had (has) my back; more than that, they showed me that how I behaved when I was at the peak of my PND was symptommatic of mental illness. The resentment towards my partner is very well a chapter in the PND playbook of sending a parent into despair. Other chapters include rage screaming, making you feel like you can't cope, tension and jaw clenching, rigid schedules, nap anxiety, and frantic online searches when you are convinced your baby's saliva is showing signs of a rare disease and you are the only one that is seeing it.

The playbook for PND may be tailored to our individual situation, yet the chapters are always the same. It's just that most people don't even realise these chapters exist: instead, they think they are: the angry mother who wonders why she cannot stand to be with her children any longer. The stressed mum who needs a break but won't allow herself one. The mother, quick to anger being woken during the night, who becomes harsh and stern in tone in reply to the kid's cry of being scared of the dark. The mum who cannot stand to listen to the kid whimpering for one more second or else she will hit the roof. The mum who becomes irrationally annoyed with friends when they dare suggest a lunch date midday, when they *should* know that's the time baby has a nap.

All normal in their abnormality. All pages in the PND book of how to fuck up your happiness. **Never a part of the fabric that makes you, who you are.** No matter how hard you want to believe it. It's more a part of the fabric weaved into the blanket of parenthood, and, if mixed with the right conditions, can form a big old cocoon of mental illness wrapped tightly around you.

I see her - me - that mother rage screaming at the 3-year-old. I see her in online posts, mothers confessing their yelling during the morning rush, getting everyone ready for school. Losing her temper when the kid didn't have his shoe on despite mum warning, num-erous times, it's time to leave. I see that mother, apologising, looking for validity, as she bares her soul to the masses. She can see why she snapped, yet I feel parents don't know the pressure they are truly under. It's not only the shoes that set her off, but there will also be a back catalogue of stressors contributing to the guttural roar of a mother on the edge; neglect, trauma, stress, and often a mental illness that has yet to be named or faced. I see the actions of most people as a result of what they are dealing with, knowingly or not. And if only they knew the iceberg under that tip, then maybe they would cut themselves some slack.

I forgave myself for screaming at my daughter, on several occa-sions. But it does nothing to settle the pain, to settle the worry that I have damaged her in some way. I understand, yet do not justify, my actions. My screams had been the result of too much weight upon my shoulders. Feeling the voices of too many narrators telling me how best to live my life, how best to raise our daughter. A full display of everything lurking underneath my actions. I hope my daughter will see this, and more importantly, that I hope *society* will see it, so that we can begin to support parents better on their journey, rather than squeezing them to the point they release their inner anger by blood-curdling screams directed at their own, defenceless offspring.

Chapter 21

My Greatest Realisation in The Fight Against PND:

You are not special. Nor are you unique.

I mean that in the nicest way possible. Hear me out…

When the Mind Demons of shitty mental health come round, keg in hand, ready to set up a rave in your brain for the foreseeable future, they do so, using a blanket of protection under which you internalise everything they tell you and keep it secret. They make you believe everything you feel, everything you say, everything you think, is *who you are*. Your **definition**. And since you think of yourself as such a worthless piece of shit and a monster of a mother, you won't dare tell another soul.

You won't tell them you screamed at your kid. You won't tell them you would rather stab your eye with a hot, Peppa Pig shaped rod than bake with your child. You won't tell anyone how crushed you feel in the darkness. You won't tell anyone how you cry yourself to sleep when you are alone with your thoughts. You won't tell a soul that you feel relief when you are child free for an hour, and dread picking them up afterwards. You won't tell anyone how jealous you are of others; the childfree couples, able to satisfy their wishes whenever they feel like it. You believe you are the only one with these thoughts and so you suffer in silence. Boy, does mental illness **THRIVE** when we feel alone.

This veil of secrecy made me believe I was the only one with these thoughts. I was the only parent who saw their baby as a chore. *Who would think such a thing?* Only a *terrible* person. Once I believed the lies of the Mind Demons, it was not too difficult for them to beat me with the stick of shame and guilt. Until I was lying there, defenceless, being beaten to death in my own mind. When their claws of evil were entrenched within my skin, poison seemed to seep from them, infecting my entire body. Physically on some days; lethargy preventing my feet from crossing the front door for the third day in a row. My head ached from the constant muscle tension and strain. Carrying around a head full of chatter and bitterness is no easy task, draining me as if straight from my soul. Life became too hard, requiring just that bit too much energy on the greyest days.

Once the mind is subjected to abuse from within, it's a hard task to pull yourself out, to muster any drive or will to fight for yourself. But there is strength and unity in numbers. When mental health is concerned, it pays dividends to know **you aren't the only one.**

Speaking Up

It takes enormous strength to stand on that soap box, pulling the mic to your mouth, ready to speak your truth when you believe everyone around will stop and stare. After all, you are the *only* parent, on a planet, of billions of people, who has ever had the despicable thought of, *'I wish I never had children'*.

But here's the secret: you, and I, ain't *THAT* special.

You haven't been cast in the Matrix; you are not 'The One'. Wondering if you should have had a child is arguably one of the most common thoughts a parent will have at some point. Whether in jest when the baby is playing ultimate cockblock when mum really needs that *'back massage'*, or whether that thought originates when you are rocking in front of the washing machine, trying to drown out the sound of your screaming baby when you just can't take being a parent for a minute longer.

You are not unique. Your thoughts are not unique. Those cruel Mind Demons are not so clever that they can come up with original content. Sure, they tailor it to you and your circumstances, but the general theme is always the same: self-worth, self-pity, sadness, rage, resentment and regret. To name a few of their greatest hits.

To some degree, we all experience intrusive thoughts of the same genre, be that in parenthood or when we are being tormented in our mental illness. Yet the key to being released from their weight is to speak up and to speak honestly, for I can almost guarantee that someone, somewhere, will relate to everything you say. Or better, they will return your vulnerability in the form of validation by simply saying, *"me too".*

Ripping My Mental Illness Apart, One Post at A Time

Once I realised that I was not entirely in control of the hands turning the cogs of my mind and actions, it became easier to release the guilt and shame associated with it.

The more I shared my parenthood journey online via blogging and social media, the more I understood that I wasn't alone in my thoughts. Even the most intimate, detailed, personalised thoughts, someone else had experienced it too. Bizarre, considering they are *my* thoughts. How could a person, on the other side of the world, relate so much to my internal monologue? And then another person said the same. Then another. Then another. The answer: the only common factor here was that they were all parents. All of whom, had experienced ill mental health, whether they knew it or not.

Post-natal anxiety and depression seemed to be the common denominators in those who related with my words. That was interesting. That was liberating. My thoughts, my issues, the very tools my demons used to tease me with on a daily basis, were never mine. They are all part of post-natal depression, and **not who I am**. So, I spoke my words a little louder, a little closer to the bone, and the Mind Demons didn't much like that.

When I spoke out, the words seemed to rip a little flesh from them - slowly at first - then my confidence grew and my words sharpened, honing right to the core of an issue. At the same time, the Mind Demons began to disintegrate. I had found their weakness and no longer was I afraid to share the lies they had told me. I knew what they had been telling me for years was false, and no longer did I need to feel the pain of them. Not from any of their lies. That's not to say I can disclose all of the lies and rid myself of the upset they cause me. Some of them, especially those that lie close to my body image and self-worth, no matter how many times I voice them, still echo in my ear from time to time. They still linger around me, waiting for that silence in the shower to zip into my mind when I run my hand over the sagging and stretched skin on my stomach. They lie in wait, hoping I have had a poor night's sleep and fancy a dip in the pool of self-destruction. Sometimes I do let them flutter around my mind. But now I am quick to seek comfort from those closest to me. I'm aware of intrusive thoughts, but I'm not immune to their power.

Still, I will take that awareness over being beaten by them blindly. That is progress in itself.

The truth is, once you see mental illness for what it is - an *illness* and not a personality trait - then you begin to rock its infrastructure.

The realisation that I had an illness as opposed to thinking this is just who I was now, ripped the darkness from me, by the roots. Some of those roots may have been strong, that tree had many rings and roots that run deep, clenching with all their might. But, in time, they could still be removed. Cut down at first, then left to rot while I focused on planting better, more serving greenery. Confidence is crucial. I needed to know and understand that those dark thoughts do not belong to me. Therefore, I need not feel anything associated with them. No guilt. No shame. No judgement. The only thing I needed to take from them, is the drive to find out **why** they held power over me, and how to rid myself of that grip.

I am The Captain Now

Many of my thoughts originated from poor self-worth. I mean really, why would I think I was any less of a human, based purely on what I presumed my partner thought of my body post-partum? This constant mental drain was only exacerbated by the sexualisation and objectification of women in society, if not the root of my poor self-worth at the time; the change in body from pre-baby into a body that can, and should, be 'fixed' according to each advert I came across on social media.

Under my radar, my mental illness took my worth and placed it into the hands of someone else, forcing me to equate my body as a measure of self-worth. In return I was left feeling inadequate, ugly and destroyed. Unable to have sex with my partner, for I felt the touch of my body repulsed him, that he only kept me in the relationship to be used as a piece of meat. That thought pissed me off so much, as it was one I felt I could not control, nor did I know **why** it was so powerful.

Then it clicked - *I* was the one in control of my self-worth. I could stand in front of the mirror and big-up my body instead of (wrongly) second guessing what my partner thought about it. *"Fake it till you make it"*, they say. So, I did. The strange thing is, I didn't hate my body, I never have. I worried purely about what my partner thought of it, of me. Along the way, I muddied my self-worth into those thoughts. Once I made the connection that my body image was warped, and body image doesn't equate to my value in any way, shape or form, then another weight was pulled from my neck. With this realisation, I heard those slimy bastard Mind Demons fall to ash a little more. And that's when I truly understood the value of self-love.

Chapter 22

Beating Postnatal Depression

I've been asked many times how I recovered, how I beat PND. Honestly, I don't like sharing my personal 'plan' to better health. Not that I'm shy - as you've seen with my never-ending desire to reference my 5th labia, any chance I get!

The reason for my secrecy is protection for those seeking answers, wanting to find a way out of the darkness guided by my rope. My healing cable is a privileged one; I live in a country with free healthcare and medication, and in a city in which kindness and compassion bolsters people to create free-to-use mental health charities. I am fortunate in the relationships surrounding me. Friends willing to tell me I am being hurtful, yet to take the time I need. My daughter, even at a young age, wrapping her arms around me in support. And my partner. What do I say about him that will do the last 6 years of our journey any form of justice? Without him, I wouldn't be here. That is a fact.

I was given everything I ever needed to succeed in the battle against PND. I had people pushing me in the background, old friends and new, who watched tears drip from my face as I sat at their kitchen table, reliving the pain of the past whilst writing this book.

I have been abundantly blessed throughout this whole journey and I know it. So, when someone asks me how they can get better, I freeze in my privilege. Not everyone has access to a GP, even less with access to free medication. If they do have the service; it can be a trial and error merry-go round of therapy, drugs, and self-discovery - lasting years, if not a lifetime.

Most women who reach out to me note that their partner is aloof, distant or absent entirely; with family ostracising them on account of their (often undiagnosed) mental illness. Women are told to 'get on with it', as they drown in the ocean of motherhood. Me telling her to reach out to someone she trusts just isn't an option, as noted by the private message sent to a stranger online, desperately seeking some way out of her torment. Even if there is a loving partner at her side, they aren't always equipped to hear the piercing words that mental illness attacks with, much less understand them. People lose friends and family during parenthood. Past traumas or abuse have a nasty habit of surfacing once we are tasked with being the responsible adult to another human. It can all cause tension, embarrassment, denial and, ultimately, isolation for those who want healing via sharing the truth.

With all that being said, I do believe there are some perspectives, in which I have learnt and try to live by each day, that can help others who are walking under the heavy cloud of depression. First and foremost, ultimately the most valuable skill in my conquest against PND, is understanding and practicing self-love.

Self-Love

"Self-love." *something from the 60s*, I scoffed. *"A pile of shite"* - as we Scots say. Although I'm not sure "self-love" was the term the therapist used, or if she covertly packaged it up in a tougher wrapper. One that wouldn't make me eye-roll, because I'm that *hardcore, lone wolf,* who feels more at peace in the world of verbal insults than compliments. But self-love was exactly the pill she sneaked down my neck and into the space that should have been warm and fuzzy, decorated with love and admiration, deep within me.

Don't get me wrong, her methods were brutal. More often than not, I cried during those sessions. Sitting in the car afterwards, wondering how I would pull myself together in the time it took me to drive to work. I don't have enough fingers to count the number of times I called into work sick, citing I was drained and unfit for work, needing a day or two to recuperate from the gut extraction that week. The only feeling I can liken it to be is the empty, numb feeling the day after attending a funeral of someone you dearly love, depleted of everything, with no energy left to feel happy or sad.

I soon learnt that self-love wasn't standing in front of the mirror, reciting affirmations that I was strong and powerful, pulling taut the sagging skin that once grew my child. It doesn't mean that you big-up yourself on the daily, then walk away as if you have done the hard work and your mind just needs to catch up. There's no point building yourself up constantly if when that mirror is out of reach, you are a real bitch to yourself.

You need to accept and love every single part of what makes you, **you**. All the good you carry, and <u>all</u> the 'dark' that you want to be free from. You need to take it all, with **no judgment**. To almost become an observer in your thoughts and actions, allowing them to flow without self-chastising if there is a blip along the road. Seeing yourself 'warts and all', without self-scolding, is the first step to understanding self-love and applying it.

You need to extend the warmth of unconditional love to yourself when you have screamed at your baby, or when you have thrown your partner out of the car after telling him (again) your relationship is over. You need to give yourself support when you've pressed 'send' on that snide message to your best friend. That is the unconditional self-love needed to pull yourself out of the dark, and to give yourself the grace you need to say that it's okay to call it quits, and lay in your bed for the day with no mental judgement.

We spend so much time in that head of ours, so we really need to make sure the loudest voice in there is that of our ally, our best friend. Cheering the shit out of us, even when our painting looks like a five-year-old has done it, with their toes, while wearing a blindfold. We need that inner voice to be the overly excited, slightly tipsy, woman in the pub bathroom who cannot stop complimenting our outfit or professing that our hair looks SO amazing, despite it being in desperate need of a wash and blow-dry.

Be *that person*, and be it to yourself.

It's really not easy to get to that loving head space, especially when we have built up an area of dedicated self-hate. So I want to break it down further, get right into the belly of 'love'. There are a few elements in curating a caring, loud voice of self-love within ourselves. So strap on that oxygen tank because we are about to go in deep here.

Forgiveness

We don't get the flu and apologise profusely we are ill and in need of care. Well, there is always the fourth day of feeling like death when you begin to feel a bit sorry for yourself, doing that snotty, ugly cry, blurting out you are so sorry you are ill, and how grateful you are for all the tasteless soup and god-awful Lemsip. You have a wee cry to yourself, while being told it's okay, and get some sleep (you drama queen), everything will be better tomorrow.

When it comes to mental health, we apologise non-stop for our illness. Or not, in some cases. Only to then breakdown and apologise through the tears when we see the horror in our wake. Many times, after a lengthy breakdown session, I would be overcome with emotion and apologies. At times, the pain and remorse would be so powerful, so intense, that all I could do was sob into my hands, saying *"I'm sorry. I'm so sorry"*. I felt like I was the burden. I was the one bringing so much tension and hurt into our family. The truth is I was never the burden; I was merely a conduit for the darkness, nothing more than a vessel for depression to do its dirty work, while I felt helpless under its control.

Often, I didn't see what I was doing or how I was impacting the home. How could I, when it was my 'normal', and my reality? So warped into believing I was justified in my actions, and this was how I should behave. Angry and full of temper; quick to empty my vile on whoever prompted it to pour. That lady deserved my middle finger as I raced past her in my car, rushing and running late to collect my child after work. She was a snail behind the wheel. **'Move the fuck over'**, I thought, get out of the fast lane (which is not the correct name of the lane, I know), it's for people who need to get past incompetent drivers like yourself. Rage pouring from me as I shoved my finger to the window, making sure she saw *exactly* how pissed off I was. I behaved like a major bitch. At times now, I still do. Yet this behaviour only arises when I deplete my reserves, and what better an illness can deplete mental reserves than depression?

I began to realise I was not the master of my own mind. More importantly, I wasn't always in **control** of my own mind. No one in their happy, right mind would think it okay to speed past another car, all the while making sure the driver saw their middle finger being pushed as close to the window as possible. Another time, I seriously considered mounting the pavement to bypass cars queuing at traffic lights. I was **livid** waiting in traffic, especially when I needed to collect my daughter after work. The safety of other people wasn't my concern at that moment because I felt justified in my rage. Who in their right mind would even consider driving down a pedestrian sidewalk just to get around traffic, and for no real reason other than they had had enough of driving that day?!

I could sit and dwell all day on my actions and words. The harsh things I've said, the snide comments and painful remarks. But where would that get me? Possibly, right back down Depression Avenue. Mind Demons feed off pain, and dwelling on things that have passed, making your toes curl while you mentally relive giving some innocent lady the finger, seems pretty painful to me.

I don't deny I have behaved wrongly, but I'm not ashamed of it. I choose to see that I was under the influence of a warped mind, tremendous stress, and a point of view that was hell-bent on self-destruction. I choose to forgive myself, to love myself for all that I had done. I apologised to my partner, to my friends, and always to my daughter. To her the most. Every single one of them gave me the compassion and love I deserved, and so I let it in. *Really* let it in. *"You don't need to be sorry",* they told me. The best thing they could have said, as it is the truth.

I'm sorry depression grew within me and stole time that I will never reclaim. I'm sorry I was so mean to myself for so long. I wasn't firing on all cylinders while PND rampaged through my mind; no one is at full mast when battling with mental illness. So, I forgave myself for everything I said or thought during that time. I released that heavy baggage from around my neck; it is a weight that none of us need bear.

Understanding and Acceptance

To take responsibility for your actions without becoming crippled by them is the **hardest** thing to do. You need to fully realise what your actions have done, how they have impacted other people, accept it, sit with it, then put the whip of self-lashing down. You can be forever sorry you acted the way you did, but you cannot harbour the self-berating forever. The best way to do this, is to understand where the behaviours, thoughts and actions originate from. Then accept it for all that is it. Your pain, your trauma, the reason for your actions. Whatever you may find, you need to accept and make your peace with how this impacts you and your behaviour.

My therapist had me lie on her chair, covered me with a blanket, and mentally took me on a journey. I was going to meet someone that day: that person was me, as a child. Having no idea what she was up to - honestly thinking that delving into the mind was erring on a pile of nonsense - still, I diligently obeyed. I like to think I'm an open person, a trait I've had to build. I'll give anything a go. (Much to my partner's delight!)

As I focused on my breathing, pushing aside how stupid I felt while enjoying the space to possibly have a nap when I should have been working, I listened intently to my therapist's instructions. Some-where along the line - in-between becoming mindful of my thoughts, bringing them out of the food list for the supermarket and back to the commanding voice of my therapist - I stumbled upon a young child, aged between 5 and 8 years old. Unlike the happy child I remember myself to be, this child was very much in need of love, a hug, comfort, someone to tell her everything is okay.

Being the adult in the situation, I hugged that poor child, with every ounce of compassion I had. Sitting in the warmth and safety of the therapist's chair, I began to cry. The emotion from the child seemed to overwhelm my body. I could feel every bit of sadness within her. How lost she felt and with a deep longing to be held. I saw this child cowering in a foetal position, curled into a protective ball. Not allowing anyone in or out, only suffering with a tremendous pain that she could not place... yet she knew love to be the key to unlocking it. She wanted to be loved so badly, yet for some reason wouldn't allow it, nor give it.

Surrounded by greenery in my mental haven, where lush grass is bordered by colourful flowers next to a stream of fresh running water, I leant down to this child. Opening my arms and heart to her, she took my hand as I pulled her to my chest. As we hugged, I was instructed to imagine a healing white light above us; pure in form, calming and unifying. As the light shone around us, my time was up and I had to leave the haven, but not before my therapist informed me that this child lived within **me** and I was to always allow her space. Within that space, I was to allow her love and grace, **always**. No matter what. No matter what she did. I was to accept who she was, how she got there, and more importantly, that she was a *part of me* and **deserved** love.

As the therapist counted down from ten to one, the cue I was to leave my mind haven, I lay in the chair completely still. Heavy in emotion, I couldn't seem to stop the tears from falling. Weighted tears that seemed to signify I was being released of something, while becoming at one with something else. I couldn't quite understand it. I was in pain for the child, but that child is me? It all seemed a bit bat-shit, but I knew the truth. I could *feel* the truth. Something inside of me knew I was accepting myself for who I was, as I welcomed and comforted the child I had met in my haven. I was accepting me. All of me. The ugly and all. For that little girl was me at my core; a vulnerable human acting out on account of her pain, desperately needing love and compassion to heal her wounds. Needing to be felt, seen and understood, before she can be fully accepted and welcomed into the love she so desperately needed in order to regain her strength.

That plot twist the therapist threw in at the end blew my mind for several days. It released a hurt within me that I no longer needed to hold, at least not alone. I became at one with the pain that depression had caused. I broke through those mental barriers my illness had created; I walked right up to myself, and mentally voiced it was okay, everything was okay, and it will be okay.

I had mentally embraced my vulnerable self, whose form took on that of one most people would agree needs the greatest amount of nourishment. A form that no one could deny was innocent; a product of events and circumstance, that forced her to act in ways of self-preservation and hurt. We wouldn't hate on a child acting out if we knew the extent of hurt that child had been suffering. We would extend only love, warmth and patience. And as that child was me, the sentiment still stood. I was to extend the same understanding, acceptance and warmth I gave to the child, to myself, as they - we - are the same entity. What a wily one that therapist was, I thought. *Very clever.*

From then on, everything became clear. Most of my frustration, anger and upset came from within. The shame associated with my temper came from unmet needs, pent up over time, communicated in snarls rather than words. It seems logical now to think if you become stifled and unheard, you might look to other methods of communication that demand attention. A rage scream won't go unnoticed, so I used it to signal I was becoming maxed out, stressed and depleted in the world of parenthood.

I understood my behaviours and actions; I knew they came from a place of upset, exuding from me in the form of rage, depression and often reclusiveness. I knew no one wanted to behave like that, but what I failed to see is that I needed to accept it as part of me, as part of my history, and my future. My depression created many a memory I wish I could forget, bringing with it pain, which in turn fed back into the cycle of lashing out and creating more life events that I need to shake out of my head. If I continued to ignore all that depression had created within me, if I tried to challenge it without acknowledging the most integral part of me, it would only cause further suffering.

I was at the source of it all; the rage, the depression, the insecurity, the pain, the isolation and the torment. I was that little girl in there who needed love and support, understanding and acceptance. I came to realise I would be unable to move forward if I didn't love me entirely. There is no one else on this planet who could give the love and acceptance to the little girl inside me. There was no other place I would find peace than for it to come from within myself. The only way to do that was to accept and understand **all** of me. To hug that child, frightened by the monster in her head, and let her know it was okay, she was in a safe and loving space now. Together we would beat those Mind Demons.

It all boiled down to loving **all** areas of me... even those that I wished I could remove and trade up for a better model. But we cannot remove elements within ourselves, at least not through hate. The only way to beat the Mind Demons was to smother them in complete unconditional love, understanding and acceptance, imm-ensely reducing their chance to fill my mind with nasty, intrusive thoughts. The Mind Demons will struggle to make intrusive thoughts stick once you have made peace with yourself. Once you and that inner child understand each other completely and know there is nothing that will infiltrate the respect you have for each other.

I understood why I behaved as I did, and why I can still behave in that manner now. But I can't allow it to eat me from the inside, to chomp and bite that inner child. An internal chatter of hate, self-deprecation and disgust, only makes the plight harder. There is no one sorrier on this earth, no one more in pain, no one more longing that time machines existed than the mother who screamed at her newborn baby. There is no one sorrier, and gut wrenchingly pained, that they told their partner they weren't in love with him, than me. There is no one more capable of reprimanding me, than me. I know what I've done and said; I know the malicious thoughts behind my behaviours. Believe me when I say, I **know** the demon that dwells within the core of my depression. And I accept them. **All**.

Everything that happened in the previous 6 years, and everything that is yet to come; I accept it. I don't want to accept that it's a high probability I will lose my shit and scream at my child again. I don't want to accept I will say cruel things to my partner in the life we will share together. I'd rather not have these traits wired within me, deeply so, that changing them will be a lengthy, if not a lifelong, journey. But I do take them with me, in kindness, using them only as a gauge of my mental status and nothing more. No fuel for self-bashing, no fuel for being a shit mother, no fuel for hating myself, to the point of believing I'm unfit for life, let alone motherhood.

I understand, accept and provide myself with unconditional self-love, the best I can. I remind myself of the abundance surrounding me, the love my family extend to me always. They find me worthy of love, as should I. I love myself enough to know no matter how much I love my daughter, being told about Minecraft for 3 straight hours is still boring as shit. I love myself enough to know as a human, I have breaking points, needs and wants, and **none** of them come at the expense of motherhood. I love myself enough to know that life will throw me curveballs every so often and test everything I learned in therapy. Becoming frustrated, yelling, crying, or lashing out, doesn't mean I'm failing or neglecting all the years of growth I've been through. The only time I'll fail is if I let go of being kind to myself or forgetting to practice self-love with all the grace I deserve.

If I, ever again, sit in front of that washing machine and scream at myself *"What is wrong with me?!"*, after a meltdown about empty food cupboards, then I'll know I need help. And you know what? I still wouldn't judge myself. A little bit of compassion goes a long way, especially if you apply it to yourself.

Boundaries

After all that hippie-dippy, self-love, finding yourself - accepting the warts and all - you still don't get to sit down and have a nice quiet cup of tea, thinking you have completed your mission. Fuck no! Parents never get to sit and rest. All that hard work will go to waste if you don't protect it. And the best way to do that is by setting up some pretty clear, much needed, never to be compromised, boundaries.

If you don't want to do something, then don't do it. If you don't want to listen to something, then don't listen. Easy, eh? Not always. People have opinions on everything, so it can feel impossible to shake the voice of others out of your head. The closer they are to you, seemingly the more powerful their approval. Plus, for me, there seems to always be that voice of 'what if' or 'what will people think' or 'what is the best thing to do… *for other people'*. All that constant questioning and confusion threatened to upset the apple cart once I had filled it with delicious, happy fruits from all my time in therapy. So I devised a pretty simple logic to keep my mental health on the positive end of the scale.

My secret to a happier life:

'I do not give a shit. I do what keeps me happy'

I'm not absolved of all insecurities, but I am confident in my needs, wants and limits. **I am confident in my boundaries**. I learnt the *very* hard way what happens to my mind when I don't respect my wishes or needs.

We often seek approval and security in others, wanting them to tell us we are doing it right and meeting their standards, almost living a life through the eyes of others. That didn't align with me. It doesn't align with many happy people.

Once I knew I had the power to accept myself, it seemed only fitting that I should nurture and protect myself to aid my acceptance and healing. I didn't need anyone to tell me I was a great parent, although the sentiment is still greatly appreciated to hear. We are all in need of a boost from time to time. When I believed I was the best parent to my daughter, just as true as I believe the sun will rise and set, I no longer entertained the opinion of anything to the contrary. Unsolicited advice from others dripped off me, unable to stick to my new Teflon coating. I didn't need to hear why my daughter should be doing XY and Z at this age, nor need I let that into my mind to paint a portrait of why this meant I was a poor parent.

No longer did I need to read the words of 'Mummy Bloggers' on social media, who used filters to express their gratitude at being a mother. Meanwhile, the truth behind the lens was of a mother screaming her face off, just like the rest of us. No longer did I need to entertain something that made me feel anything less than happy; not until I became completely confident in my new 'I am worthy' status, at least.

I have so many boundaries set up around me I could make a thrilling TV game show, daring anyone to get through the rein-forced steel maze into my psyche. Even if they did make it, I'm too fucking zen in just *living*, to be annoyed by their opinion.

' *You do you* ' - a boundary in itself; my thoughts when someone is acting or speaking in a way that might upset me. This simple thought reminds me we are all different, and others need not impact my mind if I do not wish it. It is my shielding affirmation, reinforcing my boundaries that are set up in protection.

What I'm protecting is me, which is linked to my family. I can never allow the beast of depression to roam free again. My boundaries are just that: **mine**. A reflection of learning; my needs having nothing to do with other people. As I say, "You do you", but I don't need to hold an audience with anyone in any way, shape or form. Not if I sense a threat for whatever reason. Especially not if that someone has upset me in the past with their words or behaviours. I owe no one but myself the reasons for my boundaries. Some things take a while to heal. While I'm getting there, distance and avoidance can be the best tactics.

In time, these boundaries will change. The more I practise, the more the mind-boggling words of others do little to upset me. I could write a whole other book on what not to say to a mother who has chosen to breastfeed her baby. The content of such conversations are very much still logged up there in my mind, words that placed fear and insecurity within me at the time when I was feeding my daughter. But they do little to bother me now. Now that I know better and **"do not give a shit"**.

Boundaries are one of the best acts of self-love. Knowing and appreciating yourself, so much so, that you value you enough to be protected. My boundaries are more than insurance policies, protecting me when something goes wrong. They ensure nothing will go wrong in the first place. I won't be in a situation where I feel uncomfortable as I won't attend at all, or I won't allow the situation past my barrier of giving a fuck. There are times when you cannot avoid a situation, person or energy. Instead, I learnt to be present and allow it, without letting it in. Without listening to the shite being thrown at me, knowingly or not. I learnt that everyone has their issues, a reason for their behaviour. My boundaries ensure I'm ever-knowing of this, and so I allow it to pass over me. I wish I could say this barrier prevents me from losing my shit when the kid is acting like an overtired, moaning pain in the arse, but I'm not *that* zen just yet.

Boundaries are a **necessity** for protection. Saying no to a boss who asks too much, telling the partner you need more sleep, unfollowing people who make you feel less than, removing yourself from people who upset you, are all boundaries that you can, and should, put in place. With no regret or remorse. If something is making you feel like shit, then **you do not need to suffer it**. *"Off you fuck"*, a phrase I like to mentally say, affirmation-like in status. (Just try not to speak it out loud when closing the bedroom door on the kid for the night...)

These physical and mental boundaries made all the difference in my path to feeling better. They gave me the confidence to know my sanity is worth protecting at all costs. From simple boundaries that keep my everyday sanity in check, to a deeper, more personal level of protecting my energy from being drained by those who seem to suck it out of me, while filling my mind with doubt and anxiety.

I'm No Therapist, But They Helped Me

I found these 3 elements to be like pillars on which self-love could grow: understanding, acceptance and forgiveness. Almost as if they are the foundations on which I needed to build, to create a place of true self-love, allowing nothing other than grace for myself; surrounded by so much healing light, in which darkness could never overshadow.

Ultimately, my path to overcoming PND - teasing out the kinks in need of love and facing them head on - all came from within. I never found the task daunting; to be the creator and destructor all in one, knowing only I had the ability to stop it. At times I was scared. There would be breakdowns that I couldn't explain, or if I did, I had no idea how to 'fix' the problem. Believing I was so broken and beyond repair that maybe it would be best to remove myself from the equation and resign to the scrap heap of 'fucked up and no good'.

I will be forever grateful my partner convinced me otherwise and that I had so much trust and faith in his words I decided to try and fix the issue. I am stubborn in nature, combined nicely with my dad's belief that if something is broken, you can fix it, no problem. At first, I tried medication, which helped to an extent, yet for my particular breed of demon, they would never have brought them to their knees. Next, I went to therapy. A warm and comforting stranger looked me in the face and asked me to explain why I hated myself so much. She made it sound so simple and easy; I was ill, not broken. My head needed a bit of rewiring to see things, see myself, for who I really was. I was surrounded by people telling me I was worth the fight. I was not the beast I saw in the mirror. I was in there, hurting the most out of everyone. If I could just be a little kinder to myself, I would see the way out.

There are various ways to fix your mind, to remove the unwanted visitors. Everyone will have their own elixir, a way to ignite the flame, guiding them out of the dark. But if you don't practise the art of self-love, no matter how "hippie" you think it to be, then you may as well make sure you pack a family sized pack of Lucozade for your next round of mental fights with the Mind Demons. For you will have a *very long* and *very hard* fight winning that contest, struggling to find the light in your fatigued state, if you don't have your own back.

Chapter 23

I (You) Have the Power

Each night, since battling PND, pushing those Mind Demons into a cage far from earshot, I close my eyes and thank the universe for my blessings as I recite everything I am grateful for that day. Even if that blessing was my ability to walk away, locking myself in the bathroom to avoid losing my temper with the attitude filled 6-year-old.

I am lucky, but I never forget to acknowledge the person who orchestrated the whole event. The one who worked hard to avoid the threat of losing her life, and the life of others. The one who stepped a tepid foot into the sea of battling her demons; supported, but ultimately on her own. Under all that luck, under all that privilege, there is still a woman who fought hard to be where she is today. A woman who dared to believe in her worth enough, that she made the brave choice to push herself out there, nervously following in the footsteps of all the other brave souls who made that leap and sought help. **That person was me**. The mother so consumed by PND that she never thought she would be happy, ever again.

You Are Your Own Superpower

I was given the tools to beat PND and I used them. Granted, at some points I had them forced upon me. If it wasn't for being booted up the arse to take medication or to attend therapy, I'm sure my journey would have been *very* different. I had all the support a person could ever need to beat PND. But I also had all the hatred a person needed to stop themselves from ever being happy again too. As much as medication, therapy, and the empathetic support of others surrounding me gave a blanket protection of space and time, it was **me** who did the dirty work. It was me who fought with my own mind on a daily basis. It was me who got better, who healed, and who will continue to develop my self-awareness so that I will never entertain the idea of taking the mother from my child ever again.

It is **YOU** who holds the power of beating PND, or any mind torment you may be under, as scary and overwhelming as that can seem. You are the one in control of what mental environment you allow your mind to create. The choice is yours; whether you beat yourself up believing every dickhead notion your mind wants to throw at you, or you can let those thoughts slide on down and out of your mind, into the abyss where they belong. Allowing you the freedom to begin filling your mind with better serving thoughts, and not ones that make you cower in the corner of your own bedroom, consumed by guilt for not living up to the expectation of a 'perfect human'. (Which is about as real as the idea that my 5th labia will ever fuse back together with her pant mates...)

If someone had told me that beating PND was possible, and I held the power to do it while I was in the thick of my battle, the eye-roll would have been astronomical, changing the course of the planetary system in its magnitude. I wasn't open to the notion of positivity or being the one to control my own 'destiny'. In truth, I was an angry little gremlin, who thought all mothers who loved their baby, only 'claimed' to do so in order to save face. A view I do still hold to be fair. I thought people who preached 'healing' and 'self-love' to be pretentious, full of shit, arrogant, ego driven narcissists. Again, the shoe still fits for some. I hated the mothers who told me *"It gets better"*, or *"I've been where you are"*. **'Good for fucking you'**, I thought. They didn't know me or my struggle; they didn't know the beast I held inside, the rage and anger, the desire to smash the self-destruct button instead of gently disarming it. Who the fuck are these people to tell ME who I am or what will make me better? *Arseholes.*

I was too angry and arrogant in my illness, with a head stuck firmly in the clouds of confusion, unable to let people in for fear of… something. Being hurt, vulnerable, mocked, belittled? Take your pick. At some point, there is nothing else for it but to get over yourself. At some point, you need to let other people in, listen to their wisdom and accept there are other realities out there, other than the one swirling in your head. At some point, you need to wake up, take a big fucking breath, and know **you** are the one who can change your world. Whether that is in therapy, using medication, meditation, sport, art, whatever medium you use, **YOU** are the one who holds the power. Albeit, it may not always feel like this is true, but you really do hold the power to change your mind.

Vulnerability Heals

It's not easy to step out into the big blinding light of mental healing. It can often be a scorching place of extreme discomfort, matched only in intensity by its vulnerability. No one likes to wander alone, hence the gut-wrenching pain of loneliness in parenthood.

During the first two year of motherhood, when my PND was on its 'A-Game' of blinkering the truth from my eyes, I came across a

Buzzfeed video on Postnatal Depression. As I watched the short video, my heart burst from within me. Sitting on my bed, with the laptop perched on my knees, my eyes nipped as I watched the women on screen. Through my tears came validation; a digital hug of acceptance and realisation. It was called 'Moms Talk About Their Postpartum Depression' (see page274 for website), where a handful of new mothers shared how they felt in the months after childbirth, each with their own personal take on this precious time, and how it related to their hidden mental health.

I resonated with each mother's story, with one woman saying she felt emotionally numb after the birth of her baby. But it was another mother in particular who broke me; I saw my own reflection in her. This mother, like me, had picked up her baby and screamed into their face. Breaking down as she relives the awful moment, I broke down too. Watching the video, I wept because I related with her words and her pain. I felt seen and validated, the first time I realised other mothers felt as I did and that I may in fact be mentally ill, or not as close to 'fine' as I projected to be to the outside world. I saw then that the pleas of my partner were true; I was ill and in desperate need of help. All in an instant, this horrible act of screaming at my newborn baby wasn't the act of me; it was the act of PND. When the tears of realisation dried, their salt left a bitter sting, boiling my blood in the process.

I'm not sure if I've mentioned that I'm prone to a bit of anger and rage… realising I was mentally ill was no exception. How could this be an illness of parenthood, such a prevalent one, in which no one spoke of? An illness I knew nothing about. Worse, I was made to feel every emotion imaginable about being a 'poor mother', when this was never true! I was ill; it wasn't a reflection of me as a parent. I was outraged for myself. For my partner. For our daughter. And for those women on the screen who represented all mothers being unnecessarily whipped on a daily basis by their own mind;

alone in the darkness, enabled vastly by society and our projection of what parenthood is.

The women in the video gave me the courage to open my laptop, create a blog, and to start sharing the *real* side of parenthood; the side we tend to neglect or skim over to avoid room for judgment from others.

I was *fucking livid* learning about the term 'Post-Natal Depression', a world ever-present under our nose, yet its stink concealed in taboo and fear. All this shit running through my head, constantly, didn't need to be there. The mothers on the screen told me that. As they spoke about their experience, statistics flashed on the screen before them. "1 in 7 mothers suffer with PND". *'1 in 7 my arse'*, I thought, as I typed in the name of my blog into a free hosting site. Struck by the bravery of these women, overcome with injustice, I was determined to rid myself of the mind-shackles that I, alongside PND, had created. In doing so, I wanted to help other parents out there too. I wanted to tell them how I felt, and just how angry I was that my dream of being a 'happy new mother' was stolen from me. I wanted them to know I didn't choose to feel like this, and they didn't need to accept feeling like that either. There *is* a way out from the bullshit of PND. There are people out there who sympathise with us, and there is a wee angry Scottish mum who would not put up with the weight of PND pulling her, or anyone else, down.

HonestK Changed My Life

I was pretty nervous creating my blog, feeling a bit stupid too. I worried about what people would think of me. I wasn't worried they would judge my posts or the content; I was confident and felt assured that my feelings were valid regarding my PND and parenthood. Following the Buzzfeed video, I found a whole online world of parent bloggers, some of whom suffered from mental illness and wrote about it in relation to parenthood. Sharing my mind was never the problem. Creating a 'brand' and having the audacity to believe I was worthy enough to carve out a space to share my views, was the problem.

Settling for the name *'HonestK'*, I was happy not to be identified as a 'Mummy' or 'Parent Blogger', despite all of my content stemming from that very subject. Mummy bloggers really tore my ass. They bugged me - a lot. Social media was filled with these perfect mothers, with the perfect house, husband and children; their captions reading how they had a brilliant day at the beach or that they couldn't believe how lucky they were to have such beautiful, saintly children - *#blessed*. And sure, the dream comes true for a lot of people. The law of probability teaches us that out there, somewhere, there is that mum who loves every single second with her children and has life all figured out. I have no quarrel there. It just seemed to be that *ALL* of these mothers liked to hang around on social media, using *#gifted* now and again. It's not hard to see why mothers feel like a failure when their social media feed is filled with 'perfection'.

I wasn't a Mummy Blogger. I didn't want to be lost in that void of filtered pictures and feather filled flat lays. Each to their own I always say, and that I do believe. I mean no stones to be thrown. But there was a desperate need for an army of real. Too much of the media portrayed parenthood in a golden light of gratefulness, hushing anything contrary to the belief that it was the pinnacle of life. All I saw was damaging stereotypes that parenthood was 'hard', yet everyone was so caught up in baby smiles that none of the 'hard' had any impact.

But I knew the truth. I knew there was another side to this malarkey that no one was speaking. I had sisters-in-law who told me, in solidarity, that this shit was hard, and no one tells you *how* hard.

One of them had suffered at the hands of PND too, stealing those once in a lifetime moments from her. Disrupting relationships, creating scarring moments that would be etched into her mind, just as much as the day she gave birth would be. A side to her life I never saw, a side the family worked through behind closed doors, like many parents do. Like I was doing. They gave me love and support, knowing exactly how hard this struggle was. This only made me more pissed that we had all been fed a bullshit notion of what it means to be a mother, when in reality we are all behind the scenes doing damage control to our fellow mothers.

I published my first blog in March 2017, proclaiming that I was here to share the truth on account of being dragged into motherhood by the scruff, struggling to find my feet in the process. I wanted to share how my life had been stolen from me by PND, to anyone willing to read my words. I wasn't ashamed to share my experience; I didn't give a shit if anyone read my words and disagreed. I was too hurt and angry to care. Feeling robbed of the happy life I was promised, I wanted to express myself exactly as I was: alone. Upset. Depressed. And utterly confused by the hoodwink of parenthood.

As a natural progression of the blog, I created social media accounts with the *'HonestK'* brand, diligently following a 'how to grow your blog' guide where it said the best way to get your words out there was, well, to share them, of course. I did feel like a bit of a fool, worried what my family and friends would think of me. *'Who did I think I was creating a 'brand' on social media to punt my blogs?'*, the main drag-me-down thought as I typed in my username on all the social media platforms, just like the guide advised. It was never my content that bothered me; it was more about how others would perceive me, or if they thought I was firing above my station. But I wasn't. I was simply a mother - a pissed off one - on a mission to mind-dump her crazy in digital form. To help myself, and to help the other mothers like me, searching online for the 'minority' of mothers who suffered at the hands of PND.

Being a fuddy old millennial, I didn't like Instagram (IG) when I first opened the app. *What the hell was this? Just a place for pictures? How boring,* I thought. But the guide said to create accounts on all social media platforms and then use them to show off my blog, so I did.

At first, my IG feed was full of the filtered, picture-perfect, 'Mum Bloggers', creating their own brand, built on family days out, skincare reviews and the best baby gadgets for under £50. Not before long, it dawned on me that as kind and supportive as they are, they are not here to make friends. Nor are they there to share how they find parenthood. Everyone's prerogative of course, however, they did nothing for my self-esteem. They did nothing to help rid my mind of the torment it was under, and it appeared other people felt the same way. It took me years to curate a healthy place on IG, cutting out the accounts that didn't bring me joy, while following more accounts that spoke about motherhood in the same light that I saw it.

In time, IG turned into my social media home, a place I felt safe and comfortable to share my day-to-day life in all its rage and beauty. If I had a breakdown on account of a rough day with the kid, I shared it. If I found myself wondering if parenthood was worth it all, I shared it. If I got mad at the inequality in parenthood, society, and just about any other sector of life, I shared it. I held the phone to my face, without a second thought, and ranted my way through my grievance.

Following what I presumed to be just me venting **A LOT**, my message box began to fill. Mothers and fathers expressing the same concerns as me. Thanking me for speaking out, thanking me for making them feel less alone by highlighting the struggles we all go through, and that they wished more people would share. Without knowing it, I had created a support network; seemingly a bunch of 'strangers' who always had my back, and I, theirs. People who listened to my mind, told me it was more than okay to feel this way and helped me navigate my way out of the dark.

I owe much of my life to these 'strangers' online; those who commented under my blogs, sharing with me how brave I am, and how they felt 'seen' in my words. To those who told me I was not alone under my IG posts, taking the fear off my back, that I wasn't actually crazy, and parenthood really **WAS** this mental! To the people who sent me messages or emails in support of what I wrote, striking up conversations that would lead to meet-ups and years of friendship.

Social media gets a lot to slack, not least from me, but it was (still is) my saving grace. The string netting I landed upon when I fell from the tightrope of life while balancing motherhood on my head. These people have always 'seen' me; they always knew exactly what to say to keep me going. Most of all, they created a safe online space for me to share everything, so I could get back on track with my mental health.

My Sat Nav Out of The Dark

Social media and my blog gave me something to focus on - as if parenting and working full-time wasn't enough! But I loved it. Sinking my teeth right into my new hobby, drawing up notes of future blogs; what I wanted to say, and what other topics bugged my ass. I spent hours online, speaking to all my new friends, reading and commenting on the blogs of others. Then sinking far too many hours into social media, being obsessed with the new connections I had made. Taking time to reply to everyone who commented or messaged me that day. It took my mind off what was going on around me. The pressures of working, being a mother, a partner, and attending therapy weekly. I loved writing, I loved sharing, and I loved the community of people who made me wish we all lived in a big old island of parents who just *'get it'*.

I spoke with my therapist about the blog. It was during a time of uncertainty in my workplace - yet another area of stress in my life I didn't want to deal with. My therapist encouraged me to write, to keep going, to keep the fire alive. It was something I was so passionate about, and it was helping to break down the barriers within myself. As I wrote, I made sense of many things: the way I felt, the emotions running through me, and, most importantly, *why*. My voice is honest, but my fingers are pure in their integrity, often running out with the pace of my mind. They knew what needed to be cleansed from me in order to heal.

The more I attended therapy, intertwining lessons with my home life, the more the Mind Demons withered away, as I wrote my heart into these blog posts. Everything seemed to combine tremendously, giving me a greater understanding of myself, motherhood, and my life. Followers online gave me support and strength when I was struggling. I spoke to my partner with more clarity and confidence. I looked at my daughter in awe, finally realising that I helped create this magnificent little human, and I deserved to love and enjoy every single inch of her.

I found myself online and in the words of those whom I shared my struggles in parenthood. I expressed myself in the way we should all be able to express ourselves, and I healed as a result. Taking the nervous plunge to share my thoughts online is right up there with the strength of my partner when it comes to the top reasons I'm a happy and healthy mother today. I don't think I will ever stop healing, or ever stop monitoring my mental health. I'm beyond grateful that I have an ever-ready tribe of people beside me, to help me see through the muggy times. Just as parenthood can be a lonely place, healing can also be lonely. I'm forever thankful I had people there to support me as I walked the path to better mental health, as it is very rarely, a simple, straight line.

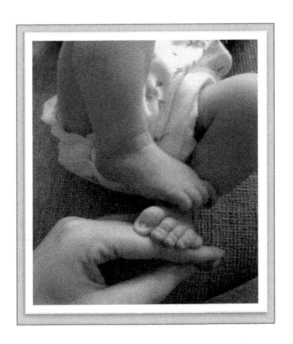

Chapter 24

Hidden Grief

By the time my daughter was 3 and a half years old, I was well on my way to dealing with PND. The mood swings had levelled out. I was an open book to everyone and anyone willing to listen, and the intrusive thoughts had become but whimpers in my mind whenever the Mind Demons thought they could dig back into my world. I don't believe I will ever be 'cured' of my mental illness. In some respects, I hope I never will be. It keeps me learning, talking and sharing. There are always, and will always be, elements of me that need to be brought into the light from time to time. (My quick temper and sharp tongue, to name the two prominent remnants of PND that I still carry with me.) But for the most part, I consider myself a survivor of PND - regarding its symptoms at least.

Yet the story doesn't end there. There is no checklist and completion goal here. Getting over the symptoms of mental illness is only the halfway mark. What I was about to learn is that the after-math can be just as brutal as living the illness - for me at least. I was about to come head-on with the life I had lived for years, the things I missed and the terrible heartache of everything stolen from me.

The Online House of Horrors

Before my daughter's fourth birthday, I decided to get an online Cloud account to save the vast and ever-expanding wealth of pictures clogging up my phone memory. I do enjoy spending an unhealthy amount of time on social media, creating funny snapshots of my life to share with friends and anyone willing to listen to my drivel. When Snapchat was all the rage, my daughter loved to create videos using the funny filters. Needless to say, I have videos a plenty of her pretending to lick the screen while digital dog ears hang from her head. She did look very cute to be fair.

On Instagram, I share the quick snaps of *'I can't believe I caught that!'*, as my kid tells viewers her father *"left the fucking heating on"*, standing there at the prime young age of 3, or thereabouts. Cursing while I gasp at her side, proud as punch she used the words in grand context, and rightly so. Why the fuck was the heating on all day, mid-summer, while no one was home?

As you can imagine, the 64GB of memory on my phone is severely bursting into a sweat as I save yet another classic snippet of life. Or just the bog-standard pictures that don't mean much to others, but as a mum, the snap embodies a memory that I never wish to lose.

Although some memories from these pictures, I wish I could lose.

Feeling the dread of not being able to hold onto these magical moments while wanting to capture more pictures, I opened an online storage service that would save everything and anything captured on my phone, uploading it onto the mystical and magical world of online Clouds. So that will be the nude pics out the window then… no one wants those babies automatically saved on the hackable world of digital clouds. I mean, I'm fairly certain a floppy maw tit isn't on the menu for creepers, and I don't judge, but I'll save myself the embarrassment and keep them behind locked doors. Apparently, a

244

locked door is the only thing that can contain them these days, as I discovered when I leaned over to tie my daughter's shoelace. A giggle peaked out her tight lips, her eyes giving away the cause of the hilarity. An escaping tit, just the one, pulled out the bra by gravity as I was bending. Clearly visible to wee pervs that eyeball down the gaping neckline when you are doing a great act of kindness, such as tying their laces. Took that like a bullet so I did. I joined in the laugh, hiding my horror of now being the owner of stretched tit-sacks that have transitioned from a solid to a liquid-like state, manoeuvring to fit whatever environment they are in, and even seeping out if they can. I told my daughter to keep her eyes off my nipples as she began to laugh, or else I would bite her nipples clean off. What a great body boost that was - my first nip-slip on account of freedom fighting titties. What they lack in fullness, they more than make up for with tenacity in their apparent never-ending bid for freedom, that's for sure.

What I didn't realise as I typed my email into the Cloud service, was that I had created this online Cloud before. I don't actually understand how it knows me, or what I've done, or when I must have created this account that linked it to previous phones, but when I logged in, I was met with hundreds of photos and videos, all from years ago; random in order and random as to why I may have saved them.

Some right crackers appeared. Videos of friends that they best wished forgotten, more than likely the *exact* reason I saved them at the time. A fair few of my girlfriends at the most unflattering chin angles as they proceed to pull a range of faces while telling me that I was a creep, and *"creeping was my game"*. Completely true, but I wasn't the one creeping down the phone looking like a potato. I see the reason I saved that bad-boy. Clips from nights out reminded me of the carefree nights my partner and I once shared as a couple. Most of the clips were full of disgustingly loud techno music (my heaven), in a dark club, filled only with coloured lights and the faces of strangers, who would be thankful that I didn't have my flash on.

As I scrolled deeper into the Cloud service, I was taken by surprise to find clips of my daughter that I thought I had lost to the Gods of Apple and Android when I switched phones soon after her birth. There she was in all her tiny, wonderful, newborn, glory. In a short, less than 15 seconds long video of her at few weeks old, I caught the moment she was suffering a bout of the hiccups. Her eyes stare at me in wonder as her tiny frame pulses out teeny judders. Thin petite fingers move without refinement as she became aware she is the master of these strange things on the end of her hand. Although there is a high probability it is wind, it looks as though she is smiling at me. It's a beautiful short clip of my baby as we sit in bed; mother amazed by her tiny little creation, enjoying a moment of bonding after a feed. That's what it looks like, that's what it should have been. Every time I am confronted with pictures of my newborn baby, I'm happy for a fleeting second - then I burst into tears.

The Painful Void of PND

That's not my baby.

That wasn't my life.

The woman holding that phone is so very intensely ill. There was no bond between my daughter and me, only transactions of instinct, keeping her alive and well as I diligently completed my 'mum' work to the best of my abilities. At the time, I didn't think she loved me either. All she seemed to need from me were things; every cry and moan was for me. It was the opposite of Stockholm Syndrome; I saw myself as a skivvy to her demands, a person she tolerated to fulfil her needs, no bond or adoration. If she could ring a bell, she would have, and then beat me after I had finished serving her wishes. I felt like I meant nothing to her, nothing special. Nothing at all like that mother and daughter bond I had imagined. And she certainly wasn't rainbow and butterflies to me either.

It's a rare occasion that I scroll back to 2015 on my phone and look at the pictures of her as a newborn baby. It's rare that I even go back as far as when she was two years old, let alone into the Thunderdome itself. Back to that time when everything was stolen from me; the weeks after her birth when my PND was in its infancy, yet causing the most destruction, both within my mind and my relationships. I never go back to these pictures - they are far too painful. Even writing about the pain brings hot tears to my eyes.

Not to say I avoid these pictures all together; I do scroll back to those weeks and try my best to fill them with a new feeling. I stare at the huge chubby cheeks of my adorable baby and try to feel the love and bond that mothers are told to experience. Almost like a weird and utterly futile form of Cognitive Behavioural Therapy, I longed to rewire my mind into forgetting the bad and only seeing the good. Then it struck me: that was never going to happen, nor should I want it to. I needed to confront the pain. I needed to confront the grief of losing my newborn baby to PND.

Hesitant to use the term 'losing' a baby, when I very well have my child by my side today, I use it to explain the hurt and sorrow, and exactly how it feels within me. I did lose years of my daughter's life to mental illness. There are so many memories I do not have. For years, I looked at other mothers holding their babies, kissing them on the head, sniffing the youth from their scalps. It hurt me to see other mothers in love with their children, for I never had that. Not for a long time. I'd say she was about 18 months old before I felt something that resembled 'love' more than it resembled 'instinct'. That moment you catch yourself staring at this mini-human, in complete adoration and overwhelming affection, opting to watch her moves and play rather than watching the TV or reading a book. Those moments in which you find yourself simply watching, so deeply in love with this little marvel of your creation.

I didn't get to enjoy those moments I caught on camera of her at a young age. I question who I took these snippets for, or why I thought the need to pull my camera out in the first place. Many of them I sent to friends, as suggested by the location of the folder. I was playing the role of a perfect mother, after all. But I don't remember being overly in awe with my baby that I felt the need to capture moments with her. My memories are very much of anguish, terror and doom.

Sometimes I question if I did actually love her. Or if I have somehow created a false narrative of what happened all those years ago. It would be nice to think that I took those short videos of her life because I wanted to capture everything; a digital memory that could last forever, never wanting to forget this time in my life. Sadly, that's just not the case. Looking at her few-weeks-old sleeping face, the pull in my stomach and lump in my throat, created entirely of pure grief and distraught, suggests that my memory is correct.

I did not love my baby.

I missed those precious weeks and months of her life; a time I will never get to relive or recreate. And I cannot stress how **heartbroken** this makes me feel. To this day, and for the rest of them I presume, I will always grieve that loss. It will always pain me to see those pictures of a cute baby and know the photographer behind the lens is suffering in mental anguish, feeling at a loss, a failure, not knowing that her life is about to fall about around her, not knowing that these are not the days of her life. These will be the darkest days, lost to PND, that she will yearn to relive once she is able to love.

For a long time, I was unable to look at the pictures, avoiding them completely. That had to change when I decided to share my thoughts on parenthood and mental health on social media. Wanting to make my blogs and Instagram posts unique to me, I opted for using my personal back catalogue of pictures as opposed to stock images online. As I wrote about my mental health and how it affected my ability to love (amongst other things), it seemed only right that I chose a picture of myself with my daughter, to which there are limited numbers. Sometimes, I would be too preoccupied with finishing a blog, bringing it to completion, ready to post, that selecting a picture was just part of the process. I could quickly scroll back to that point in my life and select the image that fitted both the post and format of the blog. There was very little emotional connection to the picture, as that energy had already been spent within the words on the screen.

When it came to posting about my journey on Instagram, where any picture can be cropped and used, I began to spend a little longer in the dreaded newborn picture section. Often, through tear-filled blurry eyes, I would quickly do my best to find a decent picture to complement my words, posting it to social media, vowing to take more up-to-date 'Insta worthy' pictures of myself and my daughter. I didn't want to keep visiting the pain of the newborn section, I also didn't want to keep sharing the *intimacy* of this section. To the outsider, these pictures seemed beautiful and adorable - the classic image of a loving mother and daughter. Yet this was an image I wanted to make **very clear** was not there, as much as it pained me to say it. I couldn't share these pictures and not share the truth behind them. I wouldn't contribute to the false narrative of motherhood that helps to create mental illness in the first place.

I continued to share as many of these pictures as I could, each with a painful tale behind them. The image of me and my daughter lying in bed, her, weeks old, and me, behind her, looking fresh and pretty, *that* was the worst day of my life, the day I pushed her away from me and screamed with resentment that I hated her. And so, I told it as it was. Each picture in the early years of motherhood comes with its own horrid memory, a breakdown or emotional scar in each of them. Sorrow nestled in the background of my daughter's gummy smile. Relationship strain and intrusive thoughts paint the wall in videos of her laughing as she bounced in her Jumperoo. My partner, looking into his phone in the background, while our daughter play-fully laughs as she bounces; his actions reiterate the disconnect that grew between us. How passive and detached we had both become within the 6 months of our daughter's life.

Not one of the early pictures and videos fill me with anything other than pain. A horrible, gut wrenching, empty void, which almost contradicts itself as it is filled with a yearning pain that shakes the rhythm of my heart. Taking with it my breath and any illusion I have that this time was anything other than pain and darkness.

A Picture Screams a Thousand Pains

For years I couldn't place what the pain was, where this emotion was coming from. Whatever it was, I tried my best to avoid it, to avoid the pictures. No sooner had a picture opened than my eyes would start to fill - not ideal when reminiscing with your partner about how cheeky our daughter looked on her first birthday. I hid my upset as much as possible; I was embarrassed by my own pain. My partner didn't look at these pictures and burst into tears, and he had been hurt and lived the trauma alongside me. If I did hint tow-ards my feelings, they were misunderstood, unintentionally, and pushed to the side in favour of, *'it's not all bad'*. But for me, **it was**. That whole time is steeped in a hurt, so it must have been *'that bad'*. Why else would I cry each time I looked at my smiling toddler as she displayed her best checked shirt and dungaree combo, with her fine golden-brown hair clipped to the side, showcasing her enormous, beautiful eyes?

What I was feeling was grief. A missed opportunity. The death of the mother I thought I would be. A baby taken from my expectations. An instant love that was replaced with rage and frustration. Something I will never get back - and I wanted it. Something I miss, so I grieve it. **I grieve my baby when I look at those pictures**. And I grieve for myself. To have lived through that time, so unaware of what was going on around, and within me. I want so much to see these pictures through the eyes of my partner. His memory isn't as tainted as mine. It pains him, yet he chooses to focus on the positives; that we made it through that time and we have a hilarious and gorgeous daughter who adores us completely. He chose to see the happy child in those pictures, whereas I felt I had no say in the matter; no choice other than to see the sadness in them all, pulled only to the loss they represent and the mother behind the phone, who is like so many mothers out there, ill and alone.

As much as I tried to make peace with my journey into parenthood and all that was taken, I knew the gut punch in these pictures represented something I had to heal. So, I opened up to myself, acknowledging that whatever emotion I was feeling was valid. Allowing myself to become upset, listening to what I had been trying to conceal, even to myself.

Taking whatever words filled my fingers, I wrote a post about my grief. Not knowing, nor caring what the reaction may be, I let my mind speak truthfully. I hated that I never got to love my daughter; that I never got to sniff her head and enjoy her smiles. I grieved all that I had missed, all that was stolen from me, all while I was physically there, yet never mentally present. Bawling my eyes out, I confronted the architect of my pain: **grief**. I allowed it to fill within me, then spill straight out again. Finally allowing the unknown pain that had made my heart tremble when I scroll into the deep of my online storage, I took the grief and wrote it into its rightful place of being felt and released. I finally grieved the baby that I did not, and could not, love.

Living With Grief

I think there is an assumption that people who experience mental illness get better (or not) and move on with life. What we may fail to see is the pain and trauma it can cause in its path; how these scars can run deep and cut just as painfully as the illness itself.

If there is one commodity in life we can never experience again, it's time. Ruthlessly so. I do not want to go back to those early years of my daughter's life to change them, for they forged the path I am on now. A path, I'd like to think, has improved me as a person, and a person who can improve the suffering of others with my story. However, I would like to go back to that time as a ghost of the future. To have the ability to stand over my daughter's crib and stare at her with nothing other than pure love. I'd like to enjoy each milestone and 'first' as the pleasure they are and should have been, rather than worrying about if and when they would come, and what impact this would have on our daughter's life. I would love to go back and hold my sleeping baby, tight against my chest, in the place she always wanted to be… yet I felt too fearful to let her rest upon me in case something terrible happened. I would love to hold and dance with my baby because I *want* to, not because I felt I *had* to, in some attempt to make her feel as though I loved her. I'd love to see my baby for the pleasure that she was; to hold her as the loving, adoring, healthy mother that I am now.

I would give anything to return to the first few months of my baby and love her, completely. To hold her without the constant intrusive thoughts spinning within my mind. But that time has passed, never to be repeated. They say a mother's love is like no other, but her grief is thrice as powerful. And so, I live with this heartache. This grief intertwined with my love. Forever.

Chapter 25

Happily Ever After?

Years after the initial visit to the doctor, taking medication, attending therapy, and now sharing my mental health in great detail online, our family life was still unsteady. Arguments changed from the depression-filled *'leave me'*, *'get out'*, *'save yourself'*, to a pair of love-struck humans, with a child, who both had some serious wounds from life and parenthood in need of healing. But they wanted to walk that path together, with as much love and respect as they could give each other.

Frustration was always the undertone of our relationship as we each worked through the Pandora's Box that parenthood had completely blown open. Not only had we to navigate bringing a child into the world and the daily structures needed to do so, but we also, unexpectedly, opened the gate to the past, dealing with issues of our own now brought into the light, as a result of parenthood.

With a lot of *'whys'*, come a lot of answers, each one to be explored, then placed in the appropriate folder.

Why was my first instinct to become angry when woken during the night?

Why does noise trigger me?

Why do I worry about being abandoned?

All of these questions placed more strain on our relationship, as we worked through the backlog of cargo we each carried with us. Although the bickering ended and we united as a couple (I dare to say we could defeat anything in our unity), we didn't make it out of our time with PND without some deep, **DEEP** wounds. My scars are clear to see, dealing with the loss I'll never recuperate from, learning the power of my mind, being scared to learn my life can change without me even realising it. My scar is my depression and the hurt that came with it; its immense power and the authority it can command over my life, even *taking* my life if it wished to do so. I am afraid of my own mind. Or rather, I now give my mind the huge respect it deserves, as it alone has the force to take everything I have from me. Yes, I am strong enough to beat it, once at least. But I would never welcome that fight again; for the sake of my own happiness, let alone the damage it can inflict upon others.

A Hard Choice to Swallow

I'm not the only one who lives with the trauma of PND and wishes my mental health never to nosedive again. Unlike me, my partner has largely kept everything within himself, pushing the memories into a place hard to reach, yet still within range of its emotional pull. Our daughter had turned three years old when I voiced the question that had been lingering in the air for a while:

"Should we have another baby?".

It was awkward. I know my partner inside out, just as he knows me. His hesitation to answer the question told me all I needed to know. I didn't want to hear his words; I could already feel them churning in my stomach. I wanted another baby - and so did he. I knew the reason for the silence filling the room was pain rather than excitement.

"I don't think I can go through that again Kirsty." He finally replied.

Fuck. He had used my name in his reply. He only uses my name when I'm in trouble, or when he is being serious. I looked at him; I could see the last 3 years written all over his face. He was tired, beat, and hollow, experiencing what seemed like an aftershock in the midst of my healing. He was the rock who took it all, but even rocks get weather-beaten, even rocks begin to fade in the tide.

My heart sank as much as my partner's upon the sound of his answer. We both wanted a baby, but there was no guarantee I would make it out the other end alive. It was as simple as that. Moreover, our daughter was at the ripe age of social development, figuring out the world. We had been lucky that the peak of my depression was at a time she knew no better. As a baby she was hugely oblivious to her surroundings, a luxury she would not be afforded now she was 3 years old.

"I can't", my partner repeated, *"I can't go through that again"*.

I knew he was right. I respect the anguish he had endured in the past 3 years; the uncertainly, the abuse and being an on-call therapist, all while he adjusted to becoming a parent himself. It was as taxing as my journey. It wasn't right for me to stamp my foot and say I wanted another baby, or else I would regret it for the rest of my life. I knew he felt the same, yet the risk to our family was too great. We are a strong unit, but not naïve. Not anymore. And so, with heavy hearts, we agreed that now was not the time and we would *"see"* about the future. And we all know that when someone says, *"we will see."* it's pretty much a backhanded **'No. Never'**.

My mental illness had stolen the joy of my first born and now it was stealing my hopes of another child. I felt as though I was being punished for having depression; a karmic debt being paid to account for all the hurt and pain I had caused in the previous years. I knew that wasn't the case, that no one judged me for being ill, nor did my partner hold a vendetta against me. But it broke my heart. I felt powerless and remorseful all at once. I felt upset for my partner too. It was clear he wanted another child, yet was too exhausted and fraught from the time we had just moved past. I felt like I had let him down, as though I was the one preventing him from having the family he wished for. Also, I was so sorry for our family, our daughter. She was going through a phase of wanting someone to play with her all the time, feeling lonely when either one of us refused her plea to play for the 5th hour that day. We wanted a sibling for her, to complete our family. But it was not to be. On account of the beast that resided within me. On account of me.

This was the first time in our relationship that we didn't agree. The first time one of us said no with a very real and reasonable reason for the roadblock. There was no directed hurt or resentment; I knew why this choice was made. I knew in time I would make my peace with it, but at that moment I was heartbroken and alone, knowing that although my illness wasn't my choice, it was still me who was preventing us from having another child.

Chapter 26

The Last Hurrah

I have all these pictures and memories of the 'bad' times during the first few years of motherhood, and not very many of the good. Part of the problem when dealing with depression is the tendency to focus on the negative, becoming oblivious to the good. If you asked me when it was that I recovered from my depression, I would have a hard time answering that. I'd try to equate it with an increase in the good memories. But my brain had been trained for a long time to see life from only one side; to dwell in the dark, and don't dare use anything positive to bring myself up or build any form of self-confidence upon it.

When my daughter was 3 and a half years old, I remember canceling plans with friends. I had called in sick to work for the week on account of my mental health. I'm not sure what prompted this low spell, but I do remember it being out of the blue as I had been feeling much better for months. It was a blow and a stark reminder that I will never be free of depression - no one is. The undertones will always be present within me, making my mental health a life-long commitment that needs to be checked when I start to show signs of struggle.

It was January, and I was meant to be seeing a theatre show with a bunch of friends. I was worried about going out, knowing I wasn't

llᵉnⁿ

up to it, nor did I want to be around happy people when I felt so drained and numb. As I sat in the car park of the local shopping centre, I burst into tears as I messaged my friend to tell her I wouldn't be able to make it out that night. I was so upset. So sad to let people down, worried they would hate me or think I was being dramatic, or if they would even believe me when I said I wasn't feeling up to it. My partner rubbed my shoulder and reassured me everything was okay, but I couldn't get over it. I composed myself the best I could, wiped the tears from my eyes and got out of the car, making our way to the shops. As we walked, my friend sent her reply to the news of my absence. She assured me it was more than okay and I should take all the time I needed, not to worry about tonight, and she wished me to feel better soon. I felt I didn't deserve her kindness; this night was about her, a gathering to meet fellow bridesmaids before the big wedding date. I was her best friend and I was letting her down, and with such short notice.

Walking into the shopping centre, I began to well up again. I was so sick of this illness, so sick of being unduly hurt, so sick of wondering what people thought of me and when they would decide enough was enough and cut me off. I was so sick of letting the people I loved down and asking for their forgiveness while I did so. I was **so over** being depressed, 3 years into parenthood and I still didn't have a grip of myself. I had done the therapy, the medication, the sharing, the chatting, the baring my fucking soul to the world, and yet here I was, still being thrown around by the Mind Demons when I thought I had defeated them.

I didn't know it at the time, but that was the last time I called off work to deal with my depression, the last time I took a week out of society in order to wash off the grey from my skin. As if it was the last mad dash from my depression, one last chance for the Mind Demons to wedge their nails back into my mind. I didn't let the blip deter me from my healing. I took note that I would never be sure when the next bump would come, but that was it. I wasn't frightened; my mind no longer controlled me. My depression had nowhere to hide. My partner loved me. My child adored me. My boss supported me. My friends encouraged me. And my social media family ate any doubt that I was anything other than a strong and capable mother. Failing those barriers, my Mind Demons knew I would drag their sorry arse to therapy to oust them if they pissed me off enough.

A Pleasant Surprise

Just like the path into PND was unnoticed, slowly acclimatising my mind into believing my thoughts and actions were who I was, the path out of the darkness was just as discreet. The yelling became less and my tolerance of being a mother grew. I didn't snap when my daughter bugged my ass after a hard day. Instead, I included her in whatever I was doing. She became the chief potato peeler, an accolade she is very proud of, as she now runs through to the kitchen to ask if anything *"needs its skin removed"*. A bit terrifying, actually.

My thoughts in the shower focused more on the present day; what outfit I wanted to wear or if I should ask my friends for a coffee date this week, instead of the mental abuse I had been accustomed to. My morning mood was still pretty shitty as mornings are akin to the devil, but now it was only tired sarcasm at the helm, rather than spiteful venom shots laced with resentment. My humour was back with a vengeance, funny to me and always cruel to the butt of the jokes: my partner. The quick tongue was back in its rightful mode; mockery and witty as it shook off the prickles of poison it was used to firing out, just months previously.

"There you are", my partner said. *"I've missed you"*

He smiled as I mocked his inability to put a shirt on the correct way for the third day in a row. Even our daughter, at 3 and a half years old, knew when her shirt was on back to front as she joined in laughing at Daddy. His error set me up for a cascade of light-hearted banter before he left for work. After a dressing down, literally, by his daughter and her mummy - the gruesome twosome - he smiled as he kissed me.

"It's good to see you laughing". His words gave me both compliment and sorrow.

What a life we had led for those three years if he had missed this kind of mockery, I thought. Instead of some Hollywood romantic, *"I'm happy to be back"* bullshit, I teased him even further saying, *"Thank fuck I'm back. You've been dressing that bad the whole time and I didn't notice? Sort yourself out mate".*

The episodes between intrusive thoughts grew longer and longer, but they did still show up from time to time. There were still nights when I would pull away from my partner and question if he loved me. I think I will always have an element of that self-doubt and unworthiness. There's still a stone to be turned there. But we know how to deal with it now. We talk it out, or we let it pass. I no longer dwell on thoughts or let them fester. Only when I am stressed do I need to patrol and police my mind, telling intrusive thoughts to pack up and move on, they are not welcome in this neighbourhood anymore.

I'm Back Baby!

The moment I knew I was better, when I knew I had slipped back into the person that resembled me before giving birth, I was driving to work. I always had the radio on as I drove, although I didn't usually pay much attention to what I was hearing. My mind was often consumed with chores, a list of things to do, intrusive thoughts, a nagging mind telling me I was late and my boss thought poorly of me. There was such a constant chatter that I arrived at work as if on autopilot, having no recollection of how I got there.

Then one day, driving along, I began to sing. I began to bob around in my seat and really enjoy the music. Giving my best karaoke voice, I sang, smiling, I tapped my fingers on the steering wheel and I felt the music. When the song finished, I became a little sad. I love music; I love a car sing-fest that would horrify anyone unfortunate enough to ever hear my *'angelic'* voice. But I hadn't sung in the car for years. I hadn't enjoyed music for years. In fact, I didn't even think about it, or what songs I would like to listen to as I drove. I mindlessly put the radio on, as that's just what people do in the car.

It hit me then; I was enjoying something, enjoying music, really sinking into it and moving with the words. Such a simple thing, yet it meant so much that day. I was back. Carefree enough to allow myself to enjoy my 30-minute drive to work instead of dreading every minute of it. Happy enough to smile and sing. I let out a tear. What a journey I had been on, what a relief it was over. What a cruel and utterly merciless illness I had just beaten.

Chapter 27

My Confession

The honest truth is - I don't relate to many of the words I have written in this book. They will always upset me. Like the smell of a perfume that reminds you of a special holiday, these words will always take me back to that place, to those early years of mother-hood. I will always hold the ability to see through the eyes of the new mother; alone, broken, scared... and distraught in her illness. I will never lose the tears that come with wanting to hug myself as a new mother, longing to tell her things will get better, she is seen, and she is doing her best. None of it will ever leave me, nor would I want it to. But her journey seems so alien to me now, as did becoming a mother in the first place.

It has pained me so much to type these words knowing they are mine, that I lived them, that my partner lived them. *We* lived them. Yet I feel like the mother I write about is no longer me, as if I wave goodbye to her with each memory I relive, finally making my peace with a period of my life that has forever scarred me. I will always hold those scars, but much like the stretch marks on my torso, the scars fade; there, but less prominent.

I feel guilty as I nod my head in acknowledgement of the mum I used to be, as if I am abandoning her in some way, but I'm not. She is in the past, and that is where she must stay. She is my past, yet she is also someone's future, someone's present. The reason I relive my story. The reason I refuse to douse the fire within me and the determination to share my experience. People didn't leave me out in the cold when I needed them, and I'm proud to join the masses of women who refuse to let any other parent out there believe they are alone in this challenging job. That, and because I am forever pissed off at the inequality in parenthood, in society. The pain and trouble many women endure as a result of *'that's motherhood, suck it up'*. The scores of pregnant women who are silenced, ignored and belittled, setting them up to be dismissed in motherhood, just like the majority of women before her.

I will **never** shut up about all of the 'hidden' sides of parenthood. I learn something new each day that blows my mind and stokes the infuriation of *'that's so unfair'* at the same time. There is no short-age of shit we need to change in order to create a better environment for parents.

Six Years Later

I sit here today, six years on, with my daughter, my partner, and my eighteen-month-old **son**, and write these words to help other pare-nts. To show them there is hope in the dark. For them to know there is a way out. Depression may be long lasting, permanent, or always threatening to return when it sees a way in, but it need not always be controlling. My son is testament to that.

We took the risk. As a couple, we held each other as we embraced the unknown of having another child, knowing full well what one of the outcomes may be… and what a completely different story that journey turned out to be. It was the biggest risk we are glad we took. We look at our gorgeous little boy as he plays with his big sister, the gift and love we almost denied ourselves and our child-ren. That is the power of PND. Its sting runs deep. For us, it always will. We close our eyes and thank each other for pulling us through the most painful journey we have had to endure thus far. We look at our children with pride. **We did that**. We made these little people. We stuck together. We took the beast by the horns. We held each other when the fire of PND burned so strong that ending my life seemed like the lesser of two evils.

Those two absolutely gorgeous and precious souls are more than just our children. They are a symbol of our life, our commitment to each other, a testament of what it means to be there for each other. To truly see another human in the ugliest form imaginable, and to stick with them.

Always.

Forever.

My family.

My soulmates.

To Our Daughter

As I type, delete and type again, words fail to describe the lump in my throat when I think of you. How amazing, in every aspect of the word, a human could be. There are no words that will ever come close to articulating what you mean to me. But I know you can feel it, our love, our bond, our respect, just as strongly as I feel it from you to me.

Only you could show me how wrong I was in my illness. Only you had the strength to show me that you always loved me and I was always the mother you deserved, that I was worth fighting for.

For me. For you.

You are everything I aspire to be in a person, I hope I continue to grow to be more like you. Strong. Kind. Compassionate. A tiny force that knows right from wrong and isn't afraid to lay down the law.

You were my support and light when everything seemed so over-whelming. You are the reason I am here, sharing my story with the world. Not only because you helped me write it, choosing me to be your mother, but because you pulled me through it. You made me fight for us, and for all the mothers out there who are still in the dark, needing to find their light.

I love you. I wish you never need to know just how beautiful it is to say that I do, and I can, love you… *'one fifty billion'*.

My daughter.

My best friend.

My buddy.

My *'nemesis'*.

To My Partner

To say I am grateful to have met you is a gross understatement. The love and dedication you have shown to me, to our family, is an awe-inspiring force. As I look back on these words, the events we lived through together, I cannot believe my luck to have your strength holding us together, to have you as the father to our two children, to have you as my best friend, holding me when I made it almost impossible to love me. Where we would be, as a family, without you, I cannot imagine.

You are the reason we continue to be. You are the only person who saw me at my worst and loved me all the more for it. No one is a better role model to our children, to me, or to anyone witnessing mental illness. You are the strongest, most compassionate, loyal and beautiful person I have ever met.

No matter where we may be or what life throws at us, with you at my side I will always be home. I am beyond eternally thankful I get to wake with you each day, pretending to sleep so you crack first and get the kids up for the day. I'm more thankful that you know I'm pretending and let me away with it all the same.

I love you so much. Shit Bounty jokes and all.

And I can't wait till we retire so we can *finally* spend a morning in bed together with pizza and *Friends* again.

Writing A Book Is Brutal

Contrary to what you have read in this book, I don't consider myself someone who cries all that much. I am a parent, so of course, I have those timeout cries when life is pulling heavily around my shoulders, opting for the 'cry in shower' method of releasing tension when things are getting a bit too much to handle. But when it comes to Disney films, when the rest of the room are bawling their eyes out, I wonder if I have some form of undiagnosed issue as my tear ducts refuse to be peer pressured into weeping.

But this book, *large inhale, even longer exhale*, it is something else. I have cried more writing this than I feel I have done in the years up to its creation. The pain of my actions, the pain of a mother so lost and vulnerable. It kills me. The love I lost and the time I will never experience ever again, can seem too much for a human to bear. The worst part of it all is this isn't the past. This is life for parents at this moment. My tears fall for myself, but also for those mothers living my past right now. Like a collective consciousness, I weep in my own pain and ache for others all at once.

I would say it is hard to write these words, but that's not entirely true. It's easy for me to share what happened. I have only pain attached to these words. No shame, no guilt, no remorse. I share my journey for others, to bring comfort in their loneliness, to bring to light the other side of motherhood. The hardship many of us endure while feeling isolated. Wiping painful tears from my eyes means nothing in comparison to those that are still living in the belief that they are failing as a mother. So for me, these words are easy to hammer into my keyboard. Reminiscing about missing my newborn baby, not so much.

I thank you for reading my story, for coming on this journey with me. My only hope is that it helps you. That this helps someone you may know or meet in future. I hope it aids in some way to share any truth you want to release. To know that whatever you are going through, whatever you are feeling, that **you are not alone**. There is always someone in need of your words, your story and your compassion.

Thank you for letting me into your mind, and I hope, in time, you will get over my incessant referencing of my 5th labia. Last time, I promise.

Floats into the wind, surfing the clouds on her 5th labia.

Okay, *that's* the last one.

THANK YOU!

I thank every person that ever took the time out to message me 'you should write a book'. Without the boost and support, this book would not have been written. Or, maybe it would have - over 20 years. The verbal booting pushed me to start writing and the constant support and encouragement of *"just get it done!!"* was needed more than I can say.

So I thank you from the bottom of my heart. For being by my side and making me feel that I am worthy of sharing my story and that it needs to be heard.

I thank my hilarious, yet somewhat suffering friend Mhairi (IG: @the_misfit_maw), who has held my hand through the entire process, sinking hours of her time into reading and editing this book. Neither one of us with any experience of writing or editing, we both knew the importance of sharing this story, and so she willingly slogged her way through this it, ripping the arse out of my awful spelling mistakes - and made-up words. She was always there to knock me back on track when the 'I'm not good enough' worries consumed me. One of the best 'strangers' I have met through social media; a lifeline to me, and my family, during my second pregnancy and thereafter. I am extremely humbled. Not only did she give her time to me, but also her love, admiration, support and home. And a lifetime supply of Bountys.

Thank you Mhairi. You are a very special person to me, and of course to your 'Best Boy'. We love you very much.

I give a huge thanks to the literacy mastermind that is Kristina (IG: @mytinyempire_), who offered to help me work out my commas from my semicolons - a skill I am still learning, thankfully she is a kind and patient human. A long-time admirer of each other's writing, point of view and talent, she is a beautiful and supportive soul, often sending me much needed boosts of praise when I was lacking in confidence. I can't believe my luck to know such a wonderfully brilliant 'grammar polis' - who will more than likely pull me up for more grammar offences once she sees this unchecked 'thank you'.

For the wonderful book cover, I thank the very talented Alison, who kindly offered to help with its creation. I absolutely love the front cover! She completely nailed the vision I had in mind and I truly appreciate the time spent answering my messages and designing the cover.

I thank my friends and family for helping this book come to completion. The friends taking my children for the day, letting me sink 6 hours into typing my life into these words. To my brother for being my 'IT' service when this less than computer savvy fool couldn't work out the most basic of tasks. For each piece of help, I am extremely grateful; there is no way this book would have been created without it.

Last, but far from least, I thank my partner. For being the co-star in my story. For having the strength and devotion to us, our family, my vision in sharing this deeply personal and painful time of his life. I thank you for always having my back and for being my inspiration, my hero and my strength when I find myself doubting.

Find Me on Social Media

Largely, I lurk around on Instagram most days: @honestkirsty

If you enjoyed reading my journey in motherhood then let me know on Instagram, by either dropping me a message or by using the hashtag **#notallmothers**

I'm on Facebook somewhere: @honestkirsty

My Blog can be found at www.honestk.com

YouTube Channel: HonestK
Youtube.com/channel/UCh5gXWUvoLHnH35Bd1-p_WQ

References

P144 - Maternal suicide the main cause of death in new mums
        BBC News
        www.bbc.co.uk/news/av/health-46064807

P235 - Moms Talk About Their Postpartum Depression
        Buzzfeed Video
        www.youtube.com/watch?v=V64PqXKs02g